THE POETRY OF PRAISE

One of the chief functions of poetry in Antiquity, the Middle Ages and the Renaissance was to praise gods, people and things. Heroes and kings were glorified in many varieties of praise, and the arts of encomium and panegyric were codified by classical rhetoricians and later by writers on poetry. J. A. Burrow's study spans over two thousand years, from Pindar to Christopher Logue, but its main concern is with the English poetry of the Middle Ages, a period when praise poetry flourished. He argues that the 'decline of praise' in English literature since the seventeenth century has meant that modern readers and critics find it hard to judge this kind of poetry. This erudite but accessible account by a leading scholar of medieval literature shows why the poetry of praise was once so popular, and why it is still worth reading today.

J. A. BURROW is Emeritus Professor and Research Fellow at the University of Bristol. He is the author of many studies of Medieval Literature, including *Gestures and Looks in Medieval Narrative* (Cambridge, 2002).

CAMBRIDGE STUDIES IN MEDIEVAL LITERATURE

General editor
Alastair Minnis, *Yale University*

Editorial board
Zygmunt G. Barański, *University of Cambridge*
Christopher C. Baswell, *University of California, Los Angeles*
J. A. Burrow, *University of Bristol*
Mary Carruthers, *New York University*
Rita Copeland, *University of Pennsylvania*
Simon Gaunt, *King's College, London*
Steven Kruger, *City University of New York*
Nigel Palmer, *University of Oxford*
Winthrop Wetherbee, *Cornell University*
Jocelyn Wogan-Browne, *University of York*

This series of critical books seeks to cover the whole area of literature written in the major medieval languages – the main European vernaculars, and medieval Latin and Greek – during the period c. 1100–1500. Its chief aim is to publish and stimulate fresh scholarship and criticism on medieval literature, special emphasis being placed on understanding major works of poetry, prose, and drama in relation to the contemporary culture and learning which fostered them.

Recent titles in the series
Maura Nolan *John Lydgate and the Making of Public Culture*
Nicolette Zeeman *Piers Plowman and the Medieval Discourse of Desire*
Anthony Bale *The Jew in the Medieval Book: English Antisemitisms 1300–1500*
Robert J. Meyer-Lee *Poets and Power from Chaucer to Wyatt*
Isabel Davis *Writing Masculinity in the Later Middle Ages*
John M. Fyler *Language and the Declining World in Chaucer, Dante and Jean de Meun*
Matthew Giancarlo *Parliament and Literature in Late Medieval England*
D. H. Green *Women Readers in the Middle Ages*
Mary Dove *The First English Bible: The Text and Context of the Wycliffite Versions*
Jenni Nuttall *The Creation of Lancastrian Kingship: Literature, Language and Politics in Late Medieval England*
Laura Ashe *Fiction and History in England, 1066–1200*

A complete list of titles in the series can be found at the end of the volume.

THE POETRY OF PRAISE

J. A. BURROW

CAMBRIDGE
UNIVERSITY PRESS

CAMBRIDGE UNIVERSITY PRESS
Cambridge, New York, Melbourne, Madrid, Cape Town, Singapore, São Paulo, Delhi

Cambridge University Press
The Edinburgh Building, Cambridge CB2 8RU, UK

Published in the United States of America by Cambridge University Press, New York

www.cambridge.org
Information on this title: www.cambridge.org/9780521886932

First published 2008

Printed in the United Kingdom at the University Press, Cambridge

A catalogue record for this publication is available from the British Library

Library of Congress Cataloguing in Publication data
Burrow, J. A. (John Anthony)
The poetry of praise / J. A. Burrow.
p.   cm. – (Cambridge studies in medieval literature)
Includes bibliographical references and index.
ISBN 978-0-521-88693-2 (hardback)
1. Laudatory poetry, English – History and criticism.   2. English poetry – Middle
English, 1100–1500 – History and criticism.   3. English poetry – Old English,
ca. 450–1100 – History and criticism.   4. Praise in literature.   I. Title.
PR317.L38B87   2008
821.009 – dc22   2007049213

ISBN 978-0-521-88693-2 hardback

Contents

Preface

This study of praise in medieval poetry grew out of the observation that modern critics and readers (myself included) commonly find it hard to come to terms with the many varieties of eulogistic writing that are encountered there. So we either turn our eyes away from this 'poetry of praise' or else look in it too eagerly for such ironies and reservations as may accommodate it to modern tastes and values. The subject is a large one, and I have necessarily been very selective in the citing of both texts and critical discussions.

I am indebted to Colin Burrow, Thorlac Turville-Petre and Nigel Wilson, who read and commented on certain chapters of this book, and also to audiences at the universities of Bristol, Nottingham, Oxford and St Andrews. I have received valuable advice from Tony Boorman, Alastair Fowler, Bob Fowler, Ronald Hutton, Christopher Logue, Charles Martindale, Rhiannon Purdie and John Scattergood, as well as from the two anonymous publisher's readers. The Bristol University Library and its Interlibrary Loans department have done much to facilitate my work. To all these, I express my gratitude. The errors and inadequacies in this book are all my own.

Introduction: from Pindar to Pound

> O bright Apollo,
> Τίν᾽ἄνδρα, τίν᾽ἥρωα, τίνα θεόν,
> What god, man, or hero
> Shall I place a tin wreath upon!

In these lines from his poem *Hugh Selwyn Mauberley*, Ezra Pound cites words taken from the opening of the second Olympian Ode by Pindar: 'What God, what hero, aye, and what man shall we loudly praise?'[1] Pindar's ode addresses its praise to a Sicilian lord, Theron, on the occasion of his victory in an Olympic chariot race run in 476 BC; and the following lines couple Theron's name with those of a god, Zeus, and a hero, Hercules. As a model of encomiastic writing, the poem was imitated by many successors, among them Horace in an ode praising Augustus (i.xii, 'Quem virum aut heroa . . .'). Neither Pindar nor Horace displays any doubt that there was indeed a great man to be celebrated, as well as gods and heroes with whom he might appropriately be coupled. By contrast, Ezra Pound's questions clearly expect no positive answers. There are no gods or heroes any more; and the most a contemporary might deserve would be a victor's wreath of base metal. The epithet 'tin', derived from the interrogative adjectives (Τίν᾽, 'what') in Pindar's line, lowers the Greek to what

---

[1] *The Odes of Pindar*, ed. and trans. Sir John Sandys, Loeb Classical Library (Cambridge, Mass., 1915), Olympian Ode ii. Pound's Greek quotation alters Pindar's order, putting man (*andra*) first and god (*theon*) last.

I

Pound, in the same poem, characterises as the 'tawdry cheapness' of modern times: tin gods, tin heroes, tin men.

Pindar's Odes belong to that class of writings which bring poetry closest to the workings of praise as a speech-act in everyday life, with the authors addressing themselves directly to a contemporary – man or woman or god – in such forms as panegyric, love-song and hymn. But in narrative texts, too, older poets commonly speak in the language of praise, though more indirectly. They celebrate their heroes and heroines, both in their own voice and in the voices of characters in the story; and they portray worlds in which people generally, in addition to many other creatures and things, quite exceed normal expectations, as in the 'golden' world of poetry that Philip Sidney spoke of.[2] This is the superlative and magnifying manner known to Greek rhetoricians as 'auxetic', and familiar to them from the epics of Homer. The remoteness of such a manner from modern taste and practice can be appreciated in Marcel Proust's parody of Homeric auxesis, in the pretentious 'neo-Homeric manner' cultivated by Marcel's young friend Bloch. Introducing an aristocratic soldier to his sisters, Bloch says: 'I present to you the cavalier Saint-Loup, hurler of javelins, who is come for a few days from Doncières to the dwellings of polished stone, fruitful in heroes.'[3] Just so, in Homer as in much ancient and medieval epic and romance, eulogistic epithets, commonly conventional or formulaic, serve to magnify such

---

[2] 'Nature never set forth the earth in so rich tapestry as divers Poets have done, neither with plesant rivers, fruitful trees, sweet smelling flowers . . . Her world is brasen, the Poets only deliver a golden. But let those things alone and goe to man . . . and knowe whether shee have brought foorth so true a lover as *Theagines*, so constant a friende as *Pilades'*, *An Apology for Poetry*, ed. G. Gregory Smith, in *Elizabethan Critical Essays*, 2 vols. (Oxford, 1904), Vol. 1, pp. 156–7.

[3] *Within a Budding Grove: Part Two*, trans. C. K. Scott Moncrieff (London, 1949), p. 94. James Joyce has many auxetic parodies in *Ulysses*, as in his journalistic account of a public execution: 'Hard by the block stood the grim figure of the executioner . . . As he awaited the fatal signal he tested the edge of his horrible weapon by honing it upon his brawny forearm or decapitated in rapid succession a flock of sheep', *Ulysses* (London, 1937), p. 293.

things as buildings and regions, as well as brave heroes and beautiful heroines.

Homer and Pindar were early masters of the poetry of praise, many varieties of which were to flourish throughout the Middle Ages and Renaissance, in panegyrics, hymns, epics, romances, love lyrics, elegies, saints' lives, allegories and the like. Since that time – since the seventeenth century – the poetry of praise has generally been on the retreat in England as elsewhere. It has followed a course rather similar to that plotted for European fiction by Northrop Frye in his *Anatomy of Criticism*. Frye distinguished five fictional 'modes' according to 'the hero's power of action, which may be greater than ours, less, or roughly the same', proposing that 'European fiction, during the last fifteen centuries, has steadily moved its centre of gravity down the list.'[4] His list starts with myth, followed by romance and 'high mimetic', followed in turn by the low mimetic, which 'predominates in English literature from Defoe's time to the end of the eighteenth century', and finally by the 'ironic mode'. The decline of praise in English poetry maps quite well on to this schema, with Ezra Pound belonging to the last, ironic, phase. And ours is still, a century later, an age of irony. Many deepseated changes in society, politics, economics and religious belief have contributed to a culture more at home with tin men than with heroes. Readers of popular fiction, it is true, as well as filmgoers, can still very happily accept superheroes and superheroines; but literary taste generally rejects them. In poetry as in the higher fiction, what Frye calls the 'centre of gravity' has shifted. Praise is no longer a prime function of poetic activity.

I shall touch again upon these very large issues in my last chapters; but perhaps enough has been said for now to suggest why it is that many readers and critics nowadays have difficulty in coming to terms

4 Northrop Frye, *Anatomy of Criticism* (Princeton, N.J., 1957), pp. 33–5.

with laudatory writing when they encounter it in premodern poems, looking back at them as we do across such a wide modal gap. Critics often respond to this embarrassment by averting their eyes. So a recent scholar, after conceding that 'the first thing to be said about Pindar's *epinikia* [odes] is that they are poems of praise', remarks that 'praise is not an activity we rate very highly' and hurries on to look for more interesting things in the poems – more interesting than mere 'mercenary flattery'.[5] A similar bias or prejudice against praise can be detected, I believe, in many readings of medieval English poems. So it is a prime intention of the present study to pay more sympathetic attention to the auxetic character of their poetic idiom and to the laudatory function that such idiom commonly serves.

I also have a second and rather more controversial intention, directed against a current predilection for depreciatory or ironic readings of laudatory writing. It is true that the very prevalence of the language of praise in premodern times made it available for a variety of purposes, not all of them simple; and although the Latin critical tradition, as we shall see, made a sharp binary distinction between praise and blame, *laus* and *vituperatio*, it recognised that one could blame while pretending to praise ('laudis simulatione detrahere').[6] So there can be no question of doubting the existence of 'simulated' or ironic praise – which is indeed often signalled quite blatantly, as when Chaucer's Friar describes the summoner in his tale:

> He was, if I shal yeven hym his laude,
> A theef, and eek a somnour, and a baude.[7]

---

[5] William Fitzgerald, *Agonistic Poetry: The Pindaric Mode in Pindar, Horace, Hölderlin, and the English Ode* (Berkeley, Calif., 1987), p. 19. See, however, on an 'exchange economy of praise' in Pindar, Leslie Kurke, *The Traffic in Praise: Pindar and the Poetics of Social Economy* (Ithaca, N.Y., 1991). I refer to this book again in my last chapter.

[6] See below, pp. 24–5, 67.

[7] *Canterbury Tales*, III 1353–4. All citations of Chaucer are from *The Riverside Chaucer*, 3rd edn, general editor Larry D. Benson (Boston, Mass., 1987).

Here the *laus* is unmistakeably *vituperatio*. But the issue is not always as clear as that; and I shall draw attention to occasions where, in my opinion, modern critics can be found reading their own ironies and reservations into the text – as if, finding pure praise unpalatable, they add their own salt. At its worst, critics as well as students fall victim to a taste for debunking, and display what Northrop Frye called an 'ironic provincialism'.[8]

In what follows, before considering some selected areas of Old and Middle English poetry, I shall give an account of the old critical tradition that treated praise, *laus*, as chief among a poet's functions. The sheer strangeness of that idea, passed down from Antiquity to the Middle Ages and the Renaissance, serves as one reminder of how much times changed in the centuries between Pindar and Pound.

[8] Frye, *Anatomy of Criticism*, p. 62.

CHAPTER I

The poetics of praise

At one point in his *Poetics*, Aristotle takes occasion to give a brief account of the history of Greek poetry up to the time of writing, in the fourth century BC. He distinguishes two types of poet, according to their differing characteristics. Of these, 'the more dignified represented noble actions and those of noble men, the less serious those of low-class people; the one group produced at first invectives, the others songs praising gods and men'.[1] This first stage was followed, says Aristotle, by the narrative poems of Homer, among which he included the comic *Margites*, a now lost poem about a fool-hero. The *Margites* belongs to the low tradition of 'invective', while the *Iliad* and *Odyssey* belong with 'songs praising gods and men'. This schematic bit of literary history has failed to impress most readers of the *Poetics*, but it possesses a double interest for the present discussion. Aristotle sorts poems out according to a single criterion: whether they look upwards at high subjects or downwards at low ones. There is no room in his scheme for what would now seem a requisite third type, where the poet shares with his audience a horizontal view of their subject, neither up nor down.[2] Everything falls

---

[1] *Poetics*, 1448^b–1449^a, translated by D. A. Russell and M. Winterbottom in *Classical Literary Criticism* (Oxford, 1989), p. 55. In their note (p. 224), Russell and Winterbottom condemn as unhistorical both the series hymns-Homer-tragedy and the series invectives-Homer-comedy. But see n. 4 below.

[2] In this respect, Aristotle's scheme differs from that of Northrop Frye referred to in the Introduction, for in Frye's fourth mode 'the hero is one of us; we respond to a sense of

under one or other of the two original rubrics, praise or invective. This omission of a third type, however, remains characteristic of older thinking about poetry, medieval as well as ancient; nor do most of the actual poems produced in these periods seem to cry out against the omission. It is as if critics and poets alike were subject to some law of the missing middle.

Another noteworthy feature of Aristotle's historical sketch is his coupling of the two Homeric epics with 'songs praising gods and men', that is, with hymns and panegyrics. In an essay about early Greek views of poetry, the Classical scholar Gregory Nagy observes that 'all Greek literature – songs, poetry, prose – originates in *kleos*, the act of praising famous deeds'.[3] Epic and praise poetry have this *kleos* in common, though it takes different forms in each, as Nagy observes:

In the epic poetry of Homer just as in the praise poetry of Pindar, *kleos* denotes the act of praising, but in epic the praise takes place by the very process of narrating the deeds of heroes, predominantly in the third person. In praise poetry, the praise is more direct: here too *kleos* denotes that act of praising, but the praise in this case applies to the here-and-now, narrated generally in the second person.[4]

'Praise' can take many forms.

Aristotle's *Poetics* remained almost unknown in the medieval West until the thirteenth century, when a Latin translation was made from

---

his common humanity' (*Anatomy of Criticism*, p. 34). A little earlier in the *Poetics* (1448ª), Aristotle remarks that characters in poems 'must be better than are found in the world or worse or just the same' (trans. Russell and Winterbottom, p. 52); but this third possibility plays no part in his subsequent discussions.

[3] Gregory Nagy, 'Early Greek Views of Poets and Poetry', in George A. Kennedy (ed.), *The Cambridge History of Literary Criticism*, Vol. I: *Classical Criticism* (Cambridge, 1989), pp. 1–77, citing from p. 9.

[4] *Ibid.*, p. 12. Nagy comments on Aristotle's scheme more sympathetically than Russell and Winterbottom: 'It is as if praise poetry were the primordial form of epic. This is in fact what Aristotle says, that epic is descended from poetry praising gods and men' (p. 18).

an Arabic version of the Greek – a version in which, as we shall shortly see, praise figures much more prominently than it did in the original. In the meantime, however, there is another of Aristotle's writings that stands at the beginning of a more continuous intellectual tradition, his *Rhetoric*. This treatise, like the *Poetics*, became available to the West only in the thirteenth century; but it set out the main lines on which Aristotle's successors treated the subject, including the subject of praise, right up to modern times. Rhetoric taught the art of public speaking, and Aristotle distinguished three species according to how hearers were called upon to respond.[5] Two of them can be clearly distinguished by the occasions of their use: in courts of law a speaker will employ 'judicial' rhetoric to persuade judges of the guilt or innocence of the defendant, and in a political assembly he will use 'deliberative' rhetoric to support or oppose some future course of action. There remain, however, other occasions of a more miscellaneous kind where public speech has no such practical ends in view and requires no decisions of its hearers. Examples are funeral orations and speeches to greet a returning leader. It is such as these that Aristotle classes together under the heading *epideikticon*, or 'demonstrative'.[6] Praise and blame (*epainos* and *psogos*), and especially praise, are above all the business of this particular branch of rhetoric, the epideictic.

The Romans took over this threefold classification from Greek rhetoricians, employing the equivalent Latin terms, *judicialis*,

---

[5] *Rhetoric*, I.3 (1358ᵃ–1359ᵃ). For translation and commentary, see George A. Kennedy, *Aristotle on Rhetoric: A Theory of Civic Discourse* (Oxford, 1991).

[6] Aristotle's main discussion is in chapter 9 of Book I. On epideictic rhetoric in Antiquity, see Theodore C. Burgess, *Epideictic Literature* (New York, 1987), originally published in *University of Chicago Studies in Classical Philology*, 3 (1902), 89–261; D. A. Russell and N. G. Wilson (eds.), *Menander Rhetor: Edited with Translation and Commentary* (Oxford, 1981), pp. xviii–xxix; George A. Kennedy, 'The Genres of Rhetoric', in Stanley E. Porter (ed.), *Handbook of Classical Rhetoric in the Hellenistic Period, 330 B.C.–A.D. 400* (Leiden, 1997), pp. 43–50. For a more general account, see Brian Vickers, *In Defence of Rhetoric* (Oxford, 1988), pp. 53–62.

deliberativus and, for epideictic, *demonstrativus*. Medieval readers
would have encountered it in the early Latin handbooks of rhetoric
most widely studied in the schools, the anonymous *Rhetorica ad
Herennium* and the *De Inventione* of Cicero. Thus: 'Tria genera sunt
causarum quae recipere debet orator: demonstrativum, delibera-
tivum, iudiciale. Demonstrativum est quod tribuitur in alicuius personae laudem vel vituperationem' ('There are three kinds of causes
which the speaker must treat: Epideictic, Deliberative, and Judicial.
The epideictic kind is devoted to the praise or censure of some particular person').[7] The two terms *laus* and *vituperatio* recur constantly in
other Latin discussions of epideictic. In his intelligent account of the
threefold classification, Quintilian observes that the epideictic has no
monopoly of *laus* or *vituperatio*, but he is content with that traditional
characterisation nonetheless, even preferring to speak of *laudativum*
rather than *demonstrativum*.[8] The latter continued to be the regular term, however. In his *Etymologiae*, Isidore of Seville explained
that 'demonstrative' oratory is so called 'because it "demonstrates"
each thing either by praising or censuring it' ('quod unamquamque
rem aut laudando aut vituperando demonstrat').[9] Alcuin cites
Cicero's *De Inventione*: 'Demonstrativum genus est, quod tribuitur
in alicuius certae personae laudem vel vituperium' ('The demonstrative kind is devoted to the praise or censure of some particular

---

[7] *Ad C. Herennium De Ratione Dicendi*, ed. and trans. Harry Caplan, Loeb Classical Library
(Cambridge, Mass., 1964), I.ii.2. Almost the same in *De Inventione*, ed. and trans. H. M.
Hubbell, Loeb Classical Library (Cambridge, Mass., 1949), I.v.7.
[8] Quintilian, *Institutio Oratoria*, III.iv.12: 'Est igitur, ut dixi, unum genus, quo laus ac vituperatio continentur, sed est appellatum a parte meliore laudativum. (Idem alii demonstrativum
vocant)' ('There is then, as I have said, one kind concerned with praise and blame, but it is
called "laudative" after its better side. (Others call it "demonstrative")'). Cited from Quintilian, *The Orator's Education, Books 3–5*, ed. and trans. Donald A. Russell, Loeb Classical
Library (Cambridge, Mass., 2001). Quintilian goes on to explain the term *demonstrativum*:
'praise and blame demonstrate the nature of anything' (III.iv.14). I cite Quintilian, an author
largely unavailable in the Middle Ages, for his statements of common Latin rhetorical
teachings.
[9] Isidore of Seville, *Etymologies, Book II*, ed. and trans. Peter K. Marshall (Paris, 1983), II.4.5.

person').[10] The tradition continued throughout the Middle Ages and beyond. In the first vernacular English rhetoric treatise (1553), Thomas Wilson has a lengthy exposition of the 'Oracion demonstrative', which 'standeth either in praise, or dispraise of some one man, or of some one thyng, or of some one deede doen'.[11] Even as late as the 1920s, James Joyce incorporated specimens of all three types of oratory into the Aeolus episode of *Ulysses*. Epideictic is represented by passages from a newspaper report of a speech in praise of Ireland: 'in the peerless panorama of Ireland's portfolio, unmatched, despite their wellpraised prototypes in other vaunted prize regions, for very beauty . . .' etc.[12] The company assembled in the newspaper office takes a very twentieth-century view of such windy praise: 'High falutin stuff. Bladderbags', thinks Leopold Bloom, and Simon Dedalus exclaims 'Shite and onions!'

Though the rhetoricians regularly couple *vituperatio* with *laus*, they devote almost all their attention to the latter, commonly contenting themselves with remarking, as Aristotle does, that methods of dispraise can easily be inferred from what has been said about its opposite.[13] Their discussions of praise extend over a wide range of occasions and objects. Praise of individual persons or gods naturally takes pride of place. Aristotle gives quite a detailed summary of the virtues and other honourable qualities that an epideictic orator may

---

[10] Alcuin, *Dialogus de Rhetorica et Virtutibus*, in *Patrologia Latina*, Vol. 101, col. 922.

[11] Thomas Wilson, *Arte of Rhetorique*, ed. Thomas J. Derrick (New York, 1982), pp. 42–76, citing from p. 42. On Renaissance epideictic, see O. B. Hardison Jr, *The Enduring Monument: A Study of the Idea of Praise in Renaissance Literary Theory and Practice* (Westport, Conn., 1962).

[12] James Joyce, *Ulysses* (London, 1937), pp. 114–17, citing from p. 117. Judicial rhetoric is represented by a defending lawyer's speech (p. 130) and deliberative by a speech on the Irish Language movement (pp. 131–3). See Vickers, *In Defence of Rhetoric*, pp. 391–3, noting Joyce's consultation of rhetorical manuals (pp. 388–9).

[13] *Rhetoric*, 1.9.41 (1368ᵃ). Similarly *Ad Herennium*, III.vi.10: 'The topics on which praise is founded will, by their contraries, serve us as the bases for censure.' Also Cicero, *De Inventione*, II.lix.177; Quintilian, *Institutio Oratoria*, IV.vii.19–23.

single out (*Rhetoric*, 1.9.3–37). The Latin handbooks speak also of
external circumstances (descent, wealth and the like), as well as physical qualities such as beauty and strength. The *Ad Herennium* sums
up: 'Laus igitur potest esse rerum externarum, corporis, animi' ('The
following, then, can be subject to praise: External circumstances,
Physical attributes, and Qualities of character').[14] But the theory of
praise also extended to the non-human. Aristotle included here both
inanimate objects and lower animals (*Rhetoric*, 1.9.1), and Quintilian observed that buildings, cities and countries may be praised as
well as men (*Institutio*, III.vii.26–7). The range of possible subjects
is displayed in two linked Greek treatises of about AD 300 which are
devoted exclusively to epideictic. The *Peri Epideiktikon*, ascribed to
Menander, offers prescriptions for the praise of Gods, emperors and
governors, and of countries, cities and harbours, as well as advice
on how to speak eulogistically on occasions such as arrivals, departures, birthdays, marriages and funerals.[15] Another such treatise, the
Progymnasmata or 'Preliminary Exercises' formerly ascribed to Hermogenes, specifies topics of praise for a similar variety of subjects,
including here owls and olive trees. This text was translated from
the Greek by Priscian, and his Latin version, known as the *Praeex-
ercitamina*, was widely studied in medieval schools as a supplement
to Priscian's standard Grammar.[16] Writing in the sixteenth century,
Thomas Wilson follows suit. An 'Oracion demonstrative', he says,
may praise 'menne, Countreis, Citees, Places, Beastes, Hilles, Rivers,

[14] *Ad Herennium*, I.vi.10 (and see Caplan's note, p. 174). So also Cicero, *De Inventione*, II.lix.177–8.
[15] Russell and Wilson (eds.), *Menander Rhetor*, gives a Greek text and complete English translation.
[16] The *Progymnasmata* is translated complete from the Greek by C. S. Baldwin in his *Medieval Rhetoric and Poetic* (New York, 1929), pp. 23–38, with pp. 30–3 on encomia. On this type of treatise, see Russell and Wilson (eds.), *Menander Rhetor*, pp. xxv–xxix. On Hermogenes and his influence, see Annabel M. Patterson, *Hermogenes and the Renaissance: Seven Ideas of Style* (Princeton, N.J., 1970).

Houses, Castles, dedes doen by worthy men, and pollicies invented by greate warriers'.[17]

Rhetoricians devoted attention to the methods and devices by which such praise might be most eloquently expressed. Aristotle treats the matter briefly towards the end of his main discussion of epideictic (*Rhetoric*, 1.9.38–9, 1368ª). One may stress the singularity of a subject, or contrast him with ordinary mortals, or compare him with other great men – a very common method in practice, this last. Aristotle's general term for the function of such devices is *auxesis*, a term which literally means 'increase' and refers in rhetorical contexts to exaggeration.[18] An epideictic orator, when he praises something, will 'magnify' it, both in the old sense of that word ('My soul doth magnify the Lord') and in the modern sense by making it bigger. Auxesis, though not confined to the epideictic, is most at home there because, Aristotle explains, epideictic oratory addresses matters not themselves in dispute; so its business is to invest existing facts with greatness or beauty, not to argue judicially about past events or, deliberatively, about policies for the future (1.9.39, III.17.3). The Latin term corresponding to *auxesis* was *amplificatio*, and Classical Latin handbooks such as the *Ad Herennium* speak of *amplificatio* in this sense.[19] Both the Greek and the Latin terms crop up in the writings of English Renaissance rhetoricians. Thomas Wilson has the first recorded use in English of *amplification* as a rhetorical

---

[17] *Arte of Rhetorique*, ed. Derrick, p. 42.

[18] On the meaning and use of *auxesis* in Greek rhetoric, see the entry in R. Dean Anderson Jr, *Glossary of Greek Rhetorical Terms* (Leuven, 2000), pp. 26–7. Latin writers occasionally adopt the term: see the entries *s.v.* in *Thesaurus Linguae Latinae* and *Dictionary of Medieval Latin from British Sources*. The latter cites Bede, commenting on Genesis 18.11 (on Abraham and Sara): 'ad faciendam auxesim potentiae caelestis "ambo" dicit esse "seniores"' ('in order to magnify the power of heaven, he says that "both" were "old"'). The term may also refer more specifically to a gradual, step-by-step, increase of 'magnification' in a sentence: see *OED s.v. Auxesis*, quotation from Puttenham.

[19] *Ad Herennium*, II.xxx.47–9. Quintilian has a long discussion, observing that 'the whole power of the orator lies in Amplification (*augendo*) and Attenuation (*minuendo*)', *The Orator's Education, Books 6–8*, ed. and trans. Donald A. Russell, Loeb Classical Library (Cambridge, Mass., 2001), VIII.iii.89ff. See Russell's comments on p. 303.

term. He treats the subject at length, as the art of 'augmentynge' or (for dispraise) 'diminishynge': 'He that can prayse or dispraise any thynge plentifullye, is able most copiouslye to exaggerate any matter.'[20] Another rhetorician, Henry Peacham, gives a charmingly frank account of the process in his *Garden of Eloquence* (1577): 'By the figure, auxesis, the orator doth make a low dwarf a tall fellow . . . of pebble stones, pearls; and of thistles, mighty oaks.'[21]

When Aristotle spoke of *auxesis*, he evidently had in mind those occasions when an orator praises a real person or thing. In such cases, rhetorical exaggerations stand to be measured, so to speak, against the known realities of a hero, a city or whatever. But there were also occasions when rhetoricians dealt in imaginary cases, magnifying non-existent people or things; and in such exercises, auxesis is to be taken somewhat differently, as departing from some generally understood norm – say, what one would expect of an average city. So taken, auxesis plays a large part also in many old poems, poems which represent their imagined worlds in heightened or magnified form, perhaps down to the smallest details. When water is poured out in Homer's *Odyssey*, it is not from an ordinary bowl but from a 'beautiful golden ewer'. It might seem odd to speak of Homer 'praising' the bowl, but this is certainly a case of 'auxesis'. The term, along with the adjective 'auxetic', deserves to be revived; and I shall use it in the present study, since it will serve to cover cases of 'magnification' where praise as a direct speech-act is not in question, as well as cases where it is.

From its beginnings, epideictic had a closer kinship with poetry than had the other two branches of rhetoric.[22] Classical rhetoricians such

---

[20] *Arte of Rhetorique*, ed. Derrick, pp. 240–66, citing from p. 244. 'Copiousness' was a Renaissance stylistic ideal.
[21] Cited by *OED s.v. Auxesis*. See also the entry for *Auxetic*.
[22] See Burgess, *Epideictic Literature*, pp. 166–94; Russell and Wilson (eds.), *Menander Rhetor*, pp. xxxi–xxxiv; and Ruth Webb, 'Poetry and Rhetoric', in Porter (ed.), *Handbook of Classical Rhetoric*, pp. 339–69.

as Aristotle and Cicero were concerned not with literature but with speech-making, especially as practised in law courts and deliberative assemblies. But with the decline of those institutions in late Antiquity, the teaching of rhetoric came to lose many of its practical applications.[23] So epideictic, unaffected by these historical changes, acquired a greater relative importance, and it began to extend its range, addressing itself, among other things, to the composition of poetry. By about the year AD 300 the Greek rhetorician 'Hermogenes' could claim that all poetry, from Homer onwards, belonged within the province of the epideictic.[24] Hence the two arts of Rhetoric and Poetic, distinct in Aristotle's treatises, draw together to establish a rhetorical concept of poetry, in which throughout the Middle Ages epideictic values prevail. In the Latin of the medieval West, *laus* and *vituperatio* play a prominent part both in treatises on poetry and in comments on individual poets. This is one of the arguments of Curtius's great book *European Literature and the Latin Middle Ages*. As Curtius writes:

Of the oratorical genres, the epideictic oration had by far the strongest influence upon medieval poetry. Its principal subject matter is eulogy. The division of rhetoric which pertained to it was expanded and methodized by the Neo-Sophists. As subjects of eulogy this later period recognized gods, human beings, countries, cities, animals, plants (laurel, olive, rose), seasons, virtues, arts, professions. Even this list of subjects suggests how close the contact between poetry and the rhetoric of eulogy could be.[25]

Many medieval Latin writings on poetry testify to this 'contact between poetry and the rhetoric of eulogy', among them the Arts of Poetry written in the twelfth and early thirteenth centuries, notably

---

[23] See E. R. Curtius, *European Literature and the Latin Middle Ages*, trans. Willard R. Trask (London, 1953), pp. 69, 154–5.

[24] Burgess, *Epideictic Literature*, p. 93. See also Webb, 'Poetry and Rhetoric'.

[25] Curtius, *European Literature*, p. 155. His subsequent discussion of panegyrical topics includes chapters on 'Heroes and Rulers' and on 'The Ideal Landscape'.

Matthew of Vendôme's *Ars Versificatoria*, Geoffrey of Vinsauf's *Poetria Nova* and John of Garland's *Parisiana Poetria*.[26] These treatises are essentially practical guides to the writing of Latin poetry by *clerici*, so they do not go in for general statements about the art; but they betray at many points their assumption that poetic discourse specialises in *laus*, as well as its opposite. Thus, whereas at the beginning of his *Ars*, Matthew speaks of the poetic epithet as 'pertinens ad bonum vel ad malum vel ad indifferens' (1.2), there is no place in what follows for the *indifferens*. Going on to discuss types of poetic opening, Matthew characterises his first examples (of uses of zeugma) under only two heads, either praise or dispraise: *ad laudem* or *approbationem*, or else *ad opprobium*.[27] Similarly, in his extensive discussion of description, Matthew gives seven long models of *descriptio personarum* (1.50–8), five of which, he explains, 'are directed at praise' ('procedunt ad praeconium') and the other two 'ad vituperium' (1.59). His examples praise a pope, Caesar, Ulysses, Marcia Cato and Helen, while vituperation is reserved for the rogue Davus and the old hag Beroe – the description of this last inviting comparison with the adjacent encomium on the beautiful young Helen.[28] In what follows, Matthew recommends the copious piling up of epithets in laudatory descriptions especially (1.63, 71), and also in dispraise; for 'the qualities of the inner man, such as reasonableness, good faith, patience, honesty,

---

[26] The *Ars Versificatoria* and the *Poetria Nova* are edited by E. Faral in his *Les Arts Poétiques du XIIe et du XIIIe Siècle* (Paris, 1924). For John of Garland's treatise, see *The 'Parisiana Poetria' of John of Garland*, ed. and trans. Traugott Lawler (New Haven, Conn., 1974). For general descriptions and summaries, see J. J. Murphy, 'The Arts of Poetry and Prose', chapter 2 in Alastair Minnis and Ian Johnson (eds.), *The Cambridge History of Literary Criticism*, Vol. II: *The Middle Ages* (Cambridge, 2005). The rhetorical sources of these treatises are mainly the *Ad Herennium* and the *De Inventione* (Faral, *Les Arts Poétiques*, p. 99).

[27] *Ars Versificatoria*, 1.7–11 (and cf. 13). Caesar is to be praised, Verres not (1.9–10).

[28] *Ars Versificatoria*, 1.56–8. See Faral, *Les Arts Poétiques*, p. 77. 1.67 speaks of *approbatio formae* as requiring amplification particularly for female subjects. Cf. IV.18 on portrayal of women either *ad approbationem* or *ad vituperium*.

wrongdoing, pride, lustfulness and other such epithets of the inner
man, that is, the soul, are to be expressed *ad laudem vel ad vituperium*'
(1.74).

John of Garland and Geoffrey of Vinsauf treat *descriptio* more
briefly. Geoffrey gives a model portrait of a beautiful woman and her
clothes (563–621), but he dismisses the topic as 'worn out and old'
(622–3) and supplements it only with one – equally encomiastic –
description of a less common subject, a royal banquet. Description,
for Geoffrey, is just one of several methods of 'amplification';
and his comments on amplification itself, as Faral observes, concern rather lengthening than heightening: 'longius ut sit opus' ('so
that the work is longer').[29] Yet lengthening very often and very
naturally involves heightening. Indeed, it was from one of Geoffrey's examples of amplification that Chaucer derived his comic
moment of extravagant rhetorical auxesis, when the Nun's Priest
exalts the fate of Chantecleer in the lofty language of Vinsauf's
lament over the death of King Richard I.[30] Elsewhere, both Geoffrey
and John of Garland show their acquaintance with the true meaning
of amplification in Classical rhetoric. In their discussions of hyperbole (*superlatio*), they employ the technical terms *augere* and *minuere*
for increase and diminishing of a subject. So Quintilian described
hyperbole as 'decens veri superiectio: virtus eius ex diverso par,
augendi atque minuendi' ('an appropriate exaggeration of the truth.
It has equal value in the opposite functions of Amplification and

---

[29] *Poetria Nova*, l. 229. See Faral, *Les Arts Poétiques*, p. 61, and Curtius, *European Literature*,
p. 492: '*Amplificatio* as *auxesis* is elevation and belongs to the vertical dimension, *amplificatio*
as *dilatare* to the horizontal.'

[30] *Canterbury Tales*, VII 3347–54. Vinsauf's lament, an example of amplification by apostrophe, praises Richard in extravagant terms, e.g. ll. 390–4. John of Garland acknowledges
the connection between lengthening and heightening in his comment on *circumlocutio*:
'Periphrasis also extends material, and it will be necessary when we intend to praise or
blame by pointing out the virtues and good qualities or enormities and vices of people's
characters', IV.369–72, trans. Lawler.

Attenuation').[31] Geoffrey says of hyperbole: 'Mirifice laudes minuit iste vel auget; / Et placet excessus, quem laudet et auris et usus' ('This mode of expression diminishes or magnifies praises to a remarkable degree; and exaggeration is a source of pleasure when both ear and good usage commend it').[32] John of Garland employs the same terminology: 'Superlatio est oratio superans veritatem alicuius augendi minuendive causa' ('Hyperbole is an expression that goes beyond the truth, either to magnify or belittle'), giving a poetic couplet as an example: 'Sidera Parisius famoso nomine tangit, / Humanumque genus ambitus urbis habet' ('The famous name of Paris reaches to the stars, and its borders contain the human race').[33] Like rhetoricians, poets deal in what Quintilian called 'an appropriate exaggeration of the truth', departing from it either by under- or by over-praise. They too are concerned not with truth but with persuasion.

A different kind of text makes the same point in a general characterisation of poetry, with emphasis upon the persuasive effect of hyperbole. The encyclopaedic *Speculum Doctrinale* of Vincent of Beauvais, citing the Arabic authority al-Farabi, describes *poetica* thus: 'Poeticae proprium est sermonibus suis facere imaginari aliquid pulchrum vel foedum quod non est ita, ut auditor credat, et aliquid abhorreat vel appetat. Quamvis cum certum sit non ita esse in veritate, animi tamen audentium eriguntur ad horrendum vel appetendum quod imaginantur' ('The special business of poetry is, by its utterances, to make people imagine something to be more beautiful or

---

[31] *Institutio Oratoria*, VIII.vi.67. Quintilian speaks of hyperbole as a form of *amplificatio* at XVIII.iv.29.

[32] *Poetria Nova*, ll. 1020–1. Cf. ll. 1661–3.

[33] *Parisiana Poetria*, VI.298–301. Ben Jonson wrote of *superlatio*: 'There are words, that doe as much raise a style, as others can depresse it. Superlation, and overmuchnesse amplifies. It may be above faith, but never above a meane', *Discoveries* (1641), ed. G. B. Harrison (London, 1923), p. 77. Like Quintilian, Jonson requires exaggeration to be *decens*, 'never above a meane', a condition neglected by John of Garland.

repulsive than it really is, in such a way that the hearer, believing, will either shun or seek it. Although it is certainly not so in truth, yet the minds of the listeners will be roused either to shun or seek what they imagine').[34]

This doctrine, that poets deal particularly in *laus* and *vituperatio* and that the function of poetry is thereby to make virtue attractive and vice repellent, gained support in the thirteenth century from a remarkable Latin version of Aristotle's *Poetics*. In 1256 a monk living in Toledo, Hermann the German, translated into Latin the so-called 'Middle Commentary' on the *Poetics* produced in Islamic Spain by the Arab scholar Averroes (1126–98).[35] Having passed through the filters of an Arabic commentary on an Arabic translation, much of the Greek original is barely recognisable; but a notable survivor is Aristotle's little excursus on the history of poetry, discussed at the beginning of this chapter. His classification of poems there under the two rubrics of praise and invective played no significant part in the general argument of the original treatise, but Averroes takes it up and makes it a central theme.[36] He announces it at the very beginning, when he ascribes to Aristotle the following general truth: 'Omne itaque poema et omnis oratio poetica aut est vituperatio aut est laudatio', that is, 'Every poem

---

[34] Vincentius Bellovacensis, *Speculum Doctrinale* (Dvaci, 1624), facsimile (Graz, 1965), Book III, Chapter cix (column 287). See Hardison, *Enduring Monument*, pp. 13–14.

[35] The Middle Commentary is translated complete from Hermann's Latin, with a useful introduction, by O. B. Hardison in Alex Preminger, O. B. Hardison Jr and Kevin Kerrane (eds.), *Classical and Medieval Literary Criticism: Translations and Interpretations* (New York, 1974), pp. 341–82. See also A. J. Minnis and A. B. Scott, *Medieval Literary Theory and Criticism, c. 1100–c. 1375: The Commentary Tradition* (Oxford, 1988), pp. 277–307; Minnis and Johnson (eds.), *Cambridge History of Literary Criticism*, pp. 171–2, 252–5; and Gilbert Dahan, 'Notes et Textes sur la Poétique au Moyen Âge', *Archives d'Histoire Doctrinale et Littéraire du Moyen Âge*, 47 (1980), 171–239.

[36] See Hardison, in Preminger, Hardison and Kerrane (eds.), *Classical and Medieval Literary Criticism*, p. 344: 'Averroes has transposed [Aristotle's] notion that the original poetic forms were encomia and lampooning verses from Chapter 4 to Chapter 1 and converted it from an observation about primitive poems to a categorial assertion about poetry in general.'

and every poetic utterance is either blame or praise.'[37] Accordingly, Averroes treats Aristotle's main topic, tragedy, not as drama (with which medieval Arabs were unacquainted), but as *carmen laudativum* or 'poetry of praise'. Hermann must have found the many passages on this theme in his Arabic original very easy to render into the familiar terminology of Latin epideictic; nor would he have experienced any difficulty with Averroes's equally un-Aristotelian stress on the direct moral function of poetry. Poets 'intendunt instigare ad quasdam actiones que circa voluntaria consistunt et retrahere a quibusdam' ('have as their purpose to urge men on to certain actions that are subject to the will, and to dissuade them from others').[38] Such was, indeed, the standard medieval justification for poetic auxesis. Poets depart from the truth and exaggerate both their praises and their blames, but only in order that readers may be drawn to virtue and repelled from vice.[39]

Shortly after Hermann produced his translation, another rendering of the *Poetics* was made by William of Moerbecke, this time from the Greek; but it was Hermann's version that held the field for some three hundred years thereafter.[40] It was first printed in Venice, 1481, and reprinted in 1515 and several times thereafter, and as late as 1594 Torquato Tasso defended its doctrines against the

---

[37] P. 41 in the edition of the Latin text by L. Minio-Paluello: *De Arte Poetica cum Averrois Expositione*, Corpus Philosophorum Medii Aevi: Aristoteles Latinus XXXIII, 2nd edn (Leiden, 1968).

[38] Ed. Minio-Paluello, p. 43.

[39] Hermann, p. 44, speaks of poets altering their material towards either of two extremes ('ad utramque duarum extremitatum') for purposes of either praise or blame. For further discussion of Averroistic poetics, see Judson Boyce Allen, *The Ethical Poetic of the Later Middle Ages* (Toronto, 1982), pp. 19–37; and Vincent Gillespie on 'affective poetics', in Minnis and Johnson (eds.), *Cambridge History of Literary Criticism*, pp. 161–78.

[40] On Hermann's version in Renaissance Italy, see Bernard Weinberg, *A History of Literary Criticism in the Italian Renaissance*, 2 vols. (Chicago, 1961), Vol. I, pp. 352–61. Hardison (p. 347 in Preminger, Hardison and Kerrane (eds.), *Classical and Medieval Literary Criticism*) notes Coluccio Salutati's description of the poet as 'vir optimus laudandi vituperandi peritus' ('an excellent man, skilled in praising and in blaming').

attacks of Castelvetro.[41] The persistence of epideictic ways of thinking through the sixteenth century may be seen in one of the earliest
vernacular English treatises on poetry, Puttenham's *Arte of English
Poesie* (1589). Its first book, 'Of Poets and Poesie', is largely devoted
to a survey of 'all the commended fourmes of the auncient Poesie'.[42]
The author describes poets as 'in deede the trumpetters of all praise
and also of slaunder (not slaunder, but well deserved reproach)'
(p. 36); and his account of the genres of Classical poetry distinguishes accordingly. He traces the 'reprehensive' tradition from
satire to the Old and New Comedies and also (unlike Aristotle)
tragedy; but poetry had its chief origin, he says, in the 'laud, honour,
and glory of the immortall gods', to be followed by celebration of
'the worthy gests of noble princes', great men who receive 'a second degree of laude' (pp. 25, 37). He summarises the tradition of
'written laudes' thus: 'So have you how the immortall gods were
praised by hymnes, the great Princes and heroicke personages by
ballades of praise called *Encomia*, both of them by historicall reports
of great gravitie and maiestie, the inferiour persons by other slight
poemes' (p. 45).

The evidences from medieval rhetoric and poetic, considered so far,
could be supplemented from very many commentaries on individual
works; for in these too *laus* figures largely, along with *vituperatio*.
The Latin commentaries to be noticed here, with one notable exception, concern poems that are themselves in Latin. So they again must

[41] Hardison, in Preminger, Hardison and Kerrane (eds.), *Classical and Medieval Literary Criticism*, p. 348. *OED s.vv. Laudative a.* and *sb.* and *Vituperation* has quotations illustrating the persistence of such terminology.
[42] Ed. G. Gregory Smith, in his *Elizabethan Critical Essays*, 2 vols. (Oxford, 1904), Vol. II, pp. 1–193. The survey occupies pp. 25–61 (chapters X to XXX). Chapters XXIII to XXX concern occasional genres such as celebrations of births or marriages and laments for the dead. The author's better-known history of English poetry follows in chapter XXXI.

indicate only how the educated minority understood, or were supposed to understand, poetry – but including, it may be supposed, poems in the vernacular.

Epic poetry, being concerned with 'the worthy gests of noble princes', naturally invited interpretation *ad laudem*. Thus early commentaries on Virgil's *Aeneid* read it as a poem in praise of Aeneas. The fourth-century grammarian Donatus stresses this early in his commentary:

> Primus igitur et ante omnia sciendum est quod materiae genus Maro noster adgressus sit; hoc enim non nisi laudativum est, quod idcirco incognitus est et latens, quia miro artis genere laudationis ipse, dum gesta Aeneae percurreret, incidentia quoque aliarum materiarum genera complexus ostenditur, nec tamen ipsa aliena a partibus laudis; nam idcirco adsumpta sunt, ut Aeneae laudationi proficerent.

> (So first and foremost one must appreciate what kind of subject our Maro is dealing with. This is nothing other than one of praise – although the fact may be obscure and difficult to see because, with a wonderful kind of laudatory art, he evidently includes other incidental kinds of matter while recounting the deeds of Aeneas. But these are not really alien to those parts concerned with praise, for they are intended precisely to further the praise of Aeneas.)[43]

Writing about Homer's *Iliad* in the early twelfth century, Conrad of Hirsau observes that 'intentio eius tota pendit in laude Grecorum et confusione Troianorum' ('his intention is entirely centred on praise of the Greeks and the confusion of the Trojans').[44] Praise and

---

[43] Cited from *Donati Interpretationes Vergilianae*, ed. Henricus Georgius (Leipzig, 1905), by Hardison, *Enduring Monument*, p. 206, discussed on p. 33, together with similar comments by Fulgentius on Virgil's 'laudis materia'. Cf. the twelfth-century commentary on the *Aeneid* ascribed to Bernardus Silvestris, on the 'magnification' of Aeneas: Minnis and Scott, *Medieval Literary Theory and Criticism*, pp. 151–52. Gavin Douglas, in his translation of the poem, blames Chaucer for showing Aeneas in an unfavourable light, where Virgil had done all he could 'Eneas for to loif and magnify', *Virgil's Aeneid Translated into Scottish Verse*, ed. David F. C. Coldwell, 4 vols, Scottish Text Society (1957–64), Prologue, l. 21.

[44] *Accessus ad Auctores: Bernard d'Utrecht, Conrad d'Hirsau Dialogus super Auctores*, ed. R. B. C. Huygens (Leiden, 1970), p. 118.

dispraise also figure quite largely in the so-called *accessus* or introductions to individual authors produced by twelfth-century teachers
of *grammatica*.[45] Striking examples are the three introductions to
Ovid's *Heroides* printed by Huygens (pp. 29–33). All three interpret
Ovid's intention in similar terms: he wished to commend chaste and
virtuous love, as in the exemplary case of Penelope, and to repre-
hend foolish or illicit love, as in the cases of Canace or Phillis. The
general aim of the collection is to delight and instruct the reader by
praising virtue and blaming vice: 'in singulis epistolis, aut laudando
castum amorem, ut in hac: *Hanc tua Penelope*, aut vituperando inces-
tum amorem, ut in illa: *Quam nisi tu dederis*' ('in individual letters,
either praising chaste love, as in "This letter your Penelope . . .",
or attacking unchaste love, as in "Unless you give this . . .""). The
intentio auctoris is moral, and he achieves his intention *laudando* and
vituperando.[46]

Examples of this kind could easily be multiplied, but I devote
the rest of this chapter to one commentary which is of particular
interest in the present context, since it treats a vernacular text – not
in English but in Italian.[47] This is the massive Latin commentary
on Dante's *Commedia* written about 1375 by Benvenuto da Imola.[48]
In his Introduction, Benvenuto cites from the Averroistic *Poetics*
of Hermann the German: 'Omne poema et omnis oratio poetica

---

[45] Edited by Huygens; discussed and translated by Minnis and Scott, *Medieval Literary Theory and Criticism*, pp. 12–36.

[46] Huygens, p. 32. The references are to the letters of Penelope (*Heroides* I.1) and of Phaedra (IV.1). Medieval commentators make similar statements about the intention and method of satirical poetry, as in twelfth-century commentaries on Horace's *Satires*: see Suzanne Reynolds, *Medieval Reading: Grammar, Rhetoric and the Classical Text* (Cambridge, 1996), pp. 146–8.

[47] Alastair Minnis discusses late medieval commentaries on vernacular texts, variously in Latin, French, Italian and Spanish, in his book *Magister Amoris* (Oxford, 2001). He notices the paucity of commentaries on English texts (pp. 298, 314–16).

[48] *Comentum super Dantis Aldigherij Comoedium*, ed. J. P. Lacaita, 5 vols. (Florence, 1887). I refer by volume and page numbers.

aut est laudatio, aut vituperatio; omnis enim actio et omnis mos non versatur nisi circa virtutem et vicium' ('Every poem and every poetic utterance is either praise or blame; for every action and every trait of character turns on nothing but either virtue or vice').[49] To these thoughts, ascribed to 'Aristoteles in sua Poetria', Benvenuto adds observations from 'Averroes commentator': it was noble souls who first devised songs to praise (*laudare*) good actions, and the less noble who sang to condemn (*vituperare*) bad ones.[50] Benvenuto continues: 'Nullus autem poetarum scivit excellentius aut efficatius laudare et vituperare quam perfectissimus poeta Dantes; laudavit siquidem virtutes et virtuosos, vituperavit vicia et viciosos' ('No poet has known better or more effectively to praise and blame than the supreme poet Dante, for he praised virtues and virtuous people and blamed vices and the vicious') (1 8). Accordingly, Benvenuto takes pains to point out places of *laus* and *vituperatio* in the *Commedia*. There prove to be many such, for Dante had no time for those who, as he said, 'visser sanza 'nfamia e sanza lodo' ('lived without infamy and without praise') (*Inferno*, III, 36).[51] These souls, the trimmers, are unworthy even of a place in Hell, and Virgil treats them with contempt:

> Fama di loro il mondo esser non lassa;
> Misericordia e giustizia li sdegna:
> Non ragionam di lor, ma guarda e passa.

(The world does not suffer that report of them shall live. Mercy and justice disdain them. Let us not speak of them, but look, and pass on.)

Inferno, III, 49–51

---

[49] *Ibid.*, 1 8. For Hermann's words, see above, p. 18. Cf. Minnis and Johnson (eds.), *Cambridge History of Literary Criticism*, pp. 253–4.

[50] *Comentum*, ed. Lacaita, 1 8. The thought goes back to Aristotle, *Poetics*, 1448[b].

[51] Citations and translations are taken from *The Divine Comedy*, ed. and trans. Charles S. Singleton, 6 vols. (Princeton, N.J., 1970–5).

It is a case of what I earlier called the law of the missing middle in medieval poetry.

Benvenuto finds 'vituperations' throughout all three cantiche of the poem. He notices, for instance, biting *invectivae* against the Genoese in *Inferno*, XXXIII, against Italy and Florence in *Purgatorio*, VI, and against modern popes in *Paradiso*, XXVII, where St Peter himself 'invehit contra successores eius'.[52] This last passage displays Dante's mastery of the art of rhetoric at its most vituperative:

> Quelli ch'usurpa in terra il luogo mio,
>   Il luogo mio, il luogo mio che vaca
> Ne la presenza del Figliuol di Dio,
> Fatt' ha del cimitero mio cloaca
>   Del sangue e de la puzza.

(He who on earth usurps my place, my place, my place, which in the sight of the Son of God is vacant, has made my burial-ground a sewer of blood and of stench.)

Paradiso, XXVII, 22–6

Dante has also another, cooler, manner of vituperation, and this bears more directly upon the present subject, for it takes the form of ironical praise. Among the uses of irony, according to Quintilian, are 'to blame with a pretence of praise and to praise with a pretence of blame' ('laudis . . . simulatione detrahere et vituperationis laudare'). Isidore of Seville, again, says that irony can be used 'when we praise one whom we wish to blame or blame one whom we wish to praise' ('aut cum laudamus eum quem vituperare volumus, aut vituperamus quem laudare volumus').[53] Thus, when Dante apostrophises the city

[52] *Comentum*, ed. Lacaita, II 546–7, III 179, 188, V 387, 389. See also, for example, Benvenuto's comments about the attacks on simoniacs in *Inferno*, XIX (II 31), on Pisa in *Inferno*, XXXIII (II 532) and on Christian kings in *Paradiso*, XIX (V 246).
[53] Quintilian, VIII.vi.5; Isidore, *Etymologies*, ed. Marshall, II.21.41.

of Florence at the beginning of *Inferno*, XXVI, Benvenuto notes his 'invectivam et ironiam' (II, 259):

> Godi, Fiorenza, poi che se' sì grande
> Che per mare e per terra batti l'ali,
> E per lo 'nferno tuo nome si spande!

(Rejoice, O Florence, since you are so great that over sea and land you beat your wings, and your name is spread though Hell!)

Inferno, XXVI, 1–3

At the end of his fragmentary *De Vulgari Eloquentia* (II xiv 2), Dante distinguishes two kinds of poetic subjects: those 'on the right', to be treated at length *persuasorie*, *gratulanter* and *laudabiliter*, and those 'on the left', for briefer treatment *dissuasorie*, *ironice* and *contemptive*.[54] To suggest, as I do in this book, that readers are sometimes overkeen to find ironies in medieval praise poetry is not to deny the occasional presence there of ironic or 'simulated' *laus*. Perhaps, though, old poets were inclined to mark such simulations more clearly than modern critics may suppose – as Dante does in the lines just quoted ('your name is spread through Hell!').

In the course of his *Vita Nuova*, Dante reports his resolution at that time to devote future writings to the praise (*loda*) of Beatrice; and the whole *Commedia* may be understood as a final fulfilment of that intention.[55] One has only to think of the vision of Beatrice at the centre of the divine pageant in *Purgatorio*, XXX, surely unsurpassed as an auxetic glorification of another human being. But there are

---

[54] On Dante's relation to traditions of vituperative writing in satire, see Suzanne Reynolds, 'Orazio Satiro (*Inferno* IV, 89): Dante, the Roman Satirists, and the Medieval Theory of Satire', in Z. G. Baranski (ed.), *Libri Poetarum in Quattuor Species Dividuntur: Essays on Dante and 'Genre'*, Supplement to *The Italianist*, 15 (1995), 128–44.

[55] *Vita Nuova*, VIII, 8–9, in *Le Opere di Dante*, ed. M. Barbi *et al.*, 2nd edn (Florence, 1960). See William Anderson, *Dante the Maker* (London, 1980), chapter 9, '*La Vita Nuova* and the Poetry of Praise', observing of Beatrice in *Purgatorio* that 'Christian art is revealed through Beatrice as an art of praise' (p. 317).

also many praises of other persons upon which Benvenuto remarks. When Dante *personaggio* addresses Currado Malaspina in *Purgatorio*, VIII, 121–32, the commentator notes that he 'extols the glory of his house' ('extollit gloriam suae domus') (III, 242). Elsewhere (V, 144), Benvenuto observes how Cacciaguida's invective against modern Florence in *Paradiso*, XVI, gains strength from being preceded by the speaker's praise of the city as it was in his own day (*Paradiso*, XV, 97–138). Medieval theory of satire held that the praise of virtue should go along with and so strengthen the satirists' attack on vice.[56]

The greatest set-piece of the 'stilo de la loda' in the *Commedia* is the double celebration of St Francis and St Dominic which occupies Cantos XI and XII of the *Paradiso*. In the first of these cantos, the Dominican Thomas Aquinas gives a eulogistic account of the life of St Francis (XI, 40–117), followed by two terzine praising his own founder, Dominic, as a worthy colleague of Francis – words which prompt Thomas to lament, in three final terzine, the decline of his own Dominican order in recent times (XI, 124–32). The same pattern, *laus* and concluding *vituperatio*, governs Canto XII. Here the Franciscan Bonaventura praises the life of St Dominic (XII, 46–105), devotes two terzine to his own founder as a worthy colleague of Dominic and concludes with a condemnation of most modern Franciscans (XII, 112–26). The structure is chiastic, with a member of one great order of friars praising the founder of its rival and blaming only brothers of his own. This serves to insure the praise, as well as the blame, against any suspicion of partiality, as Benvenuto notices. In a comment on Canto XII, he writes: 'Et hic nota quod auctor prudenter et caute inducit unum fratrem minorem, qui laudat vitam beati Dominici, et vituperat vitam suorum fratrum minorum, ut sic eius narratio plus

[56] See Paul Miller, in A. J. Minnis (ed.), *Gower's 'Confessio Amantis': Responses and Reassessments* (Cambridge, 1983), pp. 84, 96.

habeat fidei et veritatis' ('And notice here how the author wisely and circumspectly introduces a Franciscan brother to praise the life of the blessed Dominic and blame the life of his own Franciscan brothers, so that the good faith and truth of his words may be the more evident').[57]

Francis and Dominic were very different kinds of saint, but the two panels of Dante's laudatory diptych match each other in many details. Francis rose like a sun from the east (or so Assisi appears from Perugia, XI, 43–51), whereas Dominic was born in the west, in Spain, towards the setting sun (XII, 49–51); Francis was like a seraph in his ardour, Dominic like a cherub in his wisdom; and at exactly the same point in the two cantos, lines 61–3, Francis marries Poverty and Dominic espouses Faith. These comparisons between the two princes of the church, as well as the contrasts between them and their unworthy successors, follow the ancient tradition of epideictic, going back to Aristotle's *Rhetoric*, according to which comparison and contrast figure among its chief devices.[58] In both cantos, too, the speakers employ a highly elaborate narrative style, rich in metaphor and symbol, describing events in very roundabout ways. So the identity of Poverty, whom Francis marries, first mentioned simply as a 'donna' (XI, 58), is revealed only after fourteen lines of riddling allusion: she has been without a husband for more than 1,100 years; she was undisturbed when 'he who caused fear to all the world' (i.e. Julius Caesar) approached the simple fisherman Amyclas (an episode in Lucan's *Pharsalia*); and she alone wept with Christ upon the cross. These enigmas belong to the manner that Dante characterises as 'chiuso' (literally 'closed', XI, 73), a word glossed by Benvenuto

---

[57] *Comentum*, ed. Lacaita, v 75. Benvenuto makes a similar comment on Aquinas's speech in Canto XI: 'It is a better testimony and more easily credible when rival praises rival and blames his own people' (v 56).

[58] *Rhetoric*, (1368ª). Quintilian discusses *comparatio* in his section on amplification (VIII.iv.9–14), as does Geoffrey of Vinsauf, *Poetria Nova*, ll. 241–63.

with '*obscure*', an equivalent to the term used in the troubadour
trobar clus. Such a manner has been considered in many cultures to
be appropriate for ambitious kinds of panegyric.[59]

Few modern poets would rank praise among the functions of their
art. One of them has spoken of '*Laus / et vituperatio*, the worst /
remembered, least understood of the modes.'[60] But in Dante's day
these modes were well understood. Poets such as Dante and Chaucer
cultivated the arts of praise and blame according to principles laid
down in Antiquity and transmitted through the Latin Middle Ages
mainly in books of rhetoric and poetic, and in commentaries on verse
texts. Instruction in the schools taught such writers how to go about
the magnifications entailed by the business of praise. For poets and
orators alike, *laudatio* called upon all the resources of their art –
pulling out all the stops, as Dante does in Cantos XI and XII of his
Paradiso. As Quintilian observed, to praise a subject is to magnify it
and to adorn it: 'Proprium laudis est res amplificare et ornare.'[61]

---

[59] See Ruth Finnegan, *Oral Literature in Africa* (Oxford, 1970), p. 117: 'Most [African] praise
poetry, above all the official type, seems to adopt a more or less obscure and allusive style.'

[60] Geoffrey Hill, *The Triumph of Love, A Poem* (Harmondsworth, 1999), XXIII 5–7. The
poems in this sequence lean heavily towards either *laus* (e.g. no. LV, to the Virgin) or
vituperatio (e.g. no. CXIX, to 'MacSikker *et al.*').

[61] Quintilian, *Institutio Oratoria*, III.vii.6. In his *De Doctrina Christiana*, Augustine associates
rhetorical ornament and 'pulchra et splendida dictio' especially with praise and blame in
Christian teaching: *De Doctrina Christiana*, ed. and trans. R. P. H. Green (Oxford, 1995),
Book IV, Chapters xii–xxviii.

CHAPTER 2

Old English, especially *Beowulf*

Writings such as the *Poetria Nova* of Geoffrey of Vinsauf or Hermann's Averroistic *Poetics* addressed themselves to the writing and reading of Latin poetry, and they would have been accessible only to an educated minority trained in the disciplines of grammar and rhetoric. Yet what these treatises articulate about praise as a prime function of poetry also applies widely to early poetry in the vernaculars – upon which, after all, the teachings of such as Aristotle had been partly founded in the first place. Poets composing in unlearned languages did not need to be trained in the trivium (though some certainly were) to sound the note of praise. And so they insistently do – insistently, at least, to a modern ear.

Praise of gods, rulers and heroes evidently play a prominent part in the poetry of traditional societies, whether in medieval Europe or elsewhere. Many modern studies point to this conclusion. I have earlier quoted the opinion of one Classical scholar that *kleos*, the act of praising famous deeds, dominated the poetry and song of archaic Greece.[1] In their study *The Growth of Literature*, the Chadwicks compared the early writings of Greece with those of Britain, Ireland and Iceland. They observed that in these 'island literatures' also glorification of past heroes, panegyrics on living princes and the like

---

[1] See above, p. 7.

represented 'one of the most widely distributed types of poetry'.[2]
Much the same could be said of many non-European societies. The
stress placed by Averroes on praise in his reading of Aristotle has
plausibly been attributed to that scholar's familiarity with Arabic
poetry, 'whose early forms tend heavily to invective and encomiastic
verse'.[3] In the oral poetry of modern Africa, similarly, panegyric has
played a leading part:

> In the Zulu kingdoms of South Africa, every king or chief with pretensions
> to political power had his own praiser or *imbongi* among his entourage. At
> the more elaborate courts of West African kingdoms, there were often whole
> bands of poets, minstrels and musicians, each with his specialised task, and
> all charged with the duty of supporting the present king with ceremonial
> praise of his glory and the great deeds of his ancestors.[4]

Only about 30,000 lines of Old English verse have survived, and
most of these are to be found in just four late manuscripts, all of them
probably copied in monastic or cathedral scriptoria. So the sample
available today must be supposed to be biased in favour of religious
verse, much of it drawn from sources in Latin, especially the Latin
Bible. Among the authors of such poems, some were very likely
acquainted with the Latin rhetoricians' teaching about *laus* and may
have drawn upon it in their vernacular writings; it was summarised

---

[2] H. Munro Chadwick and N. Kershaw Chadwick, *The Growth of Literature*, Vol. 1: *The Ancient Literatures of Europe* (Cambridge, 1932), p. 42. On 'celebration poetry' (the Chadwicks' Type D), see especially pp. 37–42 and 341–57. On the primacy of panegyric in medieval Wales, see Minnis and Johnson (eds.), *Cambridge History of Literary Criticism*: chapters 12 and 19. On Old Norse, see *ibid.*, pp. 351–2.

[3] O. B. Hardison, in Alex Preminger, O. B. Hardison Jr and Kevin Kerrane (eds.), *Classical and Medieval Literary Criticism: Translations and Interpretations* (New York, 1974), p. 343. Averroes incorporated pieces of Arabic poetry into his version of the Greek, as can be seen in Hardison's translation.

[4] Ruth Finnegan, *Oral Poetry: Its Nature, Significance and Social Context* (Cambridge, 1977), pp. 188–9. See index under 'praise poetry'. Chapter 5 in Finnegan's earlier book, *Oral Literature in Africa* (Oxford, 1970), is devoted to panegyric, observing that 'in its specialized form panegyric is *the* type for court poetry and is one of the most developed and elaborate poetic genres in Africa', p. 111. Jeff Opland draws parallels between Anglo-Saxon poetry and that of Southern Africa: *Anglo-Saxon Oral Poetry: A Study of the Traditions* (New Haven, Conn., 2005).

by their countryman Alcuin.[5] Traces of such learning, however, are not often easy to distinguish, since the Germanic poetic tradition of alliterative verse was itself deeply committed to the language of praise and blame – as it had been, evidently, long before there was any question of Latin influence supervening. As one scholar has written: 'The function of poetry in early Germanic society seems to have been chiefly this: to distribute praise and blame . . . The songs of the scop had the central importance of defining and reinforcing the values of society by showing praiseworthy actions and their opposites.'[6] All surviving Anglo-Saxon poems, learned and unlearned alike, belong to the alliterative tradition, and all share a similar auxetic inheritance. Poets of every sort will be found magnifying their subjects, by direct praise or by forms of eulogistic reference. In the present chapter, I first take examples from some religious pieces which treat God, Old Testament heroes, and saints. I then consider the treatment of secular figures, past and present, including Beowulf. To *Beowulf* I devote particular attention, both because the poem is so rich in the language of praise and also because its representation of the hero has provoked disagreement among modern critics, some of whom detect ironies and reservations where others see just praise.

The Middle Ages had one great example of poetry in praise of their God, in the Latin versions of the ancient Hebrew Psalter. These texts, some of which begin with the words 'Laudate Dominum', gave their name to the morning service of the Church, 'Lauds'. Anglo-Saxons referred to the Psalms as *lof-sangas*, that is, 'praise-songs'.[7] The same term can be applied to many Old English poems, including the very

---

[5] See above, pp. 9–10.

[6] John D. Niles, *Beowulf: The Poem and its Tradition* (Cambridge, Mass., 1983), p. 53. Opland's *Anglo-Saxon Oral Poetry* stresses throughout the dominance of eulogy among traditional poetic functions, e.g. pp. 260–1.

[7] See Bosworth-Toller's *Anglo-Saxon Dictionary* and Supplement, *s.v. lof-sang*. The Paris Psalter has English versions opposite the Latin. The term *lof-sang* could also be used for secular panegyrics: see pp. 71–2 below.

earliest to have survived, Cædmon's Hymn. This is worth quoting
in its entirety, for it displays in little the auxetic manner characteristic
of alliterative verse:

> Nu sculon herigean heofonrices weard,
> Meotodes meahte and his modgeþanc,
> Weorc wuldorfæder, swa he wundra gehwæs,
> Ece drihten, or onstealde.
> He ærest sceop eorðan bearnum
> Heofon to hrofe, halig scyppend;
> Þa middangeard moncynnes weard,
> Ece drihten, æfter teode
> Firum foldan, frea ælmihtig.[8]

(Now we must praise the guardian of the heavenly kingdom, the might of the
governor and the thought of his mind, the work of the father of glory, as he,
the eternal lord, originated every wonderful thing. He, the holy creator, first
created heaven as a roof for the children of earth; then afterwards he, guardian
of mankind, eternal lord and almighty ruler, prepared middle-earth, land for
men.)

Opening with a *Laudate*, this little poem 'amplifies' a simple praise
of God in both senses of that term, both sustaining and heightening it. The method, very evidently, is to designate the Creator by
a variety of words and phrases – no less than eight times in nine
lines. This method, common to alliterative poetry generally, is now
known as 'variation'. Variation served a technical purpose, inaugu-
rating patterns of alliteration in a first half-line or completing them in
a second; but it also contributed to the copiousness and redundancy
of a high poetic style. So Cædmon, without ever using the plain word
'God' itself, can praise him as eternal, holy and almighty, and glorify
him as the lord, father, creator and guardian of heaven and earth.

---

[8] Quotations from all Old English poems except *Beowulf* are taken from *The Anglo-Saxon
Poetic Records*, ed. G. P. Krapp and E. V. K. Dobbie, 6 vols. (New York, 1931–42), cited by
volume and page as *ASPR*. Thus Cædmon's Hymn is *ASPR*, vi.106.

The poem is an unusually concentrated example of an alliterative manner which provided frequent opportunities for the laudatory treatment of subjects, secular as well as religious. Very probably, in fact, the earliest Christian poets, in seventh-century England, adapted for their new *laus Dei* some of the expressions that were being used at the time by scops in their eulogistic references to kings and heroes. The formulaic character of such expressions allowed the substitution of words within them, so Christian poets could quite easily introduce epithets suitable for their divine subject. It is not a long step from 'Geata dryhten' (lord of the Geats) (*Beowulf*, l. 2576a) to Cædmon's 'ece drihten', or from 'frea Scyldinga' (lord of the Scyldings) (*Beowulf*, l. 500b) to his 'frea ælmihtig'.[9]

Among other examples of *laus Dei*, some are very much in the Cædmonian manner, as in the opening lines of the Old English *Genesis* (a poem once attributed to Cædmon himself):

> Us is riht micel ðæt we rodera weard,
> Wereda wuldorcining, wordum herigen,
> Modum lufien. He is mægna sped,
> Heafod ealra heahgesceafta,
> Frea ælmihtig.[10]

(It is very right that we should praise in words and love in our hearts the guardian of the heavens, the glorious king of hosts. He has abundance of power, the head of all high created things, the almighty ruler.)

In other kinds of poem, praise of God takes a bolder and richer form. The Advent Lyrics of the Exeter Book derive their more exotic

---

[9] Bede tells the story as a miraculous event whereby a simple man, previously incapable of the arts of song, suddenly proved able to produce a new kind of poem *ad laudem Dei* in the best vernacular manner: *Bede's Ecclesiastical History of the English People*, ed. and trans. Bertram Colgrave and R. A. B. Mynors (Oxford, 1969), IV 23. See Opland, *Anglo-Saxon Oral Poetry*, pp. 116–19.

[10] Lines 1–5, *ASPR*, I.3. The account of Creation at ll. 92–168 has many similar encomiastic expressions.

imagery from those antiphons of the church known as the Great O's, one of them addressing Christ as the divine dayspring:

> Eala earendel, engla beorhtast,
> Ofer middangeard monnum sended,
> Ond soðfæsta sunnan leoma,
> Torht ofer tunglas.[11]

(O shining light, brightest of angels, sent to men upon middle-earth, and true radiance of the sun, more brilliant than the stars.)

The half-line 'engla beorhtast' here belongs to a type of formula more often used, as we shall see, of men than of God. Perhaps, in the latter case, it was felt to imply a demeaning comparison.

Sometimes, again, poets will put praise of God into the mouths of other speakers, as later in the Advent Lyrics, where the angels in heaven glorify him as 'prince of archangels', 'ruler of victory' and 'lord of lords' (ll. 400–5). The poem *Daniel* has extended examples of this in the episode of the burning fiery furnace: the Prayer of Azarias and the Song of the Three Children.[12] In these two passages one can see how easily the laudatory manner of the Latin Bible could be rendered into the English verse of that time. Azarias prays God to let his enemies know 'quia tu es Dominus Deus solus, et gloriosus super orbem terrarum' ('that thou art the Lord, the only God, and glorious over all the world') (Daniel 3.45). The English poet amplifies these words somewhat, in the alliterative manner, and introduces the military touch so characteristic of it:

> þu ana eart ece drihten,
> Weroda waldend, woruldgesceafta,
> Sigora settend, soðfæst metod.

---

[11] The Advent Lyrics form the first part of *Christ* in the Exeter Book, *ASPR*, III.3–15. I quote ll. 104–7.

[12] *Daniel*, ll. 283–332 and 362–408, *ASPR*, I.119–22, from the Vulgate Book of Daniel 3.26–45 and 52–92. (These passages, absent from the Hebrew, are not in the Authorised Version.)

(thou alone art the eternal lord, ruler of hosts and of worldly creatures, ordainer of victories, faithful governor.)

Daniel, ll. 330–2

The Song of the Children calls upon all created things to bless, praise and exalt God. In the church office Lauds it was adopted as a canticle, known as the *Benedicite* from the opening word of each verse, thus: 'Benedicite, omnia opera Domini, Domino; laudate et superexaltate eum in saecula' ('All ye works of the Lord bless the Lord: praise and exalt him above all for ever') (Daniel 3.57). The Latin repeats the same imperative verbs in every verse, but the English poet rings alliterating variations upon them. As well as *herian*, he has *bletsian* 'bless', *domian* 'glorify', *lofian* 'praise' and *wurþian* 'honour'. This is Old English verse in its element:

> Niht somod and dæg,
> And þec landa gehwilc, leoht and þeostro,
> Herige on hade, somod hat and ceald.
> And þec, frea mihtig, forstas and snawas,
> Winterbiter weder and wolcenfaru,
> Lofige on lyfte.

(Night and day together and all lands, light and darkness, praise thee duly, both hot and cold. And frosts and snows, bitter winter weather and scudding cloud, praise thee on high, mighty ruler.)

Daniel, ll. 374–9

Daniel belongs to what is the largest single category in the surviving Old English verse corpus: Christian narrative poetry. Many of these poems, like *Daniel*, take Old Testament stories (*Genesis, Exodus, Judith* etc.), and others concern New Testament figures such as St Andrew (*Andreas*) or else non-biblical saints (*Juliana, Guthlac*). These poems all exhibit, in varying degrees, something like the 'hyperbolic' manner described by A. B. Lord in his study of

traditional heroic narrative in twentieth-century Yugoslavia.[13] For a
wide range of subjects, the poets employ superlative forms of expression long since, it would appear, established as formulaic in the idiom
of alliterative verse. One very common formula of this kind is a half-
line filler consisting of the superlative *mæst*, 'most, greatest', preceded
by some noun in the genitive plural. *Genesis* refers to Noah's ark as
'holmærna mæst' ('the greatest of sea-houses', l. 1422), and the following poem in the Junius Manuscript, *Exodus*, has many instances:
the Egyptians and Hebrews are both called 'drihtfolca mæst' ('the
greatest of peoples') (ll. 34, 322, 590); the watery deaths of the
Egyptians are 'meredeaða mæst' ('the greatest of sea-deaths')
(l. 465); and the biblical pillar of cloud, more extravagantly, is 'feld-
husa mæst' ('the greatest of field-houses') (l. 85).[14] Superlative forms
of every kind are, in fact, widespread in Old English verse generally,
often occurring in clusters. The author of *Andreas* describes paradise with such a cluster, as 'Blæda beorhtost, boldwela fægrost, /
Hama hyhtlicost' ('brightest of glories, fairest of joyful dwellings,
pleasantest of homes').[15] *Daniel* praises Babylon:

> Þæt wæs þara fæstna folcum cuðost,
> Mæst and mærost þara þe men bun.

(Of all the strongholds that men inhabit, this was the best known to the
people, the greatest and most glorious.)

ll. 691–2

On occasion, poets will amplify their praise by asserting that they
themselves have never seen or heard of a better. When St Andrew
sets out on his sea-voyage, the *Andreas* poet testifies:

[13] Albert B. Lord, *The Singer of Tales* (New York, 1965), p. 78, with examples on pp. 55, 87,
etc. Some Anglo-Saxon poems, notably Cynewulf's *Judith*, employ a more sober style.
[14] *Exodus*, ASPR, I.91–107. Cf. ll. 349, 368, 461, 500, 511, 555, 578.
[15] *Andreas*, ll. 103–4, ASPR, II.5–6.

Æfre ic ne hyrde
Þon cymlicor ceol gehladenne
Heahgestreonum.[16]

(I have never heard tell of any ship more splendidly laden with noble treasures.)

Auxesis extends in these poems over a wide range of topics –
ships, drownings, clouds and towns among them – but it has its main
focus on heroes. There are many straightforward superlatives here,
sometimes elaborated, as when the English saint Guthlac is described
as 'Se selesta bi sæm tweonum / Þara þe we on Engle æfre gefrunen'
('the best between the seas that we have ever heard of in England').[17]
More distinctive are those descriptions that assimilate their subjects
to the world of heroic poetry. Both men and women are represented as
fighting the good fight, both literally and metaphorically, against the
enemies of God. So it is not inappropriate that the poets should paint
them under what Shippey calls a '"wash" of epic dignity'.[18] They
are all, in their different ways, heroes in the same long-running epic
struggle. The poem *Andreas* is notable for praise of this sort. It opens
by lauding all the twelve apostles as 'thanes of the Lord', whose
glory reflects their courage in battle 'þonne rond ond hand / On
herefelda helm ealgodon' ('when shield and hand defended helmet
on the battlefield') (ll. 9–10). Later, speaking of Andrew himself, the
poet confesses that due glorification (*lof*) of the apostle is beyond
his powers: he simply cannot do justice to 'the hardships and the
grim battles that he endured with courage' (ll. 1478–87). Other poets
apply military language to even more unlikely subjects. Alone in his
fenland retreat, the hermit Guthlac withstands attacks from devils

[16] *Andreas*, ll. 360–2. These lines closely resemble *Beowulf*, ll. 38–40, on Scyld's funeral ship.
Andreas has versions of the same formula elsewhere: ll. 471–4, 498–500, 553–4.
[17] *Guthlac*, ll. 1359–60, *ASPR*, III.87–8.
[18] T. A. Shippey, *Old English Verse* (London, 1972), p. 124.

as 'Dryhtnes cempa, / From folctoga' ('a warrior of the Lord, a bold leader of the people') (*Guthlac*, ll. 901–2); and St Helena, in Cynewulf's version of the Invention of the Cross, can be referred to as 'guðcwen' ('warrior queen') and as 'sigecwen' ('victorious queen'), even though she plays no part in any battle.[19]

Even where the subject is as pacific as St Guthlac, this language of courage and victory in war derives its justification from the common trope of Christian heroes as *milites Christi*. But there are other occasions when the heroic 'wash' seems to be applied with less regard to the context. In *Andreas*, as evil man-eaters prepare to capture the unarmed and solitary apostle, the poet praises them as 'hildfrome' ('bold in battle') (l. 1202) and 'cene under cumblum' ('brave under banners') (l. 1204). In *Judith*, again, at the very moment when the wicked Assyrians are ignominiously running away, they are characterised as 'cynerof' ('nobly valiant').[20] It is easy to see why one critic of the poem should have suggested that 'the traditional vision of the heroic society seems to be mildly ironized or subverted in the picture of the Assyrian army'.[21] Praise of warriors in ignominious retreat as 'nobly valiant' must surely be ironical? Yet determination of such ironies and subversions in English alliterative verse, as we shall see, can be a tricky business. It was not every poet who could master the insistent alliterative idiom, with its strong set towards praise and hyperbole, and even the best of them did not always succeed in making their intended meanings clear.

---

[19] *Elene*, ll. 254, 331, 260, 997, *ASPR*, ii.66–102.   [20] *Judith*, ll. 311–12, *ASPR*, iv.108.
[21] Malcolm Godden, 'Biblical Literature: The Old Testament', in Malcolm Godden and Michael Lapidge (eds.), *The Cambridge Companion to Old English Literature* (Cambridge, 1991), pp. 206–26; citing from p. 222. See, however, Niles, *The Poem and its Tradition*, pp. 163–4, arguing that such fixed or conventional epithets belong to an 'abstract, nonrepresentational style' and so may have no particular aptness, either literal or ironical, to the occasion on which they are used.

The first poem in Geoffrey Hill's *Mercian Hymns*, published in 1971, takes the form of an imaginary panegyric recited by a court poet to the eighth-century lord of Mercia, King Offa, beginning 'King of the perennial holly-groves, the riven sandstone: overlord of the M5: architect of the historic rampart and ditch . . .'.[22] No doubt some Anglo-Saxon kings did have poets charged with singing panegyrics of this sort. The poem *Widsith* speaks of one such, a man who finds a generous patron, a lord who understands his art and seeks by its aid to enhance his own *dom*, that is, his reputation or glory.[23] In fact, however, very little evidence of vernacular royal panegyric survives from the period. Indeed, there is rather little secular poetry of any kind dealing with contemporary persons and events. Evidently those clerics concerned with the compilation of the four big manuscripts upon which most present knowledge depends were reluctant to devote parchment to such ephemera. The few surviving examples, all from late in the period, are preserved in other copies: six poems in manuscripts of the Anglo-Saxon Chronicle, together with *The Battle of Maldon*, imperfectly preserved in a few leaves (since destroyed) from an otherwise lost manuscript. The most extensive of the Chronicle pieces, in the entry for 937, is *The Battle of Brunanburh*. This opens with praise of King Athelstan and his brother Edmund, who have won 'lifelong glory' ('ealdorlangne tir') by their victory over the forces of the Vikings, Welsh and Scots. The battle itself is described in high heroic style, and the poem ends on a superlative

[22] *Mercian Hymns* (London, 1971), n. p. The poem ends with a typical modern take on such eulogising: '"I liked that", said Offa, "sing it again".' Hill derived his title from a section in Sweet's *Anglo-Saxon Reader* devoted to religious pieces from Mercia.

[23] *Widsith*, ll. 138–42, ASPR, III.153. Widsith elsewhere claims to have spread the glory (*lof*) of a queen by his own song (ll. 99–102). A life of the eighth-century royal saint Æthelbert records that he had songs about his own ancestors sung to him on a journey: Opland, *Anglo-Saxon Oral Poetry*, pp. 148–50. For an early eleventh-century panegyric of an English queen in Latin prose, see *Encomium Emmae Reginae*, ed. Alastair Campbell, with a supplementary introduction by Simon Keynes (Cambridge, 1998).

note: never, not since the Angles and Saxons first came to Britain, has there been so great a slaughter.[24] A later poem, in the Chronicle entry for 1065, celebrates a hero more to the chronicler's taste, perhaps. It records the death of Edward the Confessor, praising him as a wise and virtuous ruler, 'kyningc kystum god, clæne and milde' ('a king good in his ways, pure and generous').[25] These two poems approach more nearly than any others in the surviving corpus to the kind of praise poetry about contemporary heroes and rulers to be found in other traditional societies, Welsh or West African. One must suppose that more of the sort – perhaps very much more – has been lost.

The Battle of Maldon concerns a battle fought in 991 between East Saxon forces under their leader Byrhtnoth and the invading Vikings. The poet knows the local Essex topography of the event, and he names many individual members of Byrhtnoth's company, sometimes specifying their fathers as well. One has an opportunity here to see how praise and blame might function within a particular community, serving to support its common values by honouring some people and shaming others. Those 'steadfast' men who fulfilled their obligations on the battlefield could expect honour back home from their comrades. As Leofsunu says after the death of Byrhtnoth, with some tough-minded understatement:

> Ne þurfon me embe Sturmere stedefæste hælæð
> Wordum ætwitan nu min wine gecranc,
> Þæt ic hlafordleas ham siðie,
> Wende fram wige.[26]

---

[24] *ASPR*, VI.16–20. A short poem in the 942 entry celebrates successes against the Vikings by King Edmund, described as 'guardian of men' and 'protector of warriors'. Opland sees the influence of Norse skaldic poetry in these tenth-century encomia: *Anglo-Saxon Oral Poetry*, pp. 172–3.

[25] *The Death of Edward*, l. 23, *ASPR*, VI.26.

[26] *The Battle of Maldon*, ll. 249–52, *ASPR*, VI.14. The verb *ætwitan* 'blame' (ancestor of the weaker modern *twit*) occurs again in a similar context at l. 220.

(Steadfast men around Sturmere will have no cause to blame me now that my lord has fallen, saying that I would go home and depart from the battle without my leader.)

The poem itself would have served to articulate and publish praise of Leofsunu and his loyal comrades, like the trumpet 'Clere Laude' in Chaucer's *House of Fame*. At the same time, and like the other, black, trumpet in Chaucer's poem, *Maldon* exposes to public shame those 'children of Odda', Godric and his two brothers, who first fled from the field, leading others with them (ll. 185–201, 237–43). The poet introduces these with the scathing comment, 'Hi bugon þa fram beadwe þa þær beon noldon' ('Those who did not want to be there departed then from the battle') (l. 185). It so happens that the last line of the fragmentary text that survives shows how keen the author was that praise and blame should be apportioned to the right people. There are two men called Godric, the chief traitor and also another, Godric son of Æthelgar, who died nobly in the front ranks, of whom the poet says, 'Næs þæt na se Godric þe ða guðe forbeah' ('that was not the Godric who avoided the fight').[27] These are real people, evidently, to whom justice, one way or the other, must be done.

When *The Battle of Maldon* was first printed, in 1726, its editor described it as 'a historical fragment . . . in which the warlike virtue of Byrhtnoth the ealdorman and other Anglo-Saxons is celebrated'.[28] Clearly the poem as a whole does celebrate the home side, albeit in defeat (as the Chronicle entry reports); but questions arise about the celebration of Byrhtnoth himself. The 'noble thane of Æthelred' (l. 151) fights bravely to the end and dies commending

[27] *Maldon*, l. 325. The presence of characters sharing the same name (there are also two Eadwards, ll. 117 and 273) surely means that the author is referring to actual contemporaries. One would hardly invent such awkward coincidences.
[28] 'Fragmentum historicum . . . quo Poetice & Stylo Caedmoniano celebratur virtus bellica Beorhtnothi Ealdormanni & aliorum Anglo-Saxonum', *ASPR*, VI.xxvi–xxvii.

his soul to God; but his earlier decision to allow the Vikings passage across a defensible causeway prompts the poet to a remarkable
comment:

> Ða se eorl ongan for his ofermode
> Alyfan landes to fela laþere ðeode.

(Then the earl in his *ofermod* began to allow too much land to the hateful
people.)

ll. 89–90

In an essay published in 1953, J. R. R. Tolkien rendered these lines
more freely: 'then the earl in his overmastering pride actually yielded
ground to the enemy, as he should not have done'. He saw in them
'*severe* criticism' of the leader's conduct (his italics) and condemned
Byrhtnoth's decision as folly: 'Magnificent perhaps, but certainly
wrong. Too foolish to be heroic.'[29] But what was the alternative
course of action? The situation is a peculiar one. The Vikings, who
have landed on an islet, are evidently unable to fight their way on
to the mainland across a narrow causeway which allows little more
than a single file. They have promised to sail away if the English
will buy them off, with 'Danegeld'; but Byrhtnoth declares in reply
that this would be 'too shameful' ('to heanlic') (l. 55). The Vikings
must not be allowed to depart without a fight ('unbefohtene') (l. 57).
So, to break the deadlock, he allows them across. A consequence,
in the event, is that he himself and many of his men are killed; but
it can be said that he had no reason to foresee such a bad outcome,
which appears to have depended upon the treacherous desertions
of Godric and many others.[30] Yet the heavy word *ofermod* cannot

---

[29] J. R. R. Tolkien, 'The Homecoming of Beorhtnoth Beorhthelm's Son', in *Essays and Studies 1953* (London, 1953), 1–18; citing from pp. 16 and 13.

[30] See Katherine O'Brien O'Keefe, on pp. 118–20 of her essay 'Heroic Values and Christian Ethics', in Godden and Lapidge (eds.), *Cambridge Companion to Old English Literature*, pp. 107–25.

be argued away. Tolkien's gloss, 'overmastering pride', agrees with other uses of the word and its derivatives in Old English; but these mostly occur in specifically religious contexts, often rendering the Latin *superbia*.[31] It must denote some kind of overplus of *mod*, which itself may denote spirit, 'heart' or courage; yet its exact force here is hard to determine. Perhaps the poet, looking back with regret at the event, means that Byrhtnoth on this occasion showed too great a confidence in the powers of himself and his army – too great, as the outcome was to make clear. In cases such as this, it may be difficult to second-guess the attitudes of old poets, and the difficulty is compounded here by the loss of the poem's conclusion. 'Too foolish to be heroic'? Maybe. But traditional opinion allowed more 'folly' to heroes than to ordinary mortals, and they may be praised even when their actions had unhappy consequences. Aristotle noticed the point, in his discussion of epideictic: 'those who praise or blame do not consider whether someone has done actions that are advantageous or harmful, but often they include it even as a source of praise that he did what was honourable without regard to the cost to himself'.[32] This is a contentious issue, however, and I shall pursue it further in discussion of *Beowulf*, to which I now turn.

'Every poem and all poetic utterance is either blame or praise.' In its more than 3,000 lines, *Beowulf* offers many varied illustrations of that 'Aristotelian' dictum. Its narrator speaks highly of almost everything that he has occasion to mention, and his characters most

---

[31] See the thorough discussion by Helmut Gneuss, '*The Battle of Maldon* 89: Byrhtnoð's *ofermod* Once Again', *Studies in Philology*, 73 (1976), 117–37. Gneuss (p. 129) concludes that 'all the evidence we have points to "pride"' as the meaning in *Maldon*, while conceding that almost all other occurrences of the word are clerical in character. Taking up that objection, T. A. Shippey argues against Tolkien and Gneuss in favour of a positive representation of Byrhtnoth, in accordance with a 'heroic paradigm'. See his 'Boar and Badger: An Old English Heroic Antithesis', *Leeds Studies in English*, n.s. 16 (1985), 220–39.

[32] Aristotle, *Rhetoric*, 1.3.6 (1358^b–1359^a).

often speak highly of each other. In the present discussion, I give
a general account of the poem's auxetic idiom, reserving to the last
the treatment of Beowulf himself – for it is in the case of Beowulf
especially that modern criticism has found cause to question the
laudatory intentions of the poet.

The opening of the poem at once establishes for the narrating voice
a high laudatory register, as it traces the descent of King Hrothgar
from his noble Danish predecessors. The first of these, Scyld Scefing,
reigned for many years and imposed his authority on neighbouring
peoples: 'Þæt wæs god cyning' ('That was a good king').[33] His son,
Beowulf the Dane, also won glory, binding companions to himself
by his generosity, as a young man should: 'Swa sceal geong guma ...'
(l. 20). When Scyld dies, his followers afford him a grand sea-burial,
as followers should, laying their beloved lord in the bosom of the ship
'mærne be mæste' ('in his glory by the mast'), along with weapons,
armour and treasure. Their generosity prompts the poet to voice his
own approbation for the third time, in a common superlative form:

> Ne hyrde ic cymlicor ceol gegyrwan
> Hildewæpnum ond heaðowædum,
> Billum ond byrnum.[34]

(I have never heard of a ship adorned more beautifully with weapons of war
and battle-dress, swords and mailcoats.)

As it turns out, the ensuing action of the poem casts the Danes
and their king in a less than heroic role; for they themselves have

---

[33] *Beowulf*, l. 11. All citations are from *Beowulf: An Edition*, ed. Bruce Mitchell and Fred
C. Robinson (Oxford, 1998). The same comment is made about Hrothgar at l. 863 and
Beowulf at l. 2390, and almost the same about Hrothgar at l. 1885. For similar comments,
see *Andreas*, l. 1722, *Exodus*, l. 233 and *Daniel*, l. 7.

[34] Lines 38–40. The narrator speaks in similar terms of treasures given by Hrothgar to
Beowulf (ll. 1027–9, 1197–1200) and of the feasting Danes (ll. 1011–12). Cf. also ll. 575–7
and 1842–3.

been unable to cope with the marauding monsters, gaining relief only from a foreign visitor. At one point, indeed, their chagrin ('æfþunca') (l. 502) seems to find expression in the questioning by Unferth of Beowulf's heroic credentials – an attack which prompts Beowulf to remind him that neither he nor his fellow Danes have had any success against Grendel (ll. 590–601). But this is a highly uncharacteristic exchange. Everywhere else the poet goes out of his way to shower the Danish kingdom with expressions of praise.[35] He characterises Danes as valiant ('swiðhicgende' 919, 'hwate' 1601, 'ellenrof' 1787), praising them as always ready to fight for their lord: 'wæs se þeod tilu' ('that people was good') (l. 1250). At the feast after the killing of Grendel, again, they all behave with superlative excellence:

> Ne gefrægen ic þa mægþe maran weorode
> Ymb hyra sincgyfan sel gebæran.

(I have never heard of that people in greater numbers ever bearing themselves better around their treasure-giver.)

ll. 1011–12

At the same banquet, the song of the scop casts a shadow across the celebrations, for it records the death of a Danish leader and many of his followers in Frisia; but it concludes with the remaining Danes taking vengeance and returning home with Frisian treasure (ll. 1154–7) – an outcome that redounds to the glory of Denmark. Individual Danes are also singled out for praise.[36] When the hero first arrives at Heorot, he is received with exemplary civility by Wulfgar: 'cuþe he duguðe þeaw' ('he knew the customs of noble company') (l. 359);

---

[35] This is so, notwithstanding the strongly didactic lines (175–88) condemning the Danes as heathen – a condemnation that applies, after all, to everyone in the poem, Beowulf included, and has no apparent bearing on the way they are presented generally.

[36] Questionable exceptions are Unferth and Hrothulf. Yet the former behaves handsomely to the hero later in the story, and Hrothulf's treachery (if that is what lines 1017–19 and 1163–5 imply) lies in the future.

and Hrothgar's hall-thane later shows his courtesy ('andrysnu') (l. 1796) in attending to the visitor's every need. The retainer Æschere, though carried off by Grendel's mother, is described as a mighty and glorious warrior, much loved by Hrothgar:

> Se wæs Hroþgare hæleþa leofost
> On gesiðes had be sæm tweonum.

(He was as a companion to Hrothgar the dearest of men between the seas.)
ll. 1296–7

The expression 'be sæm tweonum', equivalent to 'throughout the earth', commonly serves to amplify superlatives in Old English verse. It is applied elsewhere in *Beowulf* to the hero himself (ll. 857–61), to Hrothgar (ll. 1684–6) and to Offa the Angle (ll. 1954–7).[37]

But the glorification of the Danes focuses above all on Hrothgar and on his great hall. Like everything else in the poem, Heorot is subject to the vicissitudes of the world, being eventually destined to end in flames; but the poet represents it throughout as supreme in its kind. It is 'the best of houses' ('husa selest') (ll. 146, 285, 935) and 'the greatest of hall-dwellings' ('healærna mæst') (l. 78). There is even, as Beowulf and his followers approach it, a visionary brightness about the building:

> Þæt wæs foremærost foldbuendum
> Receda under roderum on þæm se rica bad;
> Lixte se leoma ofer landa fela.

(That was the most glorious hall of any man dwelling under the heavens, there where the mighty one lived; the light shone out across many lands.)
ll. 309–11

---

[37] Cf. also *Guthlac*, ll. 1359–60, cited above, p. 37.

Heorot was an achievement of Hrothgar's younger days, when he himself still enjoyed honour as a warrior (ll. 64–5); but he is now old. As Beowulf and his party reflect on their way back to Geatland, he has suffered a universal fate:

> þæt wæs an cyning
> Æghwæs orleahtre oþ þæt hine yldo benam
> Mægenes wynnum se þe oft manegum scod.

(That was an exceptional king, altogether without blame, until old age, which has often done injury to many, deprived him of the joys of his strength.)

ll. 1885–7

Not that anyone can blame the old man for that. As his warriors ride back from the bloodstained mere, they speak of Beowulf's glorious feat there, but the poet is careful to guard Hrothgar against any discredit:

> Ne hie huru winedrihten wiht ne logon
> Glædne Hroðgar ac þæt wæs god cyning.

(Nor did they at all find fault with their lord and friend, the gracious Hrothgar, for that was a good king.)

ll. 862–3

Accordingly, Hrothgar's name is regularly coupled with eulogistic epithets, both by the poet and by other characters. Most often he is 'mære þeoden', 'illustrious lord';[38] and elsewhere 'old and good' (l. 279), 'brave in battle' (l. 608), 'secure in his glory' (l. 922), and the best of all Danish kings:

> Ðæm selestan be sæm tweonum
> Ðara þe on Scedenigge sceattas dælde.

---

[38] Seven times: ll. 129, 201, 345, 353, 1046, 1598, 1992. The poet uses this favourite half-line on seven other occasions, most often of Beowulf himself: ll. 797, 2572, 2721, 2788, 3141. Its application to the wicked Heremod at l. 1715 is unusual and may be read as ironical; but see n. 21 above.

(the best on earth among those who dispensed treasure in Denmark.)

ll. 1685–6

Once the poem has shifted its scene to Geatland, with Beowulf's return home (from line 1903), it largely loses that focus on people-in-places that makes Heorot and its environs so imaginable. Nor do Hygelac and his Geats have anything like the presence that engaged the poet's interest in Hrothgar and his Danes. So the poet's manner becomes less intensively laudatory. At first it might seem otherwise, as Beowulf approaches Higelac's hall on his return:

> Bold wæs betlic, bregorof cyning
> Heah in healle, Hygd swiðe geong
> Wis welþungen.

(The building was splendid, the king majestic, raised up in his hall, and the very young Hygd wise and accomplished.)

ll. 1925–7

What is more, mention of Hygelac's young queen prompts the poet, in true epideictic style, to contrast her nobility with the cruel behaviour of another queen, Thryth, of which he says, 'Ne bið swylc cwenlic þeaw' ('That is not queenly conduct').[39] But the ensuing scene of reception and gift-giving in Hygelac's (unnamed) hall seems little more than a weak rerun of the corresponding scenes in Heorot – even less vivid, in fact, than the story Beowulf goes on to tell Hygelac about his Danish adventures.

In the last part of the poem, there are many centrifugal episodes concerned with the history of the dragon's treasure, the

---

[39] Line 1940. The poet goes on to describe how Thryth was reformed by her marriage to Offa, king of the continental Angles, taking the opportunity to praise Offa as a brave and generous ruler, 'as I have heard, the best of all mankind between the seas' (ll. 1955–6). This Offa was known as an ancestor of the eighth-century Offa, king of Mercia, and it has been suggested that the *Beowulf*-poet's praise of Offa I was introduced as a compliment to Offa II: so Dorothy Whitelock, *The Audience of 'Beowulf'* (Oxford, 1951), pp. 58–64.

Geatish–Swedish wars, or Hygelac's Frisian raid.[40] But the imaginative centre of these last pages lies in the dragon's lair and its environs. Here praise and blame, glory and shame, are preeminently at issue, both for Beowulf himself and for his followers. For the latter, one can make a clear and sharp distinction, as one could in the case of Byrhtnoth's followers in *Maldon*. The eleven warriors taken by Beowulf as his companions are instructed to wait in the wings while he tackles the dragon alone; but when the encounter is going badly, all of them except Wiglaf take refuge in a neighbouring wood. These are the 'hildlaten' ('battle-slack') (l. 2846) and 'treowlogan' ('troth-breakers') (l. 2847) who later come down filled with shame ('scamiende') to where their lord lies dead, to be blamed by Wiglaf with dry understatement. Their king, he says, would have no cause to boast about the support he received from them (ll. 2864–74). He predicts for them a future 'edwitlif', that is, a shameful life subject to the vituperation of comrades – than which, he says, death would be a better fate (ll. 2890–1). Wiglaf speaks quite modestly about his own part in the dragon fight; but the poem glorifies him as 'modig' ('courageous') (ll. 2698, 2757), 'ungemete til' ('immeasurably good') (l. 2721), 'sigehreðig' ('rejoicing in victory') (l.2756), and 'hildedior' ('brave in battle') (l. 3111). Here, as very occasionally elsewhere in the poem, the exemplary case prompts the poet to make its general application explicit: 'swylc sceolde secg wesan / Þegn æt ðearfe'('A man should be like that, a thane at a time of need') (ll. 2708–9). Praise and blame, as 'Aristotle' said, serve 'to urge men on to certain actions ... and to dissuade them from others'.[41]

---

[40] Praise plays relatively little part in these episodes, though Onela figures as the best of Swedish kings (ll. 2381–4).

[41] See above, p. 19. The poet introduces three similar didactic reflections with the words 'Swa sceal', at ll. 20–5, 1534–6 and 2166–9. And cf. ll. 2291–3.

Here as in *The Battle of Maldon*, it is the case of the hero that has
proved controversial, prompting several critics over the last half-
century to find faults in him. These scholars have identified a variety
of authorial reservations concerning Beowulf's conduct, conveyed
mostly in the later part of the poem.[42] Other writers have questioned
the presence of any such criticism, stressing rather the laudatory
treatment of the hero throughout.[43] 'Celebration or critique?' – that,
according to Tom Shippey, has been 'the great divide in *Beowulf*
criticism'.[44] The variety of points at issue across this divide allows
only a selective discussion here.

No one denies, of course, that Beowulf is a hero, even if he may
be an imperfect one. Like Hrothgar, only more so, he is represented
by the poet with a profusion of strong laudatory epithets. He is,
persistently, good and glorious ('mære'), famed for his outstanding
strength, courage, nobility and wisdom. The narrator does not generally amplify upon these epithets (once at ll. 2177–89), preferring
to outsource more extensive praises to characters in the poem, and
especially Danes: their coastguard (ll. 247–51), the Danes and their
scop (ll. 856–915), Queen Wealhtheow (ll. 1221–4) and Hrothgar
(ll. 942–6, 1700–9, 1841–54). The account of the scop singing his
praises on the way back from Grendel's mere is particularly interesting, for it represents poetic *laudatio* in its most archaic oral form.[45]
His improvised verses employ the traditional auxetic devices of

---

[42] An early instance may be found in Tolkien's 1953 essay on *Maldon* (n. 29 above), pp. 16–18,
followed by John Leyerle, 'Beowulf, the Hero and the King', *Medium Aevum*, 34 (1965),
89–102. For a different approach, drawing on patristic sources, see Margaret Goldsmith,
The Mode and Meaning of 'Beowulf' (London, 1970). The most recent version to date
appears in Andy Orchard, *A Critical Companion to 'Beowulf'* (Cambridge, 2003).

[43] So T. A. Shippey, *Old English Verse*, chapter 2, and his *Beowulf* (London, 1978); or Niles,
The Poem and its Tradition.

[44] Shippey, *Beowulf*, p. 35.

[45] See Opland, *Anglo-Saxon Oral Poetry*, pp. 202–5. The line describing the scop as 'guma
gilphlæden gidda gemyndig' (868) has been translated 'a man with a memory for songs of
praise' (Niles, *The Poem and its Tradition*, p. 34). The meaning of *gilphlæden* is uncertain.

comparison and contrast, ranking Beowulf with the great dragon-slayer Sigemund and setting him off against the cruel Heremod:

> He þær eallum wearð
> Mæg Higelaces manna cynne
> Freondum gefægra; hine fyren onwod.

(He, Higelac's kinsman, grew dearer to all mankind and to his friends; crime entered him.)

ll. 913–15

One cannot doubt the encomiastic intentions of the Danish scop, in the circumstances; but some critics have suggested that the *Beowulf*-poet himself sounds a note of warning even here. Thus John Leyerle: 'The scop's account ends with the phrase *hine fyren onwod* (915), which is usually taken, with an abrupt shift in pronoun, as a reference to Heremod. But conceivably it refers to Beowulf.' So also Andy Orchard: 'While modern editors and translators go to some lengths to reassure their readers that Heremod is intended here, an Anglo-Saxon audience might have felt less confident that Beowulf and Heremod were being juxtaposed not so much as opposites as equals [*sic*].'[46] Leyerle goes on to suggest that, just as Heremod left the Danes leaderless when he went to his death, so Beowulf was to be at fault in leaving his people leaderless after the dragon fight. Certainly the poet's pronouns do shift very abruptly; but I find it inconceivable that the heavy word *fyren*, 'sin' or 'crime', could have application to the later conduct of the hero, whatever doubts may be entertained about that.

Heremod figures again in another passage of prime significance for the present discussion. This is the so-called 'sermon' that Hrothgar

---

Editors offer 'gifted with magniloquence' or 'covered with glory'; but *gilp*, commonly 'boast', may refer here to poetic amplification.

[46] Leyerle, 'Beowulf, the Hero and the King', 93; Orchard, *A Critical Companion*, p. 113.

addresses to Beowulf on their last evening together in Heorot: ll.
1700–84. His long oration falls into three parts. In the first, Hrothgar
praises the hero as a good man, wise as well as strong, who has won
fame already and who will be a great help to his own people in the
future (ll. 1700–9). He then, like his scop, introduces Heremod as
a contrast, a leader who dealt out death rather than treasure to his
followers and himself came to an unhappy end: let Beowulf learn from
his bad example (ll. 1709–24). Those who glory in their prosperity
and fail to realise how easily success and life itself can slip away
fall victim to arrogance or 'oferhygd' (ll. 1740 and 1760) and may
neglect, like Heremod, their treasure-giving (ll. 1724–68). It is not
surprising that a speech of this kind, where an old man is marking
the departure of a young one, should couple praise with advice and
even warning about the future. The Greek rhetorician Menander
says of such a farewell oration (called 'propemptic') that, as well as
praising the one who is leaving, 'it can admit advice when a superior
is sending off an inferior, e.g. a teacher his pupil, because his own
position gives him a character which makes advice appropriate'.[47]
But do Hrothgar's warnings have a bearing on the hero's actual
conduct in the last part of the poem? Some critics deny it, as Shippey
flatly does. Hrothgar's sermon, he says, 'certainly has no point in the
story; Beowulf needs the old king's speech neither as a warning for
the future nor reprimand for the past'.[48] Others, however, see the
speech as offering readers the very terms on which the subsequent
behaviour of the hero is to be judged – and, with varying degrees
of severity, found wanting. The two issues in question are failures
in gold-giving and 'oferhygd', or, as some prefer, covetousness and
pride.

---

[47] Russell and Wilson, *Menander Rhetor*, p. 127. For a medieval Latin example, see Goldsmith,
    Mode and Meaning, p. 208.
[48] Shippey, *Old English Verse*, p. 41.

Judgement on the first of these issues largely turns on the critic's conception of the poet and his audience, and hence of the particular set of values that he may be supposed to have assumed. So Margaret Goldsmith, reading the poem in the light of a monastic moral theology expounded by such authorities as Augustine and Gregory, sees Hrothgar's references to lords who fail in gold-giving as warnings against *cupiditas*. Since this term denotes any inordinate attachment to earthly things, Beowulf can hardly escape criticism;[49] for does he not on his deathbed ask for a sight of that treasure he has won from the dragon, in order, he says, that he may leave the world 'more at ease' ('seft') (l. 2749)? This is not holy dying, certainly; but neither does it exemplify that niggardliness to which Hrothgar referred. On the contrary, so far from failing as a goldgiver, Beowulf's generosity as such is acknowledged by his followers (see ll. 2635, 2652, 3009, 3034); and when, in his dying speech, he thanks God for the treasure which he now sees, it is 'because I have been able before my deathday to acquire such things for my people (*minum leodum*)' (ll. 2797–8). From a more secular, non-Augustinian, point of view, this can – and I think should – be seen as a noble example of that generous concern which binds a good leader to his followers. Nor is its nobility undercut, surely, when his people bury all the treasure that he has won in his gravemound, 'where it still exists, as useless to men as it previously was' (that is, in the dragon's barrow). For is not that a reciprocal act of equal grandeur?[50]

In any case, it will be agreed that what mainly prompted Beowulf to engage in his last and fatal fight was not the hope of winning gold but rather the imperative need to protect his kingdom from the ravages of the dragon. Here, the point at issue concerns the hero's decision to

---

[49] Goldsmith, *Mode and Meaning*, especially pp. 228–30.
[50] See particularly Niles's discussion of gift-giving as part of a general social principle of 'reciprocity': *The Poem and its Tradition*, pp. 213–23.

tackle the dragon single-handed. Does the poet endorse his conduct, even though it leads to his death? Or does he register reservations about it? One of the first critics to take up the latter possibility in modern times was J. R. R. Tolkien, whose essay on *The Battle of Maldon* coupled Beowulf with Byrhtnoth as a leader who 'wished for glory, or for a glorious death' and so 'courted disaster'.[51] Leyerle developed the thought in his essay, stressing the duty of Beowulf once he was king not to hazard himself or his people by 'rash, unreflective action' stemming from 'desire for glory' and 'excessive reliance on his personal strength'.[52] Most recently, Orchard has spoken of Beowulf's 'over-confidence' and found in Wiglaf a norm of good sense by which his lord's conduct may be judged.[53]

A passage from one of Wiglaf's speeches, cited by Orchard and others, will serve to call up the questions at issue. Beowulf is dead, and the main body of his followers, summoned to the scene by a messenger, finds Wiglaf sitting there exhausted by the fight. He addresses them:

> Oft sceall eorl monig anes willan
> Wræc adreogan swa us geworden is.
> Ne meahton we gelæran leofne þeoden
> Rices hyrde ræd ænigne,
> Þæt he ne grette goldweard þone,
> Let hyne licgean þær he longe wæs,
> Wicum wunian oð woruldende.
> Heold on heahgesceap; hord ys gesceawod,
> Grimme gegongen; wæs þæt gifeþe to swið
> Þe ðone þeodcyning þyder ontyhte.[54]

---

[51] Tolkien, 'The Homecoming of Beorhtnoth', pp. 17–18, suggesting that Beowulf shows a misplaced spirit of 'chivalry' by handicapping himself in tackling the dragon.

[52] Leyerle, 'Beowulf, the Hero and the King', pp. 94, 97. Goldsmith discusses Beowulf's 'desmesure': *Mode and Meaning*, pp. 224–7.

[53] Orchard, *A Critical Companion*, pp. 260–3.

[54] Lines 3077–86. I take the translation from S. A. J. Bradley, *Anglo-Saxon Poetry* (London, 1982), p. 492. See, however, Mitchell and Robinson's note to ll. 3079–83 in their edition,

(Often many a man has to endure misery through one man's will, as has now happened to us. We could not persuade our cherished prince, the kingdom's protector, to accept any advice that he should not approach the guardian of the gold, that he should let him lie where he long had been and keep to his haunts until the world's end; he remained obedient to his exalted destiny. The hoard stands revealed – having been painfully won; the lot which urged the king towards it was too severe.)

Wiglaf speaks first here of the grief and misery ('wræc') presently suffered by him and his companions 'through one man's will'. He wishes that things might have turned out otherwise, of course, but it was indeed the determination of Beowulf alone ('anes willan') to take on the dragon single-handed. In a poem which does not commonly devote much attention to what characters think, two long passages were earlier devoted to the thoughts that led Beowulf to act as he did – described by the poet at ll. 2345–400, and voiced by the hero himself at ll. 2426–515. Both these passages speak of past occasions where he has 'ventured' and 'survived', successes from which he derives the confidence to venture once more.[55] In this part of the poem, choices for interpretation – between critique and celebration – are quite finely balanced. Introducing the first of the passages, at ll. 2345–51, the poet says that Beowulf thought it beneath him ('oferhogode') to tackle the dragon with a large force of men, and also that, having survived so many tight spots in the past, he feared little from the encounter. The poet's verb *oferhogian* is taken here by Leyerle and Orchard to echo significantly the related noun *oferhygd*, 'arrogance', which Hrothgar used in his speech of advice and warning. So Orchard writes: 'The

suggesting that these lines mean, not that the Geats tried and failed to dissuade Beowulf, but rather that they were in no position to advise him against undertaking the fight, because he was their only hope of defence against an enemy who would not be content to 'lie where he long had been'.

[55] He refers to perils in Denmark, Frisia, Geatland and Sweden. The term for 'venturing' is *(ge)neþan*, at ll. 2350 and 2511, and for 'surviving', *gedigan* or *genesan*, at ll. 2350, 2397 and 2426.

poet again apparently undercuts his hero by implying of Beowulf's
decision (based on his self-belief) not to attack the dragon mob-
handed that it was the result of over-confidence.'[56] This is perhaps
the strongest of the cases for 'under-cutting' that have been advanced.
Yet one would not expect any hero to attack a dragon at the head of
a big military force (not a good method in any case, perhaps); and
the poet certainly allows Beowulf generous grounds for confidence
in his own individual powers. Nor does he suggest, as Leyerle holds,
that such an enterprise should not have been undertaken by a king,
or by an old man. It was indeed commonly thought that kings, like
kings in chess, should be hazarded only as a last resort – so there is
no question, in *Sir Gawain and the Green Knight*, of Arthur himself
taking up the Green Knight's challenge. But the threat to Geatland
presented by the dragon is such that only King Beowulf can handle
it, as a necessary last resort. He may be old, but he is not one who,
like King Hrothgar, has been deprived by old age of 'the joys of his
strength' (ll. 1886–7). On the contrary, as Sisam argues:

There is no suggestion that age was a disadvantage in his fight with the
dragon – that he would have done better had he been younger. He still trusts
to his own unaided strength (ll. 2540ff). The demonstration that no sword
could bear the force of his stroke is reserved for this last fight (ll. 2684ff).
The contest is beyond the power of any other man.[57]

Certainly Beowulf does prove to have underestimated the threat
presented by the dragon, for his life is not saved even by the iron
shield that he prudently orders as protection against the creature's

<hr>

[56] Orchard, *A Critical Companion*, p. 260. Cf. Leyerle, 'Beowulf, the Hero and the King', 95.
However, S. B. Greenfield points out that Hrothgar's *oferhygd* 'is connected with greed,
with hoarding, with failure of generosity in gift-giving, and *not* with scorning to have help
in battle', 'Beowulf and the Judgement of the Righteous', in Michael Lapidge and Helmut
Gneuss (eds.), *Learning and Literature in Anglo-Saxon England: Essays Presented to Peter
Clemoes* (Cambridge, 1985), pp. 393–407; citing pp. 400–1.
[57] K. Sisam, *The Structure of 'Beowulf'* (Oxford, 1965), pp. 23–4.

fiery breath. But he was not to know, what the poet has already revealed, at ll. 2341–4, that this is the occasion when he and the dragon both are fated to die. Such ignorance of future outcomes, known to both narrator and audience, is a recurring source of ironies in *Beowulf*, but 'dramatic irony' of this sort does not undercut the relative standing of individuals, since their ignorance is a universal human condition.

In the passage quoted above, Wiglaf goes on to recall how he and his companions failed to persuade Beowulf to let the dragon lie.[58] Orchard credits Wiglaf with a 'clear-sightedness and perspective hitherto denied the other characters in *Beowulf*', suggesting that he 'can be said to speak not only for the poet, but for us'.[59] Most modern readers surely will sympathise with Wiglaf's reservations; but does he speak for the poet? Dissuasions from risk, in heroic narrative, do not commonly carry the day: young Beowulf's companions, according to Unferth, failed to dissuade him from the swimming match with Breca, nor did Hygelac succeed in persuading him to leave Grendel for the Danes to tackle themselves.[60] The present case is different, of course, since Beowulf loses his life; but the sensible advice to let things be, offered by his followers, seems quite unrealistic in the existing circumstances. The dragon would hardly rest content to 'lie where he had long been'. Roused from his long dormancy, he is burning buildings, including Beowulf's own royal seat, and intends to leave nothing alive in the whole kingdom.[61] One critic,

---

[58] Lines 3079–83; but see n. 54 above on the translation.

[59] Orchard, *A Critical Companion*, p. 237. See also p. 263, on Wiglaf 'taking on the voice of the poet'. Tolkien similarly: 'There could be no more pungent criticism in a few words of "chivalry" in one of responsibility than Wiglaf's exclamation: *oft sceall eorl monig anes willan wræc adreogan*', 'The Homecoming of Beorhtnoth', p. 18.

[60] Lines 510–12 and 1992–7. Orchard is struck by 'the way in which Wiglaf effectively echoes Unferth's assertion that Beowulf is impervious to sensible advice', *A Critical Companion*, p. 262.

[61] Lines 2312–15. See Niles, *The Poem and its Tradition*, pp. 238–40.

G. N. Garmonsway, has rightly observed that 'it is one sign of the maturity of this literature that we are enabled to see how heroic attitudes appeared to others who, though sometimes involved in the action, serve in the role of chorus, to remind us of the world of common sense and nonheroic norms'; but, as Garmonsway goes on to insist, such common sense and nonheroic attitudes do not prevail.[62] Wiglaf himself may be said to concede this when he goes on to say that Beowulf 'heold on heahgesceap', that is, 'held to his high destiny'. He is subject to destiny or fate (the *gifeþe* in the next line); but it is a high destiny, and one to which he himself holds.

The poem's final scene glorifies Beowulf in death, as state funerals commonly will. His followers build a towering barrow, visible from far off on a high headland, as a monument to his greatness, and twelve noble companions ride round it lamenting and lauding the dead, 'as it is fitting that a man should praise his dead lord'. The very last lines of the poem report what they said:

> Cwædon þæt he wære wyruldcyninga
> Mannum mildust ond monðwærust,
> Leodum liðost ond lofgeornost.

(They said that of all the kings in the world he was the most generous to men and the kindest, the gentlest to his people and most eager for fame.)

These are the last of the poem's many superlatives, with the poet reporting that most typical kind of epideictic utterance, panegyric of a dead ruler. The use of indirect discourse in these concluding lines brings the poem to an unusual sort of end, which has the reader leaving the story behind with the voices of Beowulf's companions merging into the voice of the narrator himself. This merger seems to allow little

---

[62] G. N. Garmonsway, 'Anglo-Saxon Heroic Attitudes', in Jess B. Bessinger and Robert P. Creed (eds.), *Franciplegius: Medieval and Linguistic Studies in Honor of Francis Peabody Magoun, Jr.* (New York, 1965), pp. 139–46; citing from p. 142.

room for the irony that some have detected in the poem's last word, *lofgeornost*. Leyerle renders it 'too eager for praise' (not 'most eager'), and sees in it 'a fault inherent in the heroic age . . . a king's unrestrained desire for individual glory'.[63] Against this another critic, John Niles, cites earlier approving references to 'lof' (24–5, 1534–6) to suggest that 'lofgeornost' should be understood as 'a high compliment . . . intended for a man who directed his life to lofty ends'.[64] On that reading, the voices of the poet and his creations unite in a final act of *laudatio*.

'Celebration or critique?' It is not, where Beowulf and Byrhtnoth are concerned, a straightforward question. We modern readers know nothing for sure about the interpretative communities to which the poet originally spoke – aristocratic? monastic? a mixture of both? – and we lack a native speaker's feel for what exactly, in their contexts, words such as *oferhygd* or *lofgeorn* signify. We also, I would argue, need to correct for our modern predilection for ironic and diminishing readings, especially where warrior heroes are concerned. Critique is more to our taste than celebration in such cases. One can see that Orchard takes this taste for granted when he defends *Beowulf* against one reader's dismissal of it as 'boring and unattractive' in the following terms: 'But if some modern readers have failed to be impressed by *Beowulf*, it is equally clear that the poet himself is far from universally positive about the characters he has created, producing a perhaps surprising number of apparently critical or at least questionable comments, both by and of a whole range of individuals.'[65]

---

[63] Leyerle, 'The Hero and the King', p. 101. Goldsmith rejects Leyerle's translation of the word, but adds: 'Nevertheless, the word is double-edged, and may well be meant as dramatic irony, in view of Wiglaf's earlier censure of Beowulf's decision to go after the dragon', *Mode and Meaning*, p. 224. Fred C. Robinson argues against taking the word in a positive sense: *'Beowulf' and the Appositive Style* (Knoxville, Tenn., 1985), pp. 81–2.

[64] *The Poem and its Tradition*, p. 207. Shippey argues against irony here, *Beowulf*, p. 35.

[65] Orchard, *A Critical Companion*, p. 238.

Certainly the poet is not universally positive about his characters, and he does indeed find room for some 'apparently critical or at least questionable comments'. These commonly represent what Garmonsway called 'the world of common sense and nonheroic norms' – a world that will dissuade heroes from risk and lament their failure to follow such advice. Yet I believe that comments of this kind function as measures of Beowulf's superiority to the speakers – even a speaker so far from unheroic as Wiglaf – and so redound to his praise.

CHAPTER 3

Middle English

The great bulk and variety of Middle English verse – very great indeed by comparison with what survives from pre-Conquest times – make it hard to do any justice to the part played by praise in the poetry of that age, even if one sets Chaucer aside for separate treatment, as I do here. As in Old English, there are many long poems devoted to 'historical' heroes, and I shall devote the greater part of the present chapter to some of these, favouring them because, like *Beowulf*, their laudatory intentions have prompted discussion in modern criticism. These are poems about the past in which, as Gregory Nagy said of Homeric epic, 'the praise takes place by the very process of narrating the deeds of heroes'.[1] However, Nagy also speaks of a second type of praise poetry in which, as he puts it, the praise applies to the 'here-and-now', and poems of this type figure much more prominently in Middle than in Old English. Directly or indirectly, they address their *laudes* to a variety of individual subjects, male and female, human and divine, public and private, often under new influences from Latin or French writings, as in the case of love lyrics and hymns to Mary. Few of these poems have prompted modern critics to question their laudatory intentions; but I shall offer at least a sketchy account of them before turning to the 'historical' pieces.

---

[1] See above, p. 7.

61

Where praise poems of the here-and-now type concern male subjects, these most often are men of some public standing, as one
would expect; but it so happens that one of the earliest and most
sophisticated examples concerns a private person – a cleric known as
Master Nicholas of Guildford. In the thirteenth-century *Owl and the
Nightingale*, the birds of the title represent the two opposing positions suggested by their traditional characters, the grave owl and the
gay nightingale; and in their long debate they find little upon which
they can agree. But they unite in accepting Nicholas as a suitable
man to judge between them. He is first proposed, as a person of
good judgement, by the Nightingale (ll. 190–8); yet her adversary,
the Owl, readily agrees to the choice:

> Ich granti wel þat he us deme,
> Vor þeʒ he were wile breme
> And lof him were niʒtingale
> And oþer wiʒte gente and smale,
> Ich wot he is nu suþe acoled.[2]

(I'm quite happy to accept his jurisdiction over us, even though he used to
be a little bit wild at one time and was rather fond of nightingales and other
pretty little things, but I know that he's completely cooled down now.)

The Owl accepts Nicholas as arbitrator between them because he has,
she says, grown out of his youthful amorous, nightingalish phase and
is now 'ripe and fastrede' ('mature and judicious') (l. 211). But his
equally ready acceptance by the Nightingale implies a more subtle
compliment, for it suggests, by a kind of triangulation, that Nicholas
occupies a position equidistant from those occupied by the two dis-
putants. His transcendent 'ripeness' is such that he will show no
undue favour to either party; so they can fly off, as they do at the end

---

[2] Lines 201–5. Text and translation from *The Owl and the Nightingale*, ed. and trans. Neil
Cartlidge (Exeter, 2001).

of the poem, both equally happy to await his judgement – a judgement that the reader is left to imagine as exemplary in its balance
and fairmindedness. If, as seems most likely, the piece was written
by Nicholas himself, with a petitionary eye on some long-overdue
church preferment (ll. 1759–78), then a prospective patron should
have been impressed as well as amused by his artfully oblique exercise
in self-praise.[3]

Praise of contemporary kings and lords appears hardly at all in
Middle English until the turn of the thirteenth century – in part, no
doubt, because poets in the earlier period were more likely to address
such subjects in Latin or in French than in the more lowly vernacular.
Nor, by comparison with what followed in Tudor and Stuart times,
are panegyrics of this kind particularly conspicuous in the fourteenth
or even the fifteenth centuries. In most of them the eulogistic intent
is beyond question, but one early example has proved controversial.
This is an elegy for an Anglo-Irish lord, Pers de Bermingham, who in
1305 invited two hostile Irish chieftains and their followers to dinner
and killed all but one of them.[4] Earlier scholars took the poem at
face value, as elegaic praise; but in 1989 Michael Benskin proposed
that it should be read as 'not a eulogy, but a satirical indictment'
(p. 61). Certainly the measures taken by Pers against his enemies
were atrocious, and it is very hard for a modern reader to believe that

---

[3] See further J. A. Burrow, *The Ages of Man* (Oxford, 1988), pp. 169–70. I cannot accept the
ironical reading tentatively suggested by Nicolas Jacobs, '*The Owl and the Nightingale* and
the Bishops', in Myra Stokes and T. L. Burton (eds.), *Medieval Literature and Antiquities:
Studies in Honour of Basil Cottle* (Cambridge, 1987), pp. 91–8.

[4] Edited by Angela Lucas in *Anglo-Irish Poems of the Middle Ages* (Dublin, 1995), pp. 150–7. See
Michael Benskin, 'The Style and Authorship of the Kildare Poems – (1) *Pers of Bermingham*',
in J. Lachlan Mackenzie and Richard Todd (eds.), *In Other Words: Transcultural Studies in
Philology, Translation and Lexicology Presented to H. H. Meier* (Dordrecht, 1989), pp. 57–75.
For a contrary view, see Thorlac Turville-Petre, *England the Nation: Language, Literature,
and National Identity, 1290–1340* (Oxford, 1996), pp. 155–8. I am indebted to a lecture about
this poem by John Scattergood, whose forthcoming essay on it will bring further historical
evidence in support of a non-ironical reading.

any poet could have countenanced them; yet Benskin fails, I think, to demonstrate any convincing evidence of ironical intention in the text of the poem. As Turville-Petre says: 'The poet neither expresses unease nor is moved to offer any justification; he is aware of no disparity between the chivalric ideals that de Bermingham represents and the bloody treachery that he enacts' (p. 157).

About most panegyrics of this kind, however, there can be no disagreement. An early instance, lamenting the death of King Edward I in 1307, celebrates his goodness and his renown ('pris') as a warrior – so great that the poet cannot express his merits:

> Þah mi tonge were mad of stel,
>   Ant min herte y-ȝote of bras,
> Þe godnesse myht y never telle
>   Þat wiþ kyng edward was.
> Kyng, as þou art cleped conquerour,
>   In uch bataille þou hadest pris.[5]

In Lancastrian and Yorkist times, with the rising status of the English language, praises of kings and nobles become more frequent – though they never match what French poets wrote for their rulers. John Lydgate's poem about the kings of England ends with eulogy of the reigning Lancastrians (Robbins no. 1, ll. 85–105); John Audelay celebrates the newly crowned Henry VI as a 'peerless prince', while recalling the triumphs of his famous father;[6] and another poem (Robbins no. 42) laments the death of Edward VI, describing him as a nonesuch: 'The dowthiest, the worthiest, withouten comparison.'

Towards the end of the Middle Ages it becomes possible to identify writers of English whose verse is embedded in the life of royal courts

---

[5] *Historical Poems of the xivth and xvth Centuries*, ed. Rossell Hope Robbins (New York, 1959), no. 5, ll. 81–6. See the discussion by Geert de Wilde, *Anglia*, 123 (2005), 23–45. Other poems of this kind in Robbins are nos. 1, 32, 39–42, 73, 83 and 92.

[6] Robbins, no. 41. Cf. 'A Remembrance of Henry VI' by James Ryman, Robbins, no. 83.

deeply enough to warrant the description 'court poet' – John Skelton in England, for example, and William Dunbar in Scotland. Dunbar was a master of *laus* (and also of *vituperatio*), and he addresses occasions at the court of James VI in high auxetic style. Thus he welcomes the arrival in Edinburgh of an emissary from the King of France in a poem beginning:

> Renownit, ryall, right reverend and serene,
> Lord hie tryumphing in wirschip and valoure,
> Fro kyngis downe most cristin knight and kene,
> Most wyse, most valyand, moste laureat hie victour.[7]

Elsewhere, on a somewhat similar epideictic occasion, Dunbar celebrates the reception of Queen Margaret by the town of Aberdeen, a royal entry which allows him to praise, not only the queen, but also the town that greets her:

> Blyth Aberdeane, thow beriall of all tounis,
> The lamp of bewtie, bountie and blythnes.[8]

The most substantial of these 'laureate' pieces concerns the marriage of Margaret and James in 1503. This poem, commonly known as 'The Thrissill and the Rois' (Bawcutt, no. 52), symbolises Margaret by a perfect rose and James, variously, by a lion, an eagle, and a Scottish royal thistle, all in a high panegyric style. Yet one notices that elsewhere Dunbar treats the king rather more familiarly, often addressing him in his petitionary poems simply as 'Sir'; and in this

---

[7] No. 56 in *The Poems of William Dunbar*, ed. Priscilla Bawcutt, 2 vols. (Glasgow, 1998). Another poem, Bawcutt no. 23, laments the death of the same visitor, Bernard Stewart, as the 'flour of chevelrie'. I write further about Dunbar's poetry of praise and vituperation in Priscilla Bawcutt and Janet Hadley Williams (eds.), *A Companion to Medieval Scottish Poetry* (Cambridge, 2006), pp. 133–48.

[8] Bawcutt, no. 8, ll. 1–2. Praise of towns is a standard epideictic topic, as in the twelfth-century poem on Durham, *ASPR*, vi.27, discussed by M. Schlauch, 'An Old English *Encomium Urbis*', *Journal of English and Germanic Philology*, 40 (1941), 14–28.

relative lack of ceremony he resembles the English poets of the time, whose treatments of royalty never approach the fullness and extravagance of those addressed to later Tudor and Stuart monarchs. Kings may indeed be praised as wise rulers or doughty knights, but poets do not hesitate also to lecture them on their duties (as Nature does in 'The Thrissill'). For them, royalty has little of that daunting charisma which poets were to bestow on Elizabeth I. As Thomas Hoccleve put it, addressing the future Henry V, 'a kyng is but a man soul, par fay.'[9]

In Middle English overall, here-and-now praises are more often and more emphatically directed at female than at male subjects, most especially in love poems and in hymns to the Virgin. Lyrics of love offered a new opening for encomiastic writing, reflecting the post-Conquest influence of Francophone poetry, the love lyrics of the troubadours and trouvères. Early English examples, in Manuscript Harley 2253, are 'Annot and Johon' and 'The Loveliest Lady in Land'.[10] The former, glorifying a certain real or imaginary Annot, compares her successively, in five very elaborately metred stanzas, with jewels, flowers, birds, spices and heroes and heroines. It begins:

> Ichot a burde in a bour ase beryl so bryht,
> Ase saphyr in selver semly on syht,
> Ase iaspe þe gentil þat lemeþ wiþ lyht,
> Ase gernet in golde and ruby wel ryht.

Courtly love lyrics later endlessly blazon the beauties and virtues of the beloved, as in a poem written by John Lydgate, according to the

---

[9] *The Regiment of Princes*, ed. Charles R. Blyth (Kalamazoo, 1999), l. 4862. Hoccleve's addresses to Henry, as prince or king, are commonly more advisory than laudatory: *Regiment*, ll. 2017–37, and balades nos. IV, V and XV in his *Minor Poems*, ed. F. J. Furnivall, EETS e.s. 61 (1892).

[10] *English Lyrics of the XIIIth Century*, ed. Carleton Brown (Oxford, 1932), nos. 76 and 83. On the love-lyrics in the Harley Manuscript (copied in the 1330s), see Thorlac Turville-Petre, *England the Nation*, pp. 203–16.

heading in the manuscript, 'at þe request of a squyer þat served in loves court':

> Fresshe lusty beaute Ioyned with gentylesse,
> Demure, appert, glad chere with governaunce,
> Yche thing demenid by avysinesse . . .'[11]

In these poems, as in other medieval treatments of women, *laus* is sharply differentiated from the *vituperatio* that is to be found in those few pieces which represent woman as ugly and evil: 'O wicket wemen, wilfull, and variable, / Richt fals, feckle, fell, and frivolus.'[12] There seems to be no middle way.

On rare occasions, vituperation takes the form of ironic, simulated praise. 'The Lover's Mocking Reply' (Robbins, no. 209) opens by addressing a 'fresch floure, most plesant of pryse', but goes on to describe her as 'crabbed of kynde' and altogether hideous; and Hoccleve's 'Commendacion de ma Dame' (Robbins, no. 210) very obviously does not commend an equally ugly woman. Such heavy-handed ironies are unmistakable. In some other poems, however, modern criticism has claimed to find ironies of a less blatant kind. So one scholar reads 'Annot and Johon' as 'a subtle burlesque of the serious business of idealizing one's mistress'.[13] Well, one would hesitate to call the poem a sincere expression of personal feeling; but I myself can see nothing in it that would cast a shadow of doubt across its hyperbolic, idealising manner – extreme though the rhetoric

---

[11] *Secular Lyrics of the* XIVth *and* XVth *Centuries*, ed. Rossell Hope Robbins (Oxford, 1952), no. 131, with many other examples in the section 'Courtly Love Lyrics', nos. 127ff.

[12] *Ibid.*, no. 212, ll. 1–2.

[13] D. J. Ransom, *Poets at Play: Irony and Parody in the Harley Lyrics* (Norman, Okla., 1985), p. 32. Theo Stemmler questions Ransom's readings as instances of the 'ironic fallacy': 'The Problem of Parody: *Annot and John*, for Example', in Piero Boitani and Anna Torti (eds.), *Genres, Themes, and Images in English Literature: The J. A. W. Bennett Memorial Lectures* (Tübingen, 1988), pp. 156–65. See also Norman Blake, *The English Language in English Literature* (London, 1977), pp. 121–3, again rejecting a parodic interpretation.

certainly is. Geoffrey Chaucer, as one might expect, presents a more
arguable case, in his amorous balade beginning 'Madame, ye ben of
al beaute shryne' ('To Rosemounde'). This poem begins by elab-
orating its conceit of Rosemounde as the shrine of all beauty: her
brightness shines like the crystal sides of a reliquary, and her cheeks
have the colour of the rubies that might adorn such a shrine. But
Chaucer goes on, less elegantly, to speak of himself as weeping tears
by the barrel-full ('tyne') (l. 9), wrapped up in his love like a pike
in its sauce (ll. 17–18). These low images have prompted some to
read the whole poem ironically, as 'a humorous lover's complaint in
which the rhetoric is slyly pushed beyond the conventionally hyperbolic to the slightly ludicrous'.[14] Yet the humour, such as it is, hardly
qualifies the hyperbolic praise, for its object (as also in Chaucer's
'Merciles Beaute') is not the lady, but the figure of the poet-lover
himself; and the sentiments attributed to that figure are themselves
far from ridiculous. How beautifully, for instance, the second stanza
makes its return to the balade refrain:

> So curtaysly I go with love bounde
> That to myself I sey in my penaunce,
> 'Suffyseth me to love you, Rosemounde,
> Thogh ye to me ne do no daliaunce.'
>
> ll. 13–16

Like songs of love, Marian lyrics belong to the post-Conquest
period in England, where the cult of the Virgin flourished particularly
from the twelfth century on. One of the earliest, 'On God Ureisun
of Ure Lefdi', describes itself as a 'lofsong' or song of praise, and

---

[14] *The Minor Poems*, The Variorum Edition of Chaucer, Vol. v. Part One, ed. George B.
Pace and Alfred David (Norman, Okla., 1982), p. 161. Cf. discussion of the poem by
Scattergood, in A. J. Minnis with V. J. Scattergood and J. J. Smith, *The Shorter Poems*,
Oxford Guides to Chaucer (Oxford, 1995), pp. 479–80.

many of these poems are just that.[15] Drawing on French and Latin models, English *laudes Mariae* celebrate the Virgin's beauty, her nobility and her readiness to take up the cause of sinners. The mainly anonymous poems in Carleton Brown's collections range from the relative simplicity of 'Edi beo þu, Hevene Quene' to the high style of the later 'O Hie Emperice and Quene Celestiall'.[16] I shall refer in the next chapter to Chaucer's poems about Mary, a subject on which he 'wroot ful many a lyne', as his disciple Hoccleve observed (*Regiment of Princes*, l. 4987). Hoccleve himself wrote several such pieces, including one that used to be ascribed to the master himself. This poem illustrates something of the luxuriance of epithets for the Virgin, many of them drawn from liturgical sources: Mary is mother of God, empress of queens, well of pity, flower of humility and the like.[17] Such panegyric rises to a height of flamboyant virtuosity in Dunbar's 'Ballat of Our Lady' some hundred years later:

> Empryce of prys, imperatrice,
>   Bricht polist precious stane,
> Victrice of vyce, hie genitrice
>   Of Ihesu, lord soverayne,
> Our wys pavys fro enemys,
>   Agane the feyndis trayne,
> Oratrice, mediatrice, salvatrice,
>   To God gret suffragane.[18]

Praise of Mary is not confined to lyrics. In the dream poem *Pearl*, she is hailed as 'Quen of cortaysye', 'Fenyx of Arraby', 'Makeleȝ

---

[15] *English Lyrics of the xiiith Century*, ed. Brown, no. 3, ll. 8 and 14. On *lofsong*, see below p. 72. For a survey of Marian Lyrics, see Rosemary Woolf, *The English Religious Lyric in the Middle Ages* (Oxford, 1968), chapters iv, vii and viii (on praise, especially pp. 124–34).

[16] *English Lyrics of the xiiith Century*, ed. Brown, no. 60; *Religious Lyrics of the xvth Century*, ed. Carleton Brown (Oxford, 1939), no. 13.

[17] Hoccleve, *Minor Poems*, ed. Furnivall, no. x. Cf. no. vii.

[18] Ed. Bawcutt, no. 16, ll. 61–8.

Moder and myryest May'.[19] This poem is chiefly devoted, however,
to another woman, if she can be so described: the dead infant daughter
who appears to her father in a vision, rather like Beatrice in Dante's
Commedia, as a damsel now enjoying the bliss of heaven. She has
the long golden hair of a beautiful woman, but otherwise the whole
opening description (ll. 161–228) is a symphony in white, as if the
dreamer can hardly make her beauty out against the background of
the dazzling crystal cliff at the foot of which she sits. Her face is
whiter than ivory, she is dressed thoughout in pure white as befits a
bride of the Lamb (Revelation 19.8), and her clothes and crown are
adorned with 'cler quyt perle' (l. 207). The name 'Pearl' by which
she is addressed quite probably plays on the child's baptismal name
'Margery', just as Chaucer does when he names Blanche 'White' in
another poem of elegiac praise, his *Book of the Duchess*.[20] She now
fulfils the promise of perfection held out by her name. As the dreamer
declares:

> Þy beauté com never of nature;
> Pymalyon paynted never þy vys,
> Ne Arystotel nawþer by hys lettrure
> Of carped þe kynde þese propertéȝ.
>
> ll. 749–52

Here, for once, an auxetic hyperbole can be seen as literally true –
albeit only in a dream.

I now turn to some of the longer, 'historical', narrative poems. In
the prologue to *The Wars of Alexander*, the poet surveys the variety of subjects that people like to hear about as entertainment after
dinner – notable events that occurred before they or their fathers were

---

[19] *Pearl*, ed. E. V. Gordon (Oxford, 1953), ll. 425–44. Pearl herself is the speaker.
[20] See Gordon's Introduction, p. xvii. I discuss Chaucer's *Book of the Duchess* below, pp. 125–7.

born. Some enjoy stories about saints, he says, some about lovers, and:

> Sum covettis and has comforth to carpe and to lestyn
> Of curtaissy, of kny3thode, of craftis of armys,
> Of kyngis at has conquirid and ovircomyn landis.[21]

In what follows, I consider three poems of this last type, alliterative narratives set in Classical or British antiquity and chiefly concerned with the 'craftis of armys' of knights, kings and conquerors: La3amon's *Brut*, the *Morte Arthure* and the *Wars of Alexander*. The last part of the chapter will be devoted to the very different case of *Sir Gawain and the Green Knight*.

The oldest of these poems is La3amon's *Brut*, probably dating from the early thirteenth century. This recounts the whole history of the kings of Britain, mainly following the *Roman de Brut* of Wace, which is itself a version of Geoffrey of Monmouth's *Historia Regum Britanniae*.[22] As La3amon first embarks on his long narrative, he introduces it with these words:

> Nu seið mid loft-songe þe wes on leoden preost,
> Al swa þe boc spekeð þe he to bisne inom.

(Now he who was a priest among the people speaks with *loft-songe*, just as the book which he took as his original reports.)

ll. 36–7

---

[21] *The Wars of Alexander*, ed. Hoyt N. Duggan and Thorlac Turville-Petre, EETS s.s. 10 (1989), ll. 8–10.

[22] I cite the Caligula text from *La3amon: Brut*, ed. G. L. Brook and R. F. Leslie, 2 vols., EETS 250, 277 (1963, 1978), with my punctuation. The Arthurian section is edited and translated by W. R. J. Barron and S. C. Weinberg, *La3amon's 'Arthur'* (Harlow, 1989). The whole *Brut* is translated by Rosamund Allen, *Lawman: Brut* (London, 1992). For an edition and translation of Wace, see Judith Weiss, *Wace's Roman de Brut: A History of the British* (Exeter, 1999).

The compound *loft-songe* is a variant of *lofsong* meaning 'song of praise', a word already noticed here as referring to psalms and to Marian lyrics; but it has secular applications too.[23] Laȝamon uses the expression again when he describes how the British celebrated Vortimer as their king 'mid muchele loft-songe' (l. 7308), probably referring to some kind of sung panegyrics. This is one of several occasions in the narrative where characters are said to 'sing' the praises of others, and where Laȝamon seems to be imagining scenes not unlike that in *Beowulf* where the Danish scop improvises verses in praise of the hero's defeat of Grendel. The *Brut* also has one instance of vituperative song or 'hoker loð', when the British king Carric has scorn heaped on him by his subjects: 'hoker loð sungen bi laðen þan kingen' ('they sang songs of derision about the hated king') (l. 14408).[24] It is remarkable that Laȝamon should have added to his sources, as he did, these references to a kind of here-and-now poetic activity with which he can hardly have been acquainted in his Worcester diocese. But he was a man of antiquarian tastes, and he evidently knew that his own very bookish *loft-songe* had archaic precedents in the oral performances of olden times.

There are two other instances of such praise-singing in the *Brut*, both added to the sources and both referring to the chief hero of the poem, King Arthur. The first occurs as Arthur's army is on the march back to England after a successful campaign in Scotland:

> Þer sungen beornes seolcuðe leoðes
> Of Arðure þan kinge and of his here-þringen,
> And sæiden on songe to þisse worlde longe

[23] Above, pp. 31 and 68. On the word see Bosworth-Toller's *Anglo-Saxon Dictionary s.v. lof-sang* and *MED s.v. lof-song. MED* explains the form *loft* for *lof* (also found in other texts of the time) in part by the influence of *loft* 'high place'. *MED* has secular instances only from the two Laȝamon places; but the Bosworth-Toller Supplement has one, from a gloss.
[24] Wace says only that he was 'full of hatred to everyone', l. 13378.

Neore nevere-mære swulc king ase Arður þurh alle þing,
King no kæisere in nævere nare kuðõe.

(There men sang wonderful songs about King Arthur and his warriors,
proclaiming in song that there would never again while the world lasted be
a king like in every respect to Arthur, nor ever such a king or emperor in
any land whatever.)

ll. 11017–21

The redoubled negatives strengthen the hyperbole: Arthur is the very
greatest king ever, and the very greatest anywhere. A little later, on
his return from conquests abroad, his subjects welcome his arrival:

Her wes fiðelinge and song, her wes harpinge imong,
Pipen and bemen murie þer sungen.
Scopes þer sungen of Arðure þan kingen
And of þan muchele wurð-scipe þe he iwunnen hafeden.

(Here there was fiddling and singing and harping too, pipes and trumpets
sounding merrily. Bards there sang about King Arthur and about the great
honour that he had won.)

ll. 11328–31

Shortly after this same return from overseas, according to Geoffrey of Monmouth, Wace and Laʒamon, there followed a twelve-year
period of peace and tranquillity for the British. It is to these otherwise
blank years that Wace assigns all those romantic Arthurian marvels
and adventures of which British *conteurs* like to speak; but Wace himself, as a critical historian, determines to pass over such tales in silence.
Though they are, he admits, not all lies – 'Ne tut mençunge, ne tut
veir' – the *conteurs* have so embellished them that they have made them
all seem fabulous ('fable').[25] At the same point in his text, Laʒamon

---

[25] *Roman de Brut*, ll. 9793–8. Later romance writers sometimes insert their 'fables' into this
time-slot: Ad Putter, 'Finding Time for Romance: Medieval Arthurian Literary History',
Medium Aevum, 63 (1994), 1–16; also Andrew Lynch, '"Peace is Good after War": The

expands Wace's comments (ll. 11454–75). The British, he says, 'tell many kinds of lie about King Arthur' ('sugeð feole cunne lesinge bi Arðure þan kinge'); but that, he adds, is just how people are: they will praise those they love beyond their deserts, and exaggerate the faults of those that they hate. *Laus* and *vituperatio* are both subject to hyperbolic heightening, in life as in literature. Yet Laȝamon insists, more explicitly than Wace, that his own narrative allows no such departures from the truth, being based on reliable written sources:

> Ne al soh ne al les þat leod-scopes singeð,
> Ah þis is þat soððe bi Arðure þan kinge.
> Nes næver ar swulc king, swa duhti þurh alle þing,
> For þat soðe stod a þan writen hu hit is iwurðen,
> Ord from þan ænden, of Arðure þan kinge,
> No mare no lasse, buten alse his laȝen weoren.

(What minstrels sing is neither all true nor all lies, but this is the truth about King Arthur. Never before was there such a king, so valiant in all circumstances; for the truth about King Arthur, from start to finish, has been established in writings according as it happened, neither more nor less, exactly as his ways were.)

                                                              ll. 11465–70

Laȝamon here claims that his praises of Arthur are free from that hyperbole in which *conteurs* (and rhetoricians) customarily dealt. There really *was*, he insists, never such a king.

Certainly Laȝamon's poem, like Wace's, has little time for the extravagances of romance; yet it is, of course, very far from being a sober work of history. Its narrative manner is strongly auxetic throughout. It makes frequent use of intensives such as *wunder*, 'marvellously' and above all *unimete*, 'immeasurable, immeasurably', a

Narrative Seasons of English Arthurian Tradition', in Corinne Saunders, Françoise Le Saux and Neil Thomas (eds.), *Writing War: Medieval Literary Responses to Warfare* (Cambridge, 2004), pp. 127–46, at pp. 128–9.

favourite word (e.g. ll. 6258ff or 14233ff); and superlatives of all sorts abound, especially in the second half of the alliterative line. Time and again Arthur is characterised as 'aðelest kingen', the most noble of kings, with alliterative variants such as 'selest alre kinge', the best of all kings, and 'baldest alre kingen' (ll. 11066, 13065). By contrast, the treacherous Modred is 'forcuðest monnen', the most wicked of men (ll. 12711, 14119, etc.). Such epithets generally fix people in the *Brut* as either very good or very bad, with little scope for variation or change – though the Saxon leader Hengest, introduced as 'cnihtene alre feirest' at l. 6967 and still so described at 7568, becomes 'cnihte vor-cuðest', the most wicked of knights, at l. 7571. There is hardly a place for irony here, though Arthur himself employs a form of it in the mocking rhetoric of his speeches to the three leaders of the soon-to-be-defeated Saxons. Yesterday, he says, Colgrim was 'monnen alre kennest' (l. 10628), Baldulf was 'cnihten alre baldest' (10638) and Childric was 'kennest alre kingen' (10646); but now . . . ? Laȝamon supports his many superlatives of this sort with a range of more elaborate auxetic devices, such as the topoi of the inexpressible and the incomparable. So, in his elaborate account of Arthur's great Whitsun court at Caerleon (ll. 12097–341), he declares that so many people attended that it is impossible to name or count them (ll. 12159, 12165) or to describe the amount of ale and wine consumed (l. 12196). No one on earth ever saw anything like it:

> To iwissen hit is isaid and soð hit is ifunden
> Þat no isah no mon naver ær mid eorðliche monne her
> Half swa hahne ricche-dom a naver nane hepen
> Swa mid Arðure was aðeles cunnes.

(Truly it has been said and proved for a fact that no one had ever before seen here among earthly men half such lofty magnificence in any gathering of nobles as there was with Arthur.)

ll. 12221–4

In the dedication of his *Historia* to King Stephen and Robert Earl of Gloucester, Geoffrey of Monmouth announced his subject as the kings of Britain and their deeds which 'deserve to be praised for all time'.[26] Geoffrey's Norman lords might be expected to appreciate his account of the glorious early history of the country which they now ruled. The west-country priest who wrote the *Brut* can hardly have had any such readers in view, but his *loft-song* celebrates the glories of Britain just as strenuously. His set descriptions sing the praises of the island itself (ll. 618–22, 1002–9), its first conqueror, the Trojan Brutus (ll. 174–9), and many of his successors – kings who, like Arthur, maintained peace and justice at home and conquered their enemies. Before Arthur was born, Merlin prophesied his coming greatness, in a speech for which Laȝamon evidently turned from Wace to Geoffrey:[27]

> Of him scullen gleomen godliche singen,
> Of his breosten scullen æten aðele scopes,
> Scullen of his blode beornes beon drunke,
> Of his eȝene scullen fleon furene gleden,
> Ælc finger an his hond scarp stelene brond.

(Of him minstrels will sing gloriously, noble bards will feast on his breast, men will get drunk on his blood, coals of fire will fly from his eyes, and each finger of his hand will be a sharp blade of steel.)

ll. 9410–14

These extraordinary lines express, in drastic physical terms, what poets owe to great warriors: they feast on their bodies, and no doubt, like other men, drink their blood. The idea is quite alien to modern

---

[26] *The Historia Regum Britannie of Geoffrey of Monmouth*, 1, Bern, Bürgerbibliothek MS 568, ed. Neil Wright (Cambridge, 1984), 1: 'gesta eorum digna eternitate laudis'.

[27] Of the Boar: 'His breast will be food for the needy and his tongue will relieve the thirsty', ed. Wright, 115 (26). See the note in Barron and Weinberg, *Laȝaman's 'Arthur'*, p. 264.

thinking: poets have an appetite for such glorious heroes and their feats of arms.

No critic, so far as I know, has tried to suggest that *laudes* in Laȝamon's poem are other than full-throated glorification.[28] But the case is otherwise with the alliterative *Morte Arthure*, to which I now turn.

The *Morte Arthure*, written about the year 1400, gives an account of the last campaigns and the death of King Arthur, drawing freely on Wace's *Brut*.[29] In his prologue, the poet promises those who like to hear deeds of olden time a noble tale about the great knights of the Round Table and how they conquered the kingdom of Rome. Then, after a long list of Arthur's previous conquests, the action begins with the arrival at a great British Christmas feast of an embassy from Rome, summoning Arthur to appear before the Emperor to answer for his refusal to do homage or pay tribute for his lands. Although Arthur refuses the demand, he impresses the ambassador so deeply that the Roman adversary sings his praises when reporting to the Emperor: Arthur is 'whyeseste and worthyeste and wyghteste of hanndez', as well as the knightliest, comeliest and most magnificent in his hospitality (ll. 530–45). It would seem that the poem is firmly set on an encomiastic course, when even Arthur's enemies join in his praise. Yet the more than 4,000 lines that follow have given rise to differing interpretations in recent times, especially where the portrayal of the hero is concerned. The general issue is, again, 'celebration or critique?' Since the publication in 1960 of a study by William Matthews significantly entitled *The Tragedy of Arthur*, several other scholars and editors have maintained that the poem,

---

[28] Christopher Cannon, in his chapter on the *Brut*, sees its real hero in the enduring land of Britain itself and its tradition of law, contrasting with the 'fragility of kings', who come and go: *The Grounds of English Literature* (Oxford, 2004), chapter 2.

[29] I cite from the edition by Mary Hamel, *Morte Arthure: A Critical Edition* (New York and London, 1984).

so far from generally celebrating Arthur, subjects him to a variety
of critiques.[30] In what follows, I set out to counter, with a certain
amount of detail, interpretations which I regard as inappropriately
moralistic. There are three main issues: the justification of Arthur's
wars, their conduct and the hero's dream of Fortune.

What justifications might contemporary readers have seen for
Arthur's campaigns in the *Morte?* Here a distinction is to be made
between his defensive action against Roman invasion of his territories
and the later campaign within the territory of his adversary.[31] The
poem never questions Arthur's right to defend his own realm. It
dismisses the Roman ambassador's assertion that he holds his lands
only as a subject of Rome, to which he owes homage and tribute
(ll. 86–115): Arthur does concede that the British have paid tribute
in the past, but only, he claims, because his ancestors were forced to
grant it 'tenefully'.[32] The case must be different, however, once his
army has crossed into the territories of the Roman Empire; and some
scholars highlight this as the moment when Arthur ceases to have just
cause. So, Finlayson describes it as the 'point in the narrative that
Arthur's wars cease to be just defences of the Right and become

---

[30] So William Matthews, *The Tragedy of Arthur* (Berkeley, Calif., 1960); *Morte Arthure*, ed.
John Finlayson (London, 1967); Karl Heinz Göller (ed.), *The Alliterative Morte Arthure:
A Reassessment of the Poem* (Cambridge, 1981); and the edition by Mary Hamel. This last,
certainly the best edition of the poem, keeps up a running critique of Arthur and others
in its notes. More recently, see Christine Chism, *Alliterative Revivals* (Philadelphia, Pa.,
2002), pp. 189–236 ('the knightly potential for self-destruction'); and Lynch, '"Peace is
Good after War"' ('a kingdom too much at war').

[31] The border is crossed when Arthur enters Lorraine (l. 2416) to besiege Metz. I set aside
the opinion expressed by Göller, that 'there can be no doubt that the poet is saying that
every war is unjust' (Göller (ed.), *Reassessment*, p. 26, his italics). Matthews, in his *Tragedy
of Arthur*, sees Arthur as a culpably imperialistic warrior from the start.

[32] Lines 271–4. At ll. 2344–5, Arthur's message to Rome speaks of 'The taxe and þe trebutte
of tene schore wynteres / That was tenefully tynte in tym of oure elders' ('The tax and
tribute over two hundred years that was unhappily conceded in our ancestors' time'). The
poet has in mind the origins of the tribute, first granted by Cassibellanus to Julius Caesar,
but only after the British king had been betrayed to the Roman invaders by his own nephew
(Wace, *Brut*, ll. 4809–20).

wars of aggression and acquisition, the categories of unjust wars recognized by the Church and medieval military writers' (*ed. cit.*, pp. 80–1). Mary Hamel in her edition agrees: 'Up to this point in the narrative, Arthur has been at least technically [?] defending his own . . . his war-plans now become openly imperialistic' (note to ll. 2399–405). But this is to overlook another 'technical' point, noticed by Lee Patterson: the poet's insistence on 'the legitimacy of Arthur's claim on Rome', a claim based on lineage and precedent.[33] Arthur recalls that 'myne ancestres ware emperours', citing the British rulers Belyn and Brenne, who won the empire of Rome by conquest in times past, and also the Emperor Constantine.[34] So he can refer to that empire as 'myn heritage'.[35] The claim will seem shaky enough to a modern reader; but several English kings used exactly the same kind of justification for English lordship over Scotland, citing precedents from Geoffrey of Monmouth's *Historia*.[36]

Both Patterson and Elizabeth Porter, in her important article, notice another justification for Arthur the warrior, drawing attention to his resolve to cross the Mediterranean and 'revenge the Renke that on the Rode dyede' (l. 3217). He never fulfils this intention, but the poet takes pains to emphasise that among his adversaries, as well as enemies of Britain, there were many enemies of God. The Emperor of Rome is himself a heretic (l. 1307), and his armies, drawn from his extensive dominions, include many non-Christian warriors,

---

[33] Lee Patterson, *Negotiating the Past: The Historical Understanding of Medieval Literature* (Madison, Wis., 1987), p. 215.

[34] Lines 275–87. On the conquest of Rome by Belyn and Brenne, see Wace, *Brut*, ll. 3145–56. Constantine is emperor at l. 5719 there. *Morte Arthure* twice asserts that Arthur's ancestors subsequently, all except Uther Pendragon, possessed the Empire: ll. 520–1 and 1309–10.

[35] Line 643, also ll. 359 and 1309. See Elizabeth Porter, 'Chaucer's Knight, the Alliterative *Morte Arthure*, and Medieval Laws of War: A Reconsideration', *Nottingham Medieval Studies*, 27 (1983), 56–78, at 59–60.

[36] See James Simpson, *Reform and Cultural Revolution*, The Oxford English Literary History, Vol. II, 1350–1547 (Oxford, 2002), pp. 69–71.

variously described as pagans, heathens and, most often, 'Saracens'.
There are also giants, said to be engendered by devils (l. 612 etc.), as
well as witches and warlocks (l. 613). Back home, the rebel Modred
has pagans and Saracens in his army, so that Gawain, in his last
battle on the beach, can invoke the crusader promise to hearten his
followers:

> We sall for ȝone Sarazenes – I sekire ȝow my trowthe! –
> Souppe with oure Saveoure solemply in heven.

(Because of those Saracens, I promise you, we will sup with our Saviour
grandly in heaven.)

ll. 3804–5

Killing the enemies of the true God was in accordance with the
crusading ideal, and that ideal would have added just one more
justification for Arthur's campaigns – little as the argument will
appeal today.[37]

The other question about Arthur's wars concerns the conduct
of them. Karl Heinz Göller, in keeping with his anti-war reading
of the poem, speaks of its emphasis on physical violence and cruel
injuries; and one can indeed see such an emphasis in, for example,
the long description of the battle of Sessie (ll. 2058–277). The very
first encounter here leaves a victim's spleen sticking to the spear
(l. 2061), every water-crossing runs with blood (l. 2144) and men
die by the thousand (l. 2152). Yet the poet expresses nothing but his
delight in the scene, describing it as 'The faireste-fygured felde that

---

[37] See Porter, 'Chaucer's Knight', 73–6. Texts in the chronicle tradition make much of the
presence of Saracens and the like among Arthur's enemies, as in his speech in the Middle
English *Brut*: '"Go we forþ in Goddes name aȝeynes þe Romayns, þat wiþ ham ledeþ
Sarasines & Paynemes þat no maner truste þai haven to God, but oneliche oppon here
strengþ"', *The Brut*, ed. F. W. D. Brie, EETS 131, 136 (1906, 1908), p. 86. Both the other
two Christian Worthies with whom Arthur is later ranked, Charlemagne and Godfrey of
Bouillon, act against Saracens (ll. 3422–35).

fygurede was ever' (l. 2151). It seems that hyperbole here serves only to glorify hand-to-hand combat. But once Arthur has crossed into the Empire, his campaigns involve damage to non-combatants, and scholars such as Hamel have understandably been shocked by the way the king's siege-engines demolish churches and houses at the siege of Metz (Hamel's note to ll. 3038–43) and by his 'wastings' in Tuscany – 'malicious destruction', which, says Hamel, 'shows a Round Table turned to bullies and vandals' (note to l. 3159).

A sustained attempt to arrive at judgement of such conduct from a point of view that is not anachronistic has been made by Porter in her article. She sums up her conclusion as follows: 'Arthur's behaviour at Metz and throughout his campaign in Lombardy and Tuscany, when compared with contemporary records of the laws and practice of war, does not substantiate the claims made by Matthews [in his *Tragedy of Arthur*] and others that the poet intended to portray him critically' (p. 72). In the case of sieges, Porter points out, the laws of war made a vital distinction. If a town resisted to the end and was taken by assault, then it and its inhabitants were considered to lie entirely at the mercy of the attackers. The prospect of such a catastrophic outcome, it was hoped, would encourage besieged garrisons to negotiate a treaty of surrender at an earlier stage. In the siege of Metz, as described at lines 3032–67, Arthur has begun the assault and evidently has the town at his mercy, when he yields to the pleas of the Duchess of Lorraine and her ladies. He grants a 'charter of peace', calls off the assault, and treats the city with laudable magnanimity, just as if it had indeed been in a position to negotiate terms.[38] It is true, as Hamel observes, that non-combatants suffer at Metz from the barrage of missiles which preceded the assault, just as the people of Tuscany are to suffer later from British depredations. But Porter

---

[38] See Porter, 'Chaucer's Knight', 64–71.

gives evidence to show that fourteenth-century *jus in bello* actually countenanced damage to enemy civilians, on grounds of 'their contribution to the war effort and the military value of demoralizing a largely defenceless population'.[39] Certainly the author of the *Morte*, as poets will, makes more of civilian (and combatant) sufferings than lawyers or chroniclers commonly do; but it is unsafe to conclude that he intended thereby any derogation from the glory of the British victories.

Some scholars, Finlayson and Hamel among them, have identified in the poem a further critique of Arthur and his knights, directed at their occasional acts of rashness or *desmesure*.[40] At one point, a companion warns Sir Gawain against rashly engaging a superior force:

> I rede ȝe wyrke aftyre witte as wyesse men of armes,
> And warpes wylily awaye as wirchipfull knyghtes.

(I advise you to behave with good sense like a wise warrior, and steal slyly away as an honourable knight should.)

ll. 2745–6

We tend to sympathise with sensible advice on such occasions; but in this case the good sense is plainly betrayed by the impossible second line: how could an honourable knight ever steal 'wylily' away in face of his enemies? Gawain disregards the advice, just as the same hero does in face of similar advice from the guide in *Sir Gawain and the Green Knight*, and he is rewarded here with a famous victory. But on other occasions such boldness may have less happy results. A notable

---

[39] *Ibid.*, 64. Christine de Pizan says that 'only priests, students, madmen and little children can expect to remain unmolested by warfaring troops'; cited from her *Livre des faits d'armes et de chevallerie* by Françoise Le Saux, in Saunders, Le Saux and Thomas (eds.), *Writing War*, p. 102.

[40] So in the editions of Finlayson, pp. 18–20, and of Hamel, e.g. her notes to ll. 1922 (Cador), 2446–7 (Arthur), 2735 (Gawain), 3833–8 (Gawain) and 4034–9 (Arthur).

case is Gawain's later attack on Modred and his men, when he wades ashore to fight against massive odds, and loses his life in the process. At one stage (ll. 3817–37), the poet makes a number of comments to the effect that Gawain is in a frenzy, no longer controlled by reason and seemingly set on his own destruction. He compares the hero, in his berserk fury, to a 'wodewyse', or wild man of the woods (l. 3817). Hamel suggests that, by this last comparison, 'the poet indicates that in his drive for revenge Gawain has abandoned chivalry, to this point his central value, and with it all judgment and civilization' (note to l. 3817). Yet such battle-rages are by no means so alien to chivalry as Hamel seems to suggest. In the *Life of the Black Prince* by the Chandos Herald, for instance, Sir William Felton is said to charge against the Spaniards 'com hom sanz sens et sanz avis', losing his life in the process; but the Herald is far from blaming him.[41] Gawain has every reason for fury against the betrayer of his lord, and his assault might have been successful with a bit of luck (ll. 3768–9). Indeed, it inspires even Modred himself with nothing but praise for a man whom he describes as 'hardyeste of hande, happyeste in armes' (l. 3878). There are other places in the poem where characters do speak against the taking of unnecessary risks; but in heroic narrative such utterances commonly carry less weight than we may now suppose – as was the case, I argued, with Wiglaf's words about the dead hero in *Beowulf*. When Arthur exposes himself to defenders' crossbows by riding unarmed around the walls of Metz, his companion blames him for his 'foly'; but this prompts the king to a sharp retort: '"Ife thow be ferde" quod the kyng "I rede thow ryde uttere"', that is, 'if you are afraid, I suggest that you ride further off'.[42] It is a graver

---

[41] *The Life of the Black Prince by the Herald of Sir John Chandos*, ed. and trans. Mildred K. Pope and Eleanor C. Lodge (Oxford, 1910), l. 2740.

[42] Line 2438. Arthur goes on to claim that God will protect an anointed king (ll. 2446–7). In the *Estoire de la Guerre Sainte* by Ambroise, Richard I is another leader blamed by his

case when Arthur, on the eve of his last battle, rejects the advice of Sir Wycharde that he should proceed circumspectly ('warely') (l. 4026) and await reinforcements before encountering Modred's superior force. Arthur responds fiercely, with a vow to avenge the death of his knights, and leads his men on to battle and the destruction of the Round Table. Yet the prudent advice of Wycharde seems beside the point here, I think because Arthur, like the hero at the end of *Beowulf*, has now arrived at his destined end. He is 'þe feye kynge', the king doomed to die (l. 4252), driven by the fatal destiny that was announced for him by his dream of Fortune.[43]

Arthur's dream of the Wheel of Fortune comes to him at the height of his success, when he is on the brink of being crowned as emperor of Rome (ll. 3222–455). He dreams of himself as raised up on the wheel, just as he now is, and then, as he will be, thrown down from it and killed. Everyone is subject to the vicissitudes of Fortune, of course, but Arthur's dream associates him in this fate specifically with the other members of a small élite group, the Nine Worthies, that is, with the most select company of great warriors and conquerors.[44] According to the philosopher who interprets the dream, this ranks Arthur among 'þe nobileste namede in erthe' (l. 3439). Yet it is in this episode that some critics have found the poem's most decisive condemnation of Arthur, as the leader responsible through his fault or sin for the whole 'tragedy' that the narrative, in their opinion, turns out to be. So Hamel sees in it 'the poet's

---

followers for rashness but vindicated as a hero protected by God: see Saunders, Le Saux and Thomas (eds.), *Writing War*, pp. 38–40.

[43] Hamel moralises: 'Arthur's rejection of Wychard's advice is based on the same motive that impelled Gawain to lead his men to destruction, the wish to enact his vengeance personally (cf. 3741–4). Like Gawain, he fails to take into account his responsibility for those he leads' (note to ll. 4034–9).

[44] The *Morte* was apparently the first to associate the Nine Worthies with the Wheel of Fortune. There is a long account of the Worthies in *The Parlement of the Thre Ages*, ll. 297–583, discussed by M. Y. Offord on pp. xl–xlii of her edition, EETS 246 (1959).

criticism of Arthur's career of conquest and the values that underlie it'.[45]

Part of the evidence for this interpretation occurs in Arthur's own account of his dream (ll. 3227–393). He reports the words spoken by the six pre-Arthurian Worthies who have already fallen from their seat on the wheel. They all, as it were in chorus, lament that they ever enjoyed so much favour from Fortune, concluding 'And therefore derflyche I am dampnede for ever!' (l. 3277). Since the six include King David, Joshua and Judas Maccabeus, it is hard to believe that this means that they are all damned in Hell. In her article (pp. 306–7), Hamel acknowledges the difficulty of this reading, which she nevertheless supports; but H. A. Kelly has proposed what seems to be a better interpretation. Noticing that Julius Caesar later speaks of himself as 'dampnede to þe dede' (l. 3299), he suggests the same meaning for 'dampnede' at line 3277: 'condemned to die'.[46] In their individual complaints, the Worthies most often speak of themselves simply as 'lost', or as fallen from their former eminence. Only one of them, the Old Testament hero Judas Maccabeus, strikes a moral note:

> Now of my solace, I am full sodanly fallen,
> And for sake of my syn ȝone sete es me rewede.
>
> ll. 3314–15

Here for once a Worthy does clearly attribute his fall to his own fault: 'now I have suddenly fallen out of my happy state, and that seat has

---

[45] Hamel, p. 42. An earlier essay by Hamel proposes influence from the opening of Dante's *Inferno*: 'The Dream of a King: The Alliterative *Morte Arthure* and Dante', *Chaucer Review*, 14 (1980), 298–312. A cruder version of Hamel's moralising interpretation is offered by Anke Janssen in Göller (ed.), *Reassessment*, pp. 140–52, arguing that '[Arthur's] fatal end cannot be imputed to Dame Fortune's fickleness but is God's just punishment for his evil deeds' (p. 141).

[46] H. A. Kelly, 'The Non-Tragedy of Arthur', in Gregory Kratzmann and James Simpson (eds.), *Medieval English Religious and Ethical Literature: Essays in Honour of G. H. Russell* (Cambridge, 1986), pp. 92–114, citing p. 100.

been taken from me because of my sin'. Yet Arthur's account of his dream offers no other support for this moralistic interpretation of Fortune's working.[47]

The commentary by the philosopher which follows gives, as already noticed, an entirely favourable account of the Worthies; but it does also address criticism at Arthur in two places. Towards the beginning (ll. 3398–400), the philosopher says that he has dealt out death and destruction arrogantly and without good cause:

> Thow has schedde myche blode, and schalkes distroyede,
> Sakeles, in cirquytrie, in sere kynges landis.
> Schryfe the of thy schame and schape for thyn ende.

(You have shed much blood and arrogantly killed innocent men in various kings' lands. Confess your shameful deeds and prepare for your end.)

And again at the end (ll. 3452–5):

> I rede thow rekkyn and reherse unresonable dedis,
> Ore the repenttes full rathe all thi rewthe werkes;
> Mane, amende thy mode or thow myshappen,
> And mekely aske mercy for mede of thy saule!

(I advise you to reckon up and recall your wrong deeds and repent at once of all your injurious actions. Change your way of thinking for the better, man, before you come to grief, and humbly ask mercy for the benefit of your soul.)

In both these passages, the philosopher speaks the language of a Christian priest addressing any man newly faced with the prospects of death and judgement: Arthur is to 'prepare himself for his end' by repenting, confessing his sins and amending his life. In these cirumstances, no conqueror, not even one of 'the noblest named

---

[47] Kelly argues that William Matthews and his followers are mistaken in reading the *Morte* as a 'tragedy' – a term that encourages anachronistic thoughts of Aristotelian tragic flaws (p. 113).

on earth', could safely deny charges of arrogance ('cirquytrie') or the shedding of much blood. Yet this clerical critique receives little support in what follows. The poem seems happy that Arthur should react after his dream, not with grief for his sins, but with wrath ('breth', l. 3465) at news that wicked men are making trouble back in Britain; and the ensuing progress of his revenge against Modred seems to leave any moral doubts quite behind. It is a just cause, justly pursued. Hamel finds some traces of penitential awareness in these pages, most notably when Arthur laments the dead Gawain as 'sakles supprysede for syn of myn one';[48] yet one has to reckon here with the rhetoric of threnody, which will always find fault with the living rather than the dead. This can be at best no more than a one-off instance of that clerical anxiety about Arthur's soul – expressed by the philosopher and shared by some modern readers – which the poem so rarely articulates, and least of all as it approaches its end. In his last battle against the usurper, Arthur figures as a pious and prayerful Christian king, confronting an enemy largely composed of Saracens. Like Gawain before him, he even invokes the crusader promise of an instant reward in heaven for death on the battlefield (ll. 4088–91). He and his men destroy a much larger military force, and he himself wins great glory in death:

> Siche honoure never aughte none erthely knyghttez
> At theire endyng-daye bot Arthure hym selven!

(No earthly knights ever had as great honour when they died as did Arthur himself.)

ll. 4169–70

So the poem ends, as it began, in high auxetic style, glorifying King Arthur and his noble Knights of the Round Table.

---

[48] 'Guiltless, overcome because of my own sin', l. 3986. See Hamel's note to the line ('Arthur's first acknowledgement of sin since his dream'). She observes other signs of spiritual improvement in her notes on ll. 4157–60 and 4322.

In a chapter entitled 'The Tragic' in his Oxford History, James Simpson discusses some late Middle English narratives of war, including the *Morte Arthure*. He stresses 'their opposition to militarist, imperialist pretensions' and attributes that opposition to a voice which he describes as 'clerical yet secular (i. e. learned though not specifically Christian)', speaking against the military values of the aristocracy.[49] In the *Morte* itself, Simpson finds no trace of this voice up to the scene of the dream of Fortune; but at that point, he says, the poem's earlier militaristic zeal is called in question by a 'powerful and decisive intervention' from the clerical voice (p. 110). He finds a similar challenge to aristocratic glorification of war and conquest in another of the texts that he discusses: *The Wars of Alexander*.

The Wars of Alexander is a very accomplished alliterative poem, based closely on a Latin *Historia de Preliis Alexandri Magni*. Like its source, it chronicles the life of Alexander from his birth and upbringing through his campaigns against Darius and Porus to his further adventures in the East.[50] No doubt the poem would have ended, like the *Historia*, with his death by poison, but both Middle English manuscripts lack the conclusion. The poet adopts a high auxetic style throughout, as befits the story of a hero who, like King Arthur, was one of the Nine Worthies. Armies are so big that they cannot be counted, and they engage in battles of surpassing ferocity; halls and palaces are all superlatively rich and splendid; Alexander's horse Bucephalus is 'the best under heaven'; and so on. In the same hyperbolic manner, the poet introduces his hero as 'þe aȝefullest þat evir armys hauntid' ('the most formidable that ever took up arms') (l. 16); and Alexander's prowess as a warrior figures prominently in

---

[49] Simpson, *Reform and Cultural Revolution*, pp. 68, 103. His discussion of the *Morte* occupies pp. 106–10.

[50] *The Wars of Alexander*, ed. Hoyt N. Duggan and Thorlac Turville-Petre, EETS s.s. 10 (1989).

the ensuing narrative, as in the campaigns against Darius that led to his conquest of Persia. At the same time, the poet also portrays him as a man who can feel pity and show mercy, most memorably in his final exchanges with the defeated and dying Darius (ll. 3356–451). Moved to tears by 'pure pete of his payn', Alexander seeks to comfort the Persian emperor. No man, he says, should rejoice just because another has suffered at the hands of Fortune – a reference to Fortune which Darius echoes in his grateful response (at l. 3432). In his discussion of the poem, James Simpson sees in these references to Fortune and the changefulness of things a clerical challenge to Alexander's way of life and his ambitions: 'Speeches of this kind, in which enemy kings confide their shared comprehension of imperial delusion, stand at the heart of this brilliant alliterative work' (p. 116). Yet warriors hardly need clerics to remind them of the fickleness of Fortune, and they can surely speak of it as occasion arises without raising doubts about their imperial projects.

There is, however, a very strong and extended challenge to Alexander's way of life later in the poem, in the exchange of letters across the Ganges between him and the leader of the Brahmins, Dindimus.[51] In reply to Alexander's polite letter of enquiry – seeking, he says, knowledge and wisdom – Dindimus offers an account of the simple existence of the Indian sect. They live 'a lowly life and a clean' (l. 4389), following a régime of health and virtue in accordance with the dictates of nature. They eat only what they find growing, drink nothing but water, wear no clothes and have no houses, weapons or money. This is hard primitivism, a position from which praise of such as Alexander is not to be expected. And Dindimus does indeed blame him severely. So:

---

[51] *Wars*, ll. 4316–833. There is another Englishing of these exchanges in *Alexander and Dindimus*, ed. W. W. Skeat, EETS e.s. 31 (1878).

> For þi tent is all on terrandry and tourment of armes,
> In bost and in bobans in bataills and stryvys,
> A craft till oure condicions at cordis bot litill.

(For your mind is all set on dominance and military oppression, the pride
and vainglory of battles and strife, a business that agrees very little with our
ways.)

ll. 4380–2

Later in his letters, Dindimus advances a variety of other criticisms: of
covetousness, luxury, gluttony and also (the Brahmins being natural
monotheists) idolatry. Alexander responds by dismissing the Indian's
claims for the simple life: Dindimus and his followers live that way
because they are incapable of anything better. They are like beasts:

> All þis condicions I call bot comon of bestis,
> Þat has no sent in þaire saule ne savour in na gude.

(In this way of life I say that you are no better than beasts, which have no
perception in their souls nor any appetite for what is good.)

ll. 4743–4

Simpson condemns Alexander's response as 'a pure instance of Western orientalism', and sees in the Indian's criticisms a challenge that
'threatens to undo the achievement of the imperialist'.[52] Yet it is
hard to understand the Brahmin way of life as any real alternative
for Alexander and his like. Dindimus himself concedes that, even
if he were able fully to convey his message, 'it would do you no
good' (l. 4379). Indeed, if *per impossibile* Alexander were to be converted, that would be 'unhalesom' ('not good for him'?) (l. 4516).
The two men are simply poles apart. Nor can one assume, as Simpson

---

[52] Simpson, *Reform and Cultural Revolution*, p. 115. For a lengthy discussion of Western
orientalism in the poem, see Chism, *Alliterative Revivals*, pp. 111–54, speaking of 'Alexander's strange xenophobic, misogynist, semi-Oedipal quest for world conquest and historic
transcendence' (p. 147).

perhaps does, that readers faced with this opposition would be expected simply to side with Dindimus. Alexander has a case. In the words of King Lear, 'Allow not nature more than nature needs, / Man's life is cheap as beast's.' The whole episode is deeply interesting in itself, certainly, and it presents a real challenge, which neither Alexander nor the poem can be said to meet; but it seems to cast no shadow across the ensuing representation of the hero. After dictating a last letter to Dindimus, Alexander sets up a marble pillar to mark the Ganges as the easternmost point to which he has pursued his enemies, and then turns back to encounter more marvels, hardships and dangers. The English text, as we have it, breaks off at the point where Alexander in Babylon commissions a magnificent throne, inscribed with the names of all the countries he rules. No doubt the poet followed the Latin to its ending, with the death of Alexander by poison and his grand funeral. It may be that he struck a note of criticism in his final summary, as the source probably did; but there is every reason to suppose that his poem would have ended on a major chord, like the Latin, celebrating Alexander as 'conqueror of all the world in twelve years'.[53]

In his book *The Medieval Alexander*, George Cary studied the varying treatments of Alexander in medieval texts, variations which went back to sources themselves at odds in their judgements on the hero. He observes that writers were often content simply to combine their conflicting authorities, without regard for consistency of treatment. Such is the case with the Dindimus episode in the *Historia de Preliis* in its relation to the main body of the text. In this connection, Cary speaks of 'the juxtaposition of passages based

---

[53] The EETS editors summarise the remaining Latin on their p. 300. The Latin text edited by Steffens in 1975 speaks of Alexander as 'victor omnium, sed ira et luxuria victus' ('conqueror of all, but conquered by wrath and sensuality'). Manuscripts closer to the English poet's source (Gl and C³) omit *ira* but have *luxuria*. I owe this information to Professor Turville-Petre.

upon different conceptions of Alexander', undertaken, he says, 'not
from any wish to vary the conception of Alexander expressed, but
from the desire to complete the reader's knowledge of Alexander by
presenting him with all the available literature in a single volume'.[54]
The close English rendering of the *Historia* makes no attempt to
reconcile such different assessments of the hero as were to be found
there. Cary classed the *Wars* overall among those secular works of
the later Middle Ages which celebrate Alexander as 'the great, the
greatest, conqueror' (pp. 241–3), and he was surely right to do so.
But on what terms does the Brahmin's critique coexist with that
celebration? Like the *Historia*, the poem suggests no answer to this
question. This may be explained by the pre-history of these texts,
which was such that they are not unified by the overall conception of
any single author. Their dossier on Alexander included many things
to his credit, but also a few that were not. Interpretation, it seems,
can go no further than that.

Poems about war and conquest such as the *Wars* and the *Morte
Arthure* present their own challenges to modern interpretation, but
these do not arise in the last alliterative poem to be considered in
this chapter; for *Sir Gawain and the Green Knight* shows young King
Arthur and his Round Table enjoying a period of peace – during
that early interval of twelve war-free years, one may imagine, to
which Geoffrey of Monmouth and his followers refer.[55] The poem
confines itself to just one of those fabulous knightly adventures commonly assigned to that quiet time; and the outcome of this Adventure of the Green Chapel depends not at all on conventional feats

[54] George Cary, *The Medieval Alexander*, ed. D. J. A. Ross (Cambridge, 1956), p. 168.
[55] See above, p. 73 and n. 25. A prolonged period of tranquillity is suggested by the fact that,
after undertaking his adventure on New Year's Day, Gawain simply remains with Arthur
('lenges') (l. 536) until he sets off in early November.

of arms. Praise and blame are here at issue, not 'in felde þer felle men foȝt' (l. 874), but in halls and chambers during the Christmas holidays.

In *Sir Gawain*, as not in the other poems just considered, it is the sophistication and subtlety of the author that present the challenge. His staple or default style is straightforward enough, in the romance mode of representing everything as superlative, for better or worse, in its kind. Everything in Arthur's Britain is out of the ordinary, 'outtrage' (l. 29): the Green Knight himself, of course, but also feasts, armour, hunts and the rest. Bertilak's residence is 'A castel þe comlokest þat ever knyȝt aȝte' ('the most beautiful castle ever owned by a knight') (l. 767), constructed in the best late fourteenth-century style, whereas at the other extreme the Green Knight's 'chapel' seems not to be constructed at all: 'nobot an olde cave, / Or a crevisse of an olde cragge' ('nothing but an old cave, or a crevice in an old crag') (ll. 2182–3).[56] In this poem, to be old is evidently bad, just as to be new, or young, is good. This opposition appears most starkly in the two contrasting *descriptiones* that introduce Bertilak's young wife ('more beautiful than Guinevere') and the ugly old woman who accompanies her (ll. 941–69).

Yet the progress of the poem does not leave undisturbed such praises and blames. The beauty of Bertilak's wife, like everything else in his splendid castle, appears in a rather different light once her husband has explained, at the Green Chapel, what part they both played in the ugly old woman's plot against Camelot. This poet leads his readers to take *laudes personarum* with a pinch of salt. But with how much salt? Here readers differ among themselves – especially about Arthur and his court, and also about the hero himself.

---

[56] Citations are from the edition by J. R. R. Tolkien and E. V. Gordon, revised by Norman Davis (Oxford, 1967).

King Arthur and his court are introduced at the beginning of the
story with a battery of superlatives. Lines 50–9 declare that the knights
are the most renowned ever, the ladies the loveliest and Arthur the
most handsome; and they are all in their 'first age',

> Þe hapnest under heven,
> Kyng hyȝest mon of wylle;
> Hit were now gret nye to neven
> So hardy a here on hille.

(The most fortunate in the world, and the king supreme in his spirit; it
would be very hard nowadays to name such a bold company of fighting men
anywhere.)

ll. 56–9

Yet the narrative that follows presents a world where things are not
quite as simple as such unqualified praise suggests. Going out of
his way to explain why, when the Green Knight arrives, Arthur has
not yet taken his seat at the feast, the poet offers two very different
reasons. The king has made a noble vow that he will not eat until some
adventure or marvel turns up; and, at the same time, his young blood
and his 'wild' brain lead him to want to be up on his feet as much
as possible: he is 'sumquat childgered', that is, somewhat childish,
or perhaps boyish (l. 86). There is a similar doubling-up of a higher
with a lower explanation – much lower in this case – when the poet
attempts to account for the silence which first greeted the entry of
the Green Knight:

> I deme hit not al for doute,
> Bot sum for cortaysye –
> Bot let hym þat al schulde loute
> Cast unto þat wyȝe.

(I guess that this was not entirely out of fear, but somewhat out of courtesy –
allowing him to whom all owed deference [i. e. Arthur] to respond to the
man.)

ll. 246–9

As the indeterminate 'somewhats' in these two passages suggest, the First Fitt allows readers a degree of freedom in their evaluation of this Arthur and this court – somewhere between the extremes represented by pure nobility and courtesy at the high end and mere childishness and dread at the other. So it is not surprising that the very many critical studies of this poem should offer a wide variety of assessments, some leaning towards celebration and some towards critique. I can refer here to no more than two of the latter kind, one early, the other recent.[57] In his book-length study of the poem published in 1965, Larry Benson referred to lines 246–7 (just cited above) and observed: 'These refined gentlemen, more used to dances and jousts than to real fighting, do not quite know how to deal with the vigorous world of adventure that the Green Knight represents' (p. 100). They are 'courtiers rather than warriors' (p. 214): 'The world outside does not matter here; courtesy and ceremony are the most important concerns' (p. 99). A rather similar critique of the court has been offered by Christine Chism, though from a quite different, historicist, point of view. Seeing in the poem a reflection of late fourteenth-century relations between provincial Cheshire and the court of the young Richard II, Chism describes Arthur's household in terms such as were used at the time by critics of Richard's. She speaks of 'the immature young king and his coterie of young chamber knights' (p. 91), and suggests that Camelot is to be understood as representing 'a royal court becoming increasingly alienated from traditional seigneurial modes of chivalry' (p. 68).

The poem does, it is true, offer some promptings for interpretations such as these, for it catches Camelot in a less than heroic light, as a company of young men and women enjoying themselves

---

[57] Larry D. Benson, *Art and Tradition in Sir Gawain and the Green Knight* (New Brunswick, N.J., 1965); Chism, *Alliterative Revivals*, chapter 3: 'Heady Diversions: Court and Province in *Sir Gawain and the Green Knight*'. The profusion of critical comment on this and other aspects of the poem makes it impossible to go beyond the barest sampling here.

on an occasion which calls for no feats of arms. Yet the critiques just noticed invite several objections. Contemporaries did, as Chism rightly says, blame King Richard for his youth and immaturity; but in a poem where 'old' is generally an epithet *ad malum*, a 'first age' may be no bad time of life. Youth has a positive value generally in romances. Even Arthur's 'childgered' spirit harmonises easily, in the poet's double explanation, with his nobility ('nobelay', l. 91). Nor can Benson be allowed to stigmatise the knights as 'courtiers', in the weak sense that he evidently intends, as if they could not, when need arose, constitute a 'hardy here on hille'. Benson speaks disparagingly of a preoccupation with courtesy and ceremony; yet it is by courtesies and ceremonies that Arthur and Gawain prove themselves able to handle the shock of the Green Knight, masking apprehension and 'wonder' in formal speech and customary behaviour, and so upholding what the intruder challenged, that is, 'þe revel and þe renoun of þe Rounde Table' (l. 313).

This renown of the Round Table is a main point at issue in the poem, and the closing pages speak of it twice. In his words of explanation at the Green Chapel, Bertilak says that old Morgan sent him to Camelot on a mission

> For to assay þe surquidré, ȝif hit soth were
> Þat rennes of þe grete renoun of þe Rounde Table.

(To put their pride to the test and see whether it is true, what is said about the great glory of the Round Table.)

                                                                ll. 2457–8

The word *surquidré* refers here to the pride of the Round Table in its own high reputation; and it is this that Camelot treats as having been vindicated when the knights agree to adopt Gawain's green belt as a distinguished addition to the insignia of their order:

For þat watz acorded þe renoun of þe Rounde Table,
And he honoured þat hit hade evermore after,
As hit is breved in þe best boke of romaunce.

(For that was agreed as a glory for the Round Table, and its wearer to be honoured in all future times, as it is written in the best book of romance.)

ll. 2519–21

This response has prompted some critics to blame the court, one of them condemning their 'bathetic' attitude as 'trivial and inadequate'.[58] But that is to overlook the circumstances of the case. The renown of the Round Table was formally staked, in the First Fitt, on the ability of its representative to fulfil the terms and conditions of the Beheading Agreement as they were set out with legalistic precision there; and Gawain has succeeded in doing just that – turning up on the appointed day and receiving the return blow without resistance. He has, in fact, both succeeded and survived in an adventure which seemed to promise nothing but either shameful failure or certain death. It is no wonder that he should be received back at Camelot with embraces, joyful laughter and comforting words. How could it have been otherwise?

Yet for Gawain himself, of course, the case is different; and his bitter self-reproaches contribute to an unusual kind of ending, in which both praise and blame play a part. Camelot may regard the Exchange of Winnings as a private, add-on test in which their communal honour was not involved; but for the hero, his failure in it is a source of personal mortification. The standards by which he judges himself are set by his heraldic sign, the pentangle, and the poet's moral exposition of that made the highest of claims for its bearer (ll. 631–65). Gawain is like 'golde pured', and all the many virtues

---

[58] W. R. J. Barron, *'Trawthe' and Treason: The Sin of Gawain Reconsidered* (Manchester, 1980), p. 136.

represented by his sign are 'harder happed on þat haþel þen on any oþer' ('more securely fixed in that man than in any other') (l. 655). Such superlative praises are borne out by much in what follows – by Gawain's courage and hardihood on the journey north and by his conduct as a guest at Hautdesert. But his stay in that castle is overhung by the prospect of his forthcoming encounter, and it is fear of that – 'doute', again – that precipitates him into his one fault, when he breaks his word with the host by withholding the green belt. Readers have differed widely in their judgements of Gawain's fault, and understandably so; for the balance between praise and blame of the hero remains at issue to the very end of the poem. Gawain returns to Camelot resolved to wear the belt for the rest of his life as a mark of 'blame' (l. 2506; cf. 2500) and defines his fault as an act of 'trecherye' (l. 2383), 'unleuté' (l. 2499) and 'untrawþe' (ll. 2383, 2509). These terms of his explain why he should blame himself in such vituperative language, for it is 'in bytoknyng of trawþe', above all, that he bears the pentangle as his heraldic sign (l. 626). So it can be no light matter to supplement it, as he now does, with the belt as a 'token of untrawþe' (l. 2509). Yet in the scene at the chapel, the Green Knight addresses the same fault in a very different spirit:

> here yow lakked a lyttel, sir, and lewté yow wonted;
> Bot þat watz for no wylyde werke, ne wowyng nauþer,
> Bot for ȝe lufed your lyf; þe lasse I yow blame.

(You were a little at fault here, sir, and good faith was lacking in you; but that was not because of any fine workmanship or love-making either, but because you loved your life; I blame you the less.)

ll. 2366–8

Gawain has fallen short in 'lewté', fidelity to his pledged word, but only 'a lyttel' – another of the poem's indeterminate somewhats. And where Gawain has seen 'cowarddyse' (ll. 2374, 2379, 2508), his adversary sees no more than a very natural attachment to life, extenuating the fault: 'þe lasse I yow blame'. What is more, the lines just quoted follow after words of praise scarcely less wholehearted than those of the poet himself in the pentangle passage. Gawain has been 'assayed', as gold is assayed, and found by his adversary to be

> On þe fautlest freke þat ever on fote ȝede;
> As perle bi quite pese is of prys more,
> So is Gawayn, in god fayth, bi oþer gay knyȝtez.

(Quite the most faultless man that ever trod earth; just as a pearl is of greater value than a white pea, so is Gawain, for sure, by comparison with other fine knights.)

ll. 2363–5

'On þe fautlest freke' evidently means, not 'one of the most faultless men', but 'quite the most faultless man',[59] a superlative which is hardly weakened by the ensuing comparison between Gawain and other knights, who may look like pearls but are actually no better than dried peas.

The poem could have ended with some reconciliation between the divergent judgements on its outcome that are expressed by hero, companions and adversary. Gawain might have been shown yielding to the comforts offered him, rather than resolving to carry his mark of blame for ever. As it is, readers are left to arrive at their own judgement. Is the hero, as Bertilak says, 'on þe fautlest freke'? Or is he rather, as Gawain himself persists in maintaining, a chastening example of 'þe faut and þe fayntyse of þe flesch crabbed' ('the faultiness and the frailty of the perverse flesh') (l. 2435)? Yet the poem seems to

---

[59] See Davis's note to l. 137, on *one* strengthening superlatives, referring to Tauno F. Mustanoja, *A Middle English Syntax*, Part I (Helsinki, 1960): 'The meaning of *one the best man* is "the very best man"' (p. 298). Yet Mustanoja notes that towards the end of the Middle English period this type 'becomes contaminated with current partitive expressions of the type *one of the best men*' (p. 299); and such a weaker sense cannot be ruled out here.

suggest that all three parties, in their different roles, can claim justification for their differing responses: heavy self-blame from the hero, lightly qualified praise from the adversary, and a joyful welcome from the court. This is not a case where the discrepancy between blame and praise arises from the complex prehistory of a text, as with the Dindimus episode in the *Wars*. The *Gawain*-poet, working with a much freer hand, has created a situation in which discrepant judgements relate meaningfully to each other and to the positions from which they are spoken. Like his contemporary, Geoffrey Chaucer, this poet was interested in the 'voicing' of praise.

CHAPTER 4

Geoffrey Chaucer

In some lines written about fifteen years after the poet's death, John Lydgate recorded an anecdote about Chaucer which he had perhaps heard from Chaucer's own son Thomas. In celebration of what he calls Chaucer's 'well-saying', Lydgate instances his way of responding when asked by others to comment on their writings:

> For he þat was gronde of wel seying
> In al hys lyf hyndred no makyng.
> My maister Chaucer, þat founde many spot,
> Hym liste nat pinche nor gruche at every blot,
> Nor meve hym silf to perturbe his reste
> (I have herde telle) but seide alweie þe best,
> Suffring goodly of his gentilnes
> Ful many þing enbracid with rudnes.[1]

One can see here the lineaments of that inscrutable, sometimes ironical Chaucer that is so familiar from his own writings, not least in his poetry of praise. He sees faults, but does not choose to speak ill of them, lest by doing so he should 'perturb his rest'. So he always 'says the best'. No doubt poets who (like Thomas Hoccleve) submitted their work to the master's eye went away without knowing quite

---

[1] Lydgate's *Troy Book*, ed. H. Bergen, EETS e.s. 97, 103, 106, 126 (1906–20), V 3519–26. The poem was written between 1412 and 1420. Lydgate addressed a laudatory poem to Thomas Chaucer on the occasion of his leaving England (the epideictic genre 'propemticon'): no. 2 in *John Lydgate: Poems*, ed. John Norton-Smith (Oxford, 1966). On their acquaintance, see Derek Pearsall, *John Lydgate* (London, 1970), pp. 161–2.

what to make of him. Did he or did he not really think well of what they had written?

Readers of the *General Prologue* to the *Canterbury Tales* encounter a similar Chaucer, who also 'says always the best' – the affable pilgrim narrator. From the moment when the pilgrim checks in at the Tabard Inn, he strikes the note of praise:

> The chambres and the stables weren wyde,
> And wel we weren esed atte beste.
>
> 1. 28–9²

The accommodation, for horses as well as people, was absolutely first-class. And so, in their different ways, were most of his fellow pilgrims, as he goes on to describe them. He employs a whole battery of epithets in their praise, including 'fair' (9x), 'good' (15x), 'noble' (4x) and 'worthy' (11x). The Monk is a 'fair prelaat', the Reeve a 'wel good wrighte', the Pardoner a 'noble ecclesiaste' in church, and the Knight a 'worthy man' – a 'worthynesse' stressed in his case by no less than four uses of the adjective in quick succession (ll. 43, 47, 64, 68). The same kind of well-saying appears also, more unobtrusively, in the frequent use of small intensifying adverbs like 'full' and 'well'. *Ful* is Chaucer's equivalent to the modern *very* (a word not employed by him in that adverbial sense), and he uses it to strengthen adjectives and other adverbs as many as forty-eight times here. The Knight is more than just worthy, he is 'ful worthy' (l. 47); the Wife of Bath has red stockings 'ful streit yteyd, and shoes ful moyste and newe' (l. 457); the Reeve's legs are 'ful longe . . . and ful lene' (l. 591) and the smiling of the Prioress is 'ful symple and coy' (l. 119) – with no less than ten further occurrences of the word in the portrait of the Prioress, including:

---

² All quotations are from *The Riverside Chaucer*, 3rd edn, general editor Larry D. Benson (Boston, Mass., 1987).

> Ful weel she soong the service dyvyne,
> Entuned in hir nose ful semely;
> And Frenssh she spak ful faire and fetisly.
>
> ll. 22–4

The other little adverb, *wel* or *weel*, as in the first line just quoted, contributes to the narrator's persistent stress on just how good his fellow pilgrims were at everything they undertook (35x). In conjunction often with the verb *koude* 'could', it serves to magnify their many different kinds of know-how. Thus the Squire:

> Wel koude he sitte on hors and faire ryde.
> He koude songes make and wel endite,
> Juste and eek daunce, and weel purtreye and write.
>
> ll. 94–6

Most of the pilgrims, indeed, are represented as nonesuches in their particular walks of life, and eleven of them are said to have no rivals there – a version of the common auxetic device, comparison. The Shipman knows so much about navigation that 'Ther nas noon swich from Hulle to Cartage' (l. 404); the Wife of Bath is so good at cloth-making that 'She passed hem of Ypres and of Gaunt' (l. 448), and so on – of the Parson, 'A bettre preest I trowe that nowher noon ys' (l. 524), of the Pardoner, 'Ne was ther swich another pardoner' (l. 693) and of the Man of Law, 'Nowher so bisy a man as he ther nas' (l. 321).

Chaucer was certainly familiar with the sharp binary distinction drawn in treatises of rhetoric and poetic between *laus* and *vituperatio* – witness his *House of Fame*, to be considered shortly – but in the *General Prologue* it is not possible to sort all the portraits out into two such clearly contrasting categories, as Matthew of Vendôme does with his specimens of description *ad laudem* or *ad vituperium* (above, p. 15). In her study of the *General Prologue*, Jill Mann sees Chaucer as making a break here from the rhetorical tradition:

Chaucer saw the possibility of combining the two affective tendencies of admiration and vituperation – whose separation in other portraits gave an impression of artificiality – in such a way as to reproduce the complex response which we normally have to real people. The combination is not, of course, a matter of simple addition; its most frequent form, as we have seen, is the presentation of morally reprehensible traits in terms of enthusiastic appreciation. Chaucer further complicates our responses by the use of ambiguities which represent a development of medieval satiric irony, but could have been adopted with the same general aim of complicating the reader's emotional responses.[3]

Every reader of the *Prologue* will recognise something like the complexities of which Mann here speaks. If one tried to place all the portraits on a scale running from pure blame at the bottom to pure praise at the top, the five pilgrims with which the sequence concludes – Miller, Manciple, Reeve, Summoner and Pardoner – would all certainly figure somewhere near the bottom; yet even with these men, as Mann argues, there is a kind of amused delight in their varied expertise, as well as undoubted recognition of their morally reprehensible traits. And there are other portraits, such as that of the Prioress, where the 'two affective tendencies of admiration and vituperation' are much more evenly balanced and the overall effect distinctly ambiguous.

Praises in the *General Prologue* are often ironically inflected, but determination of the ironies can prove elusive. The general principle is simple enough: 'this author cannot have meant *that*' – as when Dean Swift proposed the eating of babies in order to reduce the numbers of the poor in Ireland and provide delicacies for the rich. But it is not usually as easy as that to determine what a past author cannot seriously have meant, for ironies may be wrongly imputed or missed unless one takes account of the values held by the writer and assumed

---

[3] Jill Mann, *Chaucer and Medieval Estates Satire: The Literature of Social Classes and the 'General Prologue' to the 'Canterbury Tales'* (Cambridge, 1973), p. 184.

by him in his readers, so far as they may be determined. In the case of medieval writings, this may require historical information as well as imagination – information such as that which Mann's study of the *General Prologue* provides from the 'estates literature' of the time, showing how Chaucer's portraits relate to what was then currently said about the virtues and vices of particular occupations.

By way of contrast with such historically grounded understanding of past values, I cite the ironical reading of the portrait of the Knight offered by Terry Jones in his book *Chaucer's Knight: The Portrait of a Medieval Mercenary*. Observing that the Knight's battles are fought mainly against 'heathens', Jones asks himself the following question: 'Is it credible that Chaucer – the humanist who chooses a polemical pacifist tract as his own tale – could really have believed that killing heathens was the best way of converting them to the religion of love and peace?'[4] In support of his own decisively negative answer, Jones presents well-documented accounts of the bloody campaigns in question, stressing their concern for glory and loot rather than for the religion of love and peace. Yet it seems as certain as such things can be that Jones errs in crediting Chaucer with our modern, humanist disapproval of 'killing heathens', as if that were a transhistorical value common to all people of good will, like the disapproval of eating babies. The historian Maurice Keen shows that the crusading ideology was still fully alive in the fourteenth century and concludes, against Jones, that 'what Chaucer was trying to portray in his *Prologue* was the best kind of knight of his time, one who had expressed his love of "honour" and "chivalrie" by his dedication to the noblest activity for a knight'.[5] Elizabeth Porter arrives at the same conclusion,

---

[4] Terry Jones, *Chaucer's Knight: The Portrait of a Medieval Mercenary* (London, 1980), p. 2. The polemical tract in question is Chaucer's *Melibee*.

[5] Maurice Keen, 'Chaucer's Knight, the English Aristocracy and the Crusades', in V. J. Scattergood and J. W. Sherborne (eds.), *English Court Culture in the Later Middle Ages* (London, 1983), pp. 45–61, citing from p. 57.

studying the Knight along with the Arthur of the alliterative *Morte*.
She also reads the portrait as celebratory:

> We too readily assume that Chaucer and the unknown poet of the *Morte
> Arthure* had the same preoccupations and the same ideals as late twentieth
> century liberal intellectuals. In our age the military hero has suffered an
> eclipse; neither can we espouse the ideal of war to further the cause of
> religion. It was not so in the fourteenth century. The Knight and Arthur are
> heroes created out of the needs and aspirations of their own age.[6]

The reading of the Knight by Terry Jones has understandably made
an appeal to modern readers; yet it must surely be counted among
those acts of 'ideological appropriation' noticed by Derek Pearsall in
modern criticism of the *Canterbury Tales*, interpretations 'whereby
stories that seem to promote attitudes or ideas distasteful to modern
readers are shown, through dramatic irony or ironic reconstruction,
to promote the opposite'.[7]

The 'well-saying' manner so conspicuous in the *General Prologue*
also, to a greater or lesser degree, characterises much of the rest of
Chaucer's verse. Before I turn to other works, however, something
must be said about the stylistic traditions that contributed to Chaucerian auxesis, for these do not lie in the alliterative poetry with which
this study has so far chiefly dealt. Jill Mann speaks of hyperbole as
part and parcel of what she calls Chaucer's 'romance style', and so
it is – taking the term 'romance' to refer to French poetry as well
as to the tradition of rhymed romance in English.[8] For the French,
I confine myself to a few illustrations taken from two poems which

---

[6] Elizabeth Porter, 'Chaucer's Knight, the Alliterative *Morte Arthure*, and Medieval Laws of War: A Reconsideration', *Nottingham Medieval Studies*, 27 (1983), 56–78, citing from 78.
[7] Derek Pearsall, *The Canterbury Tales* (London, 1985), p. 250. Pearsall discusses Jones on p. 116.
[8] Mann, *Chaucer and Medieval Estates Satire*, p. 12.

Chaucer certainly knew and admired, the *Roman de la Rose* of Guillaume de Lorris and the *Jugement du Roy de Behaigne* of Guillaume
de Machaut.[9]

The easiest sort of auxetic effect in these very courtly writings
comes from the frequent use of intensifying words. One of these,
mou(l)t, an adverb meaning 'very' or 'very much', functions as a
heightener in many different connections, like *ful* in Chaucer. In
Machaut's *Behaigne*, the Knight recalls his former felicity as a lover,
a time when he enjoyed 'Moult grant deduit et moult parfaite joie'
('very great pleasure and very perfect joy') (l. 585). At the beginning
of the *Roman de la Rose*, the narrator describes how he went to bed,

> et me dormoie mout forment,
> Et vi un songe en mon dormant
> Qui mout fu biaus et mout me plot.

(and I fell asleep very deeply and, as I slept, I saw a dream which was very
fine and pleased me very much.)

ll. 25–7

Another little word, *maint*, 'many', serves to magnify the quantity
rather than the quality of people and things. Machaut's poem opens
with a description of spring which has no less than six *maints* in the
first eight lines: spring is a season of 'mainte couleur' on the earth,
when Love takes possession of 'mainte dame belle . . . maint amant . . .
mainte pucelle', promising them many a new joy and many a care,
'mainte lie nouvelle / Et maint esmay'. In the *Rose*, the garden of
Delight is said to have contained 'Maint figuer et maint bon datier'
('Many a fig-tree and many a good date palm') (l. 1337); and there
were also, Lorris declares, three times more birds than in the whole

---

[9] *Le Roman de la Rose*, ed. Félix Lecoy, CFMA, Vol. 1 (Paris, 1965); *Le Jugement du Roy de
Behaigne and Remede de Fortune*, ed. James I. Wimsatt and William W. Kibler, The Chaucer
Library (Athens, Ga., 1988).

realm of France (ll. 480–1). In Machaut's poem, the Knight even
magnifies his own sorrow by claiming that it is '.c. mille fois' greater
than the Lady's – 100,000 times, quite a common auxetic multiplier.[10]

Auxesis takes a more openly rhetorical form when speakers declare
that a subject surpasses their capacity to describe it. This is the
'inexpressibility topos' discussed by Ernst Robert Curtius.[11] So in the
Rose, the speaker confesses his inability to do justice to the beauty of
the garden (ll. 1411–14), and the God of Love declares that no one
can 'conter en romanz ne en livre' the sorrows that lovers endure
(l. 2593; cf. 2949–51). Machaut's narrator cannot describe the beauty
of a bird's song (*Behaigne*, ll. 38–40), and the Knight praises his lady
in hyperbolic terms:

> On ne porroit en tout le monde eslire
> Sa pareille, ne tous li mons soffire
> Ne porroit pas, a sa beauté descripre
> Parfaitement.

(No one could find her equal in the whole wide world, nor could the whole
world suffice to describe her beauty perfectly.)

ll. 293–6

These lines combine, very naturally, the inexpressibility topos with
the other epideictic device of comparison. The lady is not only indescribably lovely, she also has no equal anywhere; she is incomparable. Hyperboles of this kind occur quite frequently in these French
poems.[12] Machaut's Knight, while conceding that Nature might pos-
sibly be able to produce the equal of his lady, says that the goddess
could do so only by taking the lady herself as a model, for she 'de
beauté toutes autres passoit' (l. 403); and he protests that no man

[10] *Behaigne*, l. 877. Other hundred thousands occur at ll. 311, 627, 817 and 1805.
[11] E. R. Curtius, *European Literature and the Latin Middle Ages*, trans. Willard R. Trask (London, 1953), pp. 159–60.
[12] For examples in Old English, see above, pp. 36–7, 44, 45 etc.

ever suffered as much as he has done from that same lady's rejection of him (ll. 103–9).

These French poets reserve their most extensive passages of praise for the formal *descriptiones personarum* so dear to the handbooks. Guillaume de Lorris has two main sets of portraits, contrasting a group of personifications that are alien to his garden of Delight, such as Hatred and Poverty, with a group of courtly denizens who enjoy its pleasures.[13] Like those of Matthew of Vendôme, and unlike those of Chaucer's *Prologue*, these descriptions devote themselves exclusively to either *vituperatio* or *laus*. The aliens are represented by ugly images on the outer side of the garden wall, while the beautiful denizens dance a *carole* within. A passage from the description of one of the latter, Largess, will illustrate *descriptio ad laudem* at its sophisticated best:

> Mes ele ot son col desfermé,
> Qu'ele avoit ilec em present
> A une dame fet present,
> N'avoit guerres, de son fermal.
> Mes ce ne li seoit pas mal
> Que la cheveçaille ert overte,
> S'avoit sa gorge descoverte
> Si que par outre la chemise
> Li blancheoit la char alise.

(But she had her neck uncovered, since she had then not long before made a gift to a lady of her brooch. Yet that suited her well, for the newly opened collar revealed her throat, so that the delicate flesh shone white through the shift.)

ll. 1164–72

Largess has declared her essential moral nature by the impulsive gift of a brooch (*fermal*), but by doing so she also opens up a seductive

---

[13] *Roman de la Rose*, ll. 139–460 and 794–1276 respectively.

glimpse of the white flesh at her neck. The lines evoke at once the beauty of the virtue and the beauty of the lady who embodies it. The Middle English translation, probably by Chaucer himself, may be rather more heavy-handed and circumstantial, but it catches in its last couplet the delicate sensuality of the image:

> And opened hadde she hir coler,
> For she right there hadde in present
> Unto a lady maad present
> Of a gold broche, ful wel wrought.
> And certys, it myssat hir nought,
> For thorough hir smokke, wrought with silk,
> The flesh was seen as whit as mylk.[14]

Guillaume de Machaut puts eulogistic description to a different use towards the end of his *Behaigne*, where the narrator proposes that the King of Bohemia, Machaut's longtime employer and patron, should judge between the two parties in the dispute, the Knight and the Lady. This proposal gives occasion (as in *The Owl and the Nightingale*) for an encomium. The passage, lines 1292–343, manages to praise the king for every possible royal and courtly virtue, employing *comparatio* in the most extreme way: the King surpasses Alexander in largess, Hector in prowess and Ovid in his knowledge of love (ll. 1296–7, 1324–7). But Machaut, like Lorris, is at his best with female subjects, and his pièce de resistance in *Behaigne* is the Knight's long speech in praise (*loenge*) of his mistress at lines 286–408, a passage upon which Chaucer was to draw heavily in his *Book of the Duchess*. The Knight opens with general praise of the lady – including the hyperbolic lines 293–6 already quoted – and then embarks upon an extended physical description, the *effictio* of the rhetoricians, descending from head to

---

[14] *The Romaunt of the Rose*, ll. 1190–6. The translator adds some heightening touches of his own. The brooch is gold and 'very well made' and the smock is of silk.

toe, as recommended by Geoffrey of Vinsauf.[15] The high point here is the very sophisticated portrayal of the lady's eyes (ll. 312–35). Her eyes speak a variety of messages, for they penetrate the Knight's heart 'Par leur rigeur et par leur bel acueil', offering both fair welcome and also *rigeur* – 'severity', perhaps. They are sharp, *agu*, as well as sweet, *doux*. In what follows, these antinomies are resolved into an image of rather daunting self-possession, as the lady is said to direct her friendly glances unerringly at those alone whom she chooses to wound (ll. 328–35).

The other main source of Chaucer's 'romance style' lies in the rhymed poetry of his own language, and especially in the English metrical romances. These exhibit, in a generally less polished form, many of the same auxetic devices to be found in the French poetic tradition, in part because of their sources in that tradition. I confine myself here to some few examples taken from two poems, both of which Chaucer may well have read, *Sir Orfeo* and the *Lybeaus Desconus* of Thomas de Chestre.[16]

Both these poems exhibit the general auxetic idiom that so suits the high world of romance, with little intensives and laudatory epithets. In *Lybeaus*, even a dwarf is said to be a 'well fayr wy3t' (l. 405); and in *Orfeo*, when Heurodis 'þis fair quene' falls asleep under 'a fair ympe tree' (ll. 70–1), she is visited by two 'fair kni3tes' (l. 135) from what is later called the 'fair cuntray' of the otherworld (l. 351). The castle of the fairy king in that otherworld prompts the poet to

[15] Geoffrey recommends that descriptions of beautiful women should begin 'a summo capitis' and conclude at ground level: *Poetria Nova*, ed. Faral, ll. 599–600.
[16] *Sir Orfeo*, ed. A. J. Bliss, 2nd edn (Oxford, 1966); *Lybeaus Desconus*, ed. M. Mills, EETS 261 (1969). Chaucer lists 'sir Lybeux' among heroes of romance in *Sir Thopas*, VII 900. The probable author of *Lybeaus*, Thomas de Chestre, seems to have been a contemporary, and perhaps an acquaintance, of Chaucer. Edward III contributed to the ransoms of Geoffrey Chaucer and 'Thomas de Chestre', both captured by the French in the campaign of 1359–60: Martin M. Crow and Clair C. Olson (eds.), *Chaucer Life-Records* (Oxford, 1966), pp. 23–4.

an extended description of its glories. It is like the court of Paradise itself, indescribably marvellous: 'No man may telle, no þenche in þouȝt, / Þe riche werk þat þer was wrouȝt' (ll. 373–4). Similarly, the enchanted castle in *Lybeaus* has pillars and walls of jasper and crystal and doors of brass: 'No rychere never þer nas / Þat he hadde seye wyth eye' (ll. 1799–800). Such romance hyperbole serves to magnify especially the beautiful women and brave knights to be found in such poems. The hero of *Lybeaus* is introduced as 'a conquerour, / Wys of wytte and whyȝt werrour / And douȝty man in dede' (ll. 4–6); and Sir Orfeo is praised, as the demands of the story require, for his incomparable skill as a harper: 'He lerned so, þer no-þing was / A better harpour in no plas' (ll. 31–2). *Orfeo* introduces its heroine at greater length, with six lines of praise capped with the inexpressibility topos:

> Þe king hadde a quen of priis
> Þat was y-cleped Dame Heurodis,
> Þe fairest levedi, for þe nones,
> Þat miȝt gon on bodi and bones,
> Ful of love and of godenisse;
> Ac no man may telle hir fairnise.
>
> ll. 51–6

In *Lybeaus*, where the hero encounters a knight who promises a prize to any comer whose lady is more beautiful than his own mistress, two stanzas are devoted to the beauty of this mistress, her red lips, golden hair, and the rest: 'Her beawte telle al / No man wyth mouþe ne myȝt' (ll. 890–1).

Derek Brewer and others have rightly stressed what Brewer calls the 'English tap-root' of Chaucer's poetry, especially in rhymed romances such as *Orfeo* and *Lybeaus*.[17] But Chaucer cannot have

---

[17] D. S. Brewer, 'The Relationship of Chaucer to the English and European Traditions', in D. S. Brewer (ed.), *Chaucer and Chaucerians* (London, 1966), pp. 1–38, citing from p. 12.

failed to register the difference in the quality of writing between
two poets such as Guillaume de Machaut and Thomas de Chestre.
Indeed, he has fun mainly at the expense of the latter type in *Sir
Thopas*, the burlesque version of a native tail-rhyme romance that
the pilgrim narrator contributes to the Canterbury entertainment. In
this very free-wheeling piece, the many infelicities and absurdities
include several passages of maladroit romance auxesis. The opening
description of the knightly hero devotes the following stanza to his
face:

> Sire Thopas wax a doghty swayn;
> Whit was his face as payndemayn,
>   His lippes rede as rose;
> His rode is lyk scarlet in grayn,
> And I yow telle in good certayn
>   He hadde a semely nose.

VII 724–9

One may wonder how Sir Thopas can display both a white face and a
scarlet complexion, but the description is evidently to be taken as an
exaggerated version of the delicate pink skin commonly attributed
to beautiful heroines, with its two constituent colours heightened by
the mundane comparisons with bread and cloth. The rose-red lips
would also belong normally to a female subject, like the knight's
mistress in *Lybeaus*. The last line makes a joke about the compulsive
ticking-off of praiseworthy features in such a *descriptio*: 'He hadde
a semely nose.' The later description of the 'fair forest' through
which Thopas rides lists the many animals, plants and birds that

See also P. M. Kean, *Chaucer and the Making of English Poetry*, Vol. 1: *Love Vision and Debate* (London, 1972), pp. 1–23; Larry D. Benson, 'The Beginnings of Chaucer's English Style', in Theodore M. Andersson and Stephen A. Barney (eds.), *Contradictions: From 'Beowulf' to Chaucer: Selected Studies of Larry D. Benson* (Aldershot, 1995), pp. 243–65; and Christopher Cannon, 'Chaucer's Style', in Piero Boitani and Jill Mann (eds.), *The Cambridge Companion to Chaucer*, 2nd edn (Cambridge, 2003), pp. 233–50.

he encounters there, with a variety of enthusiastic wrong notes: the 'wild beasts' are buck and hare, the plants are exotics not to be looked for in Flanders and the sweetly singing birds include sparrow-hawks and parrots (ll. 754–71). What little the hero manages actually to do in the aborted narrative, he does with extravagant force. He exhausts both himself and his horse by violent use of the spur:

> His faire steede in his prikynge
> So swatte that men myghte him wrynge;
> His sydes were al blood.
>
> ll. 775–7

And when he sets out at last to encounter his adversary (a giant with no less than three heads),

> His goode steede al he bistrood,
> And forth upon his wey he glood
> As sparcle out of the bronde.
>
> 903–5

Here, as elsewhere in the poem, Chaucer glances at the empty use of intensives such as *al*: Thopas bestrides all his horse, Flanders is all beyond the sea and the like.[18]

This tale of a knight who surpasses, we are told, the heroes of other 'romances of prys' (ll. 897–902) makes fun, among other things, of the hyperbolic style of romance; but for some evidence of Chaucer's more serious thinking about *laus poetica*, one must turn to an earlier work, *The House of Fame*. This dream poem concerns itself with the circulation of news and opinion. The prime agent in that process is Aeolus, god of the winds, who serves as trumpeter to the goddess Fame in her castle. Aeolus has two trumpets, which he blows at her command, and these represent respectively *laus* and *vituperatio*

---

[18] For other empty uses of 'al', see ll. 715, 719, 773, 831 and 884. For intensive uses of 'ful', see ll. 721, 742, 771 (a wood-dove singing 'ful loude and clere'), 822, 854, 865, 883 and 886.

(ll. 1573–82). The golden trumpet, with its sweet-smelling breath, is named 'Clere Laude', where the epithet *clere* denotes both the purity and the carrying-power of the *laus* that it transmits (ll. 1722–5). The foul-smelling instrument of blackened brass, used by Aeolus to publish vituperative reports, is named 'Sklaunder'. It may be noted here that Chaucer's English, like our own, lacked a fully serviceable antonym for 'praise'. In modern use, 'slander' denotes only discreditable reports that are false, and that was the leading sense also in Middle English, but the word could also at that time refer to such reports when they were true (*OED Slander* sb., senses 1 and 3). Chaucer has both types in mind here, for Aeolus blows Sklaunder not only for those who have not deserved it but also for those who have (ll. 1606–56, 1771–1810).[19]

All reports, good and bad, deserved and undeserved alike, take their origin in common talk and gossip, 'tidings', in the wicker house of Rumour, and from there they are transmitted to Fame's castle (ll. 2110–20), to be blown abroad as either praise or blame by the trumpets of Aeolus. In this process of widening publication, it is poets who play a prominent part. The castle of Fame is topped with pinnacles in the niches of which stand

> alle maner of mynstralles
> And gestiours that tellen tales
> Both of wepinge and of game,
> Of al that longeth unto Fame.
>
> ll. 1197–200

Fame's great hall, too, is full of 'hem that writen olde gestes', men like Thomas de Chestre, perhaps (l. 1515). But the dominating figures in the hall are the great Classical writers who, standing on their high

---

[19] The author of the *Arte of English Poesie* (cited above, p. 20) registers the difficulty when, recalling the *House of Fame*, he speaks of poets as trumpeters of praise and 'also of slaunder (not slaunder, but well deserved reproach)'. The common modern antonym 'blame' also fails to cover the ground.

pillars, 'bear up the fames' of the heroes of Antiquity. These include the epic poets Homer, Virgil, Statius and Lucan, who are further represented at Fame's court by their muse, Calliope. She leads her sister muses in singing the praises of the goddess: 'Heryed be thou and thy name, / Goddesse of Renoun or of Fame!' (ll. 1405–6). Thus, set in the fantastic context that Chaucer has imagined for it, *oratio poetica* figures as a prime agent in the spreading and perpetuating of good and bad reputations, 'clere laude' and 'sklaunder'.

The character of Fame in Chaucer's poem can be summed up in a line from the poem paraphrased in its first book, Virgil's *Aeneid*. Virgil's Fama, spreading the news of Dido's affair with Aeneas, is described as 'tam ficti pravique tenax quam nuntia veri' ('as ready to hold on to the untrue and discreditable as to report what is true') (IV 188). Neither goddess pays regard to truth, and both distribute good and bad reports alike quite arbitrarily. So Chaucer can describe his Fame as a sister to that other arbitrary goddess, Fortune (ll. 1547–8). When deserving people petition her for good fame, she accepts some and rejects others for reasons that the dreamer cannot begin to understand (ll. 1538–48). And even when she does happen to grant *laus* to the deserving, the praise will commonly overshoot the truth. So, when Fame addresses a group of petitioners to whom she has chosen to grant well-deserved praise, she promises them that

> ye shul han better loos,
> Right in dispit of alle your foos,
> Than worthy is, and that anoon.
>
> ll. 1667–9

The goddess who 'magnifies' in the old sense of the word (as at *House of Fame*, l. 306) also magnifies in the modern sense. In literature as in life, praise and blame are both subject to hyperbolic heightening. Laȝamon remarked on this in his *Brut* (above, p. 74), and Dante in his

Convivio gives a more specific account of the process, which he calls *dilatazione*, or 'dilating'. Such is the nature of both *fama buona* and *infamia* that they dilate as they pass from mouth to mouth, leaving truth behind in the process.[20]

It is in keeping with this very sceptical account of 'clere laude' that Chaucer's own poetry of praise should so often prove questionable – more often, indeed, than that of any other poet discussed in this study. As we shall see, Chaucer pays particular attention to the sources from which praise comes. Who is speaking? And why? These are questions that may cast a shadow, more or less deep, across the praises themselves. The speaker may, for example, be open to suspicions of partiality, as when Pandarus praises Criseyde to Troilus and Troilus to Criseyde; or he may be under the constraint of circumstances, like the narrator who praises women at the behest of the God of Love in *The Legend of Good Women*. It so happens that the *House of Fame* itself provides a striking example of how different voices, even among the great poets of Antiquity, may pass contrasting judgements on the same case. In Book I there, the account of Aeneas's life generally follows Virgil in magnifying the hero; but in the Dido episode, Chaucer draws on a different source, Ovid's *Heroides* (referred to along with the *Aeneid* at l. 379), where Ovid imagines for Dido a letter to Aeneas in which she complains of her desertion by him. Accordingly, this section of Chaucer's narrative represents Aeneas, not as the noble Virgilian hero, but as the false betrayer of an innocent woman. Much depends, evidently, on one's point of view. Yet even

---

[20] *Convivio*, I.iii.6–11, in *Le Opere di Dante*, ed. M. Barbi *et al.*, 2nd edn (Florence, 1960). See Piero Boitani, *Chaucer and the Imaginary World of Fame* (Cambridge, 1984), pp. 74–5. Chaucer represents the magnifying power of Fame also in the construction of her castle out of beryl, a precious stone that 'made wel more than hit was / To semen every thing, ywis, / As kynde thyng of Fames is' (ll. 1290–2). There are literal descriptions of such dilation in the scene at Deiphebus's house, *Troilus and Criseyde*, II 1583–9, and in *House of Fame*, 2060–75.

the wilful goddess Fame will on occasion, albeit accidentally, bestow praise where praise is unquestionably due; and Chaucer himself does that, I believe, more often than modern criticism commonly allows. His praises of the Virgin Mary suffer not at all from being voiced by two nuns in the *Canterbury Tales*; nor, or so I have argued, does the pilgrim narrator speak with any ironic reservations when he praises the Knight in the *General Prologue*.

It is such descriptions of persons that raise the most interesting critical questions; but epideictic magnification also extends to many other subjects, as the Elizabethan rhetorician observed: 'menne, Countreis, Citees, Places, Beastes, Hilles, Rivers, Houses, Castles, dedes doen by worthy men'.[21] Chaucer's *laudes* cover a similarly wide range, including flora and fauna (flowers, birds, horses), buildings (castles, houses, inns) and the like. I shall sample just a few treatments of such miscellaneous subjects before returning to the *descriptiones personarum*, leaving *Troilus and Criseyde* for discussion at the end of the chapter.

With its variety of different genres, Chaucer's poetry shows very clearly how 'magnification' varied according to the conventions of particular poetic kinds. Shorter fabliau tales generally describe the settings for their action only insofar as this is required to localise and explain what the characters do. So, in the fabliau tale of the Reeve, there is no description of the mill beyond what the plot requires; the Reeve has no time for poetic glorifications: 'this is verray sooth that I yow telle' (I 3924). Similarly, the Shipman does not waste words on the garden in which his monk meets the merchant's wife: he refers to it simply as 'the gardyn' (VII 90). It is in the dream poems and romance narratives that one should look for the amplified treatment of settings such as houses and gardens. The *Book of the Duchess*

---

[21] See above, pp. 11–12.

begins the report of its dream with an extravagant description of the birdsong that wakens the dreamer there (ll. 291–320), a passage which insists three times that no one ever heard anything so beautiful: 'Was never herd so swete a steven / But hyt had be a thyng of heven' (ll. 307–8, also 302–4 and 314–16). The hyperbolic manner persists as the dreamer enters a beautiful forest, with its profusion of flowers, trees and animals: the flowers seem seven times more numerous than stars in the sky, and not even a skilled Arabic mathematician could number the animals (ll. 405–9, 434–42). The garden in the *Parliament of Fowls* is equally wonderful (ll. 183–210). In the *House of Fame*, one finds another favourite subject of poetic amplification, buildings. The temple of Venus, the castle of Fame and the house of Rumour are all, in their different ways, incomparably marvellous. Fame's castle prompts Chaucer to his most elaborate protestation of inexpressibility. It is so wonderful

> That al the men that ben on lyve
> Ne han the kunnynge to discrive
> The beaute of that ylke place,
> Ne coude casten no compace
> Swich another for to make,
> That myght of beaute ben hys make,
> Ne so wonderlych ywrought.[22]

Well-saying of the same kind also figures in romance narratives such as the Canterbury stories of the Knight and the Squire. Although, in the *Knight's Tale*, the description of the great lists built by Theseus has a few touches of 'verray sooth' unimaginable in the *House of Fame* (even mention of cost), this is in every sense an extravagant structure, a whole mile in circumference: 'Swich a noble theatre

---

[22] *House of Fame*, ll. 1167–73, continuing to l. 1180. For the temple of Venus, see ll. 121–7 and 470–3. The house of Rumour is said to be more wonderfully and intricately made than the Cretan labyrinth, ll. 1918–23.

as it was / I dar wel seyen in this world ther nas' (I 1885–6). The
Squire's Tale has many such passages of encomiastic description, as
in its long account of Cambyuskan's birthday festivities (v 58–346).
After a feast that is 'so solempne and so ryche / That in this world
ne was ther noon it lyche' (ll. 61–2), the company retires to dance in
the King's chamber:

> Who koude telle yow the forme of daunces
> So unkouthe, and swiche fresshe contenaunces,
> Swich subtil lookyng and dissymulynges
> For drede of jalouse mennes aperceyvynges?
> No man but Launcelot, and he is deed.
>
> ll. 283–7

The narrator more than once confesses his inability to do his subject
justice (also at ll. 34–41, 61–74, 105–9, 278–82, 424), and such comments have prompted some modern readers to take the whole poem
with a large pinch of salt, as if the young Squire is to be understood
as having undertaken an ambitious and highfalutin story that proves
beyond his powers.[23] Certainly it is hard to imagine how the rest
of the complex story, as projected, could have been accommodated
within the bounds of the Canterbury collection; but earlier readers,
including Spenser and Milton, found the tale impressive for all its
fragmentary state; and some of the descriptive passages are among
Chaucer's finest, as when the people of Tartary wonder at the horse
of brass:

> For it so heigh was, and so brood and long,
> So wel proporcioned for to been strong,
> Right as it were a steede of Lumbardye;
> Therwith so horsly, and so quyk of ye,
> As it a gentil Poilleys courser were.
>
> v 191–5

---

[23] *Riverside Chaucer*, pp. 890–1, gives references.

Like everything else in this high romance, the horse is outstanding in its kind – and how vividly! 'So horsly, and so quyk of ye.'

In his discussion of the *Squire's Tale*, Pearsall defends it against approaches designed, as he says, 'to make a tale conform to modern tastes by "ironising" the narrator'.[24] I think he is right to do so. But there are other genres of narrative in the *Canterbury Tales* where one finds indisputable examples of the poetry of praise being undercut by ironies. That peculiar kind of fabliau assigned to the Merchant opens with January's determination to seek what he calls a 'blisful lyf' in marriage to a young woman, and the old man's hopes are expanded by the narrator into a long passage in praise of the married state (IV 1267–312). All critics have recognised in this a clear case of simulated *laus*. The prologue to the tale has portrayed the Merchant as a man embittered by his own experience of marriage, and his encomium leaves no doubt about his true intention in voicing it. The signs are everywhere in the sheer extravagance of the claims made for wives. A wife is 'mannes helpe and his confort, / His paradys terrestre, and his disport' (ll. 1331–2), she will never contradict or disobey her husband (ll. 1344–6), she will never be extravagant (l. 1343), and so on. The statements all run directly counter to common wisdom – such common wisdom as the context suggests – so the irony, as often in medieval writings and even in Chaucer, is very clearly signalled. It is almost as unmistakeable as in that Middle English carol which follows each stanza praising women with a contradictory burden:

> Of all creatures women be best,
> Cuius contrarium verum est.[25]

---

[24] Pearsall, *The Canterbury Tales*, p. 141, in a good discussion, pp. 140–3.
[25] No. 399 in *The Early English Carols*, ed. Richard Leighton Greene, 2nd edn (Oxford, 1977); also no. 38 in *Secular Lyrics*, ed. Robbins. The first stanza begins, 'In every place ye may well see / That women be trewe as tirtyll on tree.'

The burden of that little poem expresses in bald terms the most downright response to ironical praises: 'the contrary of that is true'. The Merchant, as Chaucer has portrayed him, cannot have intended to praise women. On the contrary. Matters are rather more complex, however, when the Merchant goes on to narrate January's wedding-feast in terms so hyperbolic that they would not have seemed out of place in the *Squire's Tale*. He describes it as an occasion of 'joye and blisse': the greatest musicians of Antiquity never made such music, Hymen never saw a happier married man, and not even Martianus Capella, author of *The Marriage of Philology and Mercury*, could have done justice to the scene. The Merchant even asserts that it was the god Bacchus who poured the wine, while Venus danced before the company 'with hire fyrbrond in hire hand' (l. 1727). Although there is obvious dramatic irony here, given the later course of the marriage, this narrative cannot be read *per contrarium*. The wedding, strangely enough, must have been that magnificent. It is as if Chaucer's poetry of praise, prompted here by a common epideictic topic, has run out of control. Pearsall characterises the effect well: 'The glittering lines that describe the wedding-feast, with their wealth of classical and mythological allusion (ll. 1709–49), are a rhetorical charade, detached from any reality to which they might refer.'[26] Chaucer makes an attempt to retrieve the passage and restore it to the realities of the Merchant's world with some rather uneasy lines at the end:

> Whan tendre youthe hath wedded stoupyng age,
> Ther is swich myrthe that it may nat be writen.
> Assayeth it youreself; than may ye witen
> If that I lye or noon in this matiere.

ll. 1738–41

[26] Pearsall, *The Canterbury Tales*, p. 205.

This narrator can well speak ironically about mismatches between youth and age, but he cannot have been 'lying' about the magnificence of the wedding. He is not like a historian who can get real things wrong.

This is one of those 'disorienting shifts of register' noticed by Helen Cooper in the *Merchant's Tale*.[27] In a later passage, though, hyperbolic description makes more and better sense. The Merchant describes the garden that January has built:

> He made a gardyn, walled al with stoon;
> So fair a gardyn woot I nowher noon.
> For, out of doute, I verraily suppose
> That he that wroot the Romance of the Rose
> Ne koude of it the beautee wel devyse;
> Ne Priapus ne myghte nat suffise,
> Though he be god of gardyns, for to telle
> The beautee of the gardyn and the welle
> That stood under a laurer alwey grene.
>
> ll. 2029–37

This is one of those places in Chaucer's poetry that seem to challenge the epideictic distinction between magnifying and diminishing, for both these contradictory impulses prove to be simultaneously at work. The ostensible point is to magnify the beauty of January's garden with the help of a version of the inexpressibility topos which implies comparison with the garden of Delight in the *Roman de la Rose*. Such hyperbole can hardly pass unquestioned in a fabliau context, and the reference to Priapus perhaps implies a particular irony, given that January's sexual activity in the garden, 'paying his wife her debt', must suffer by comparison with the courtly doings in Guillaume de Lorris's poem. Yet readers who detect – as I do here and occasionally elsewhere in the tale – a note of real lyrical intensity

[27] Helen Cooper, *The Canterbury Tales*, Oxford Guides to Chaucer (Oxford, 1989), p. 216.

in the passage will not rest content with an exclusively ironic reading
of it. They may see in the garden 'walled al with stoon' the latterday
realisation of an ancient dream that goes right back to the 'paradys
terrestre' so sarcastically compared to the married state earlier by the
Merchant (l. 332), the dream of a 'Garden of Eden just made for two',
as a twentieth-century love song had it. Many other men, including
Guillaume de Lorris, have shared in the 'fantasye' of old January. It
is something more than a mere individual folly.

There are other Canterbury tales where auxetic writing stands
out as too lofty for its subject or genre. The effect may simply be
one of comic extravagance, without any identifiable ironic point.
Such seems to be the case with the passage where the Nun's Priest
laments the capture of Chantecleer by the fox in high rhetorical
style, magnifying the event with apostrophes to Destiny, Venus and
'Gaufred, deere maister soverayn' (VII 3338–54). The last of these
refers to the elaborate lament for the death of King Richard I in
Geoffrey of Vinsauf's *Poetria Nova*.[28] The Nun's Priest expresses the
wish that he could do as much justice to the present tragic subject.
Some have seen in this obviously ridiculous allusion an ironical
comment on the inflated quality of Geoffrey's poem, or even on
the whole tradition of high auxetic rhetoric to which it belongs.[29]
But 'mock-heroic' writing such as this does not necessarily mock
anything at all; and I believe that readers who see Chaucer directing
a shaft of criticism at Vinsauf are misled by our prejudice against
epideictic eloquence. After all, when the narrator goes on to compare
the cries of the hens with the lamentations of ladies in Antiquity, the
distress of those ladies is not mocked. Nor, indeed, is the distress of

---

[28] *Poetria Nova*, ed. Faral, ll. 368–430, one of several examples of amplification by apostrophe.
[29] Discussion and references in the note on pp. 238–40 of Derek Pearsall's edition, *The Nun's
Priest's Tale*, Variorum Edition of Chaucer, Vol. II (Norman, Okla., 1984), questioning
readings that find ridicule of Vinsauf here.

the hens. This very Chaucerian bit of rhetorical magnification seems to leave both parties in the comparison intact.

In the rest of this chapter, I return to Chaucer's praise of people in his *descriptiones personarum*. I shall concentrate mainly on the more formal passages of direct description, for it is these that raise the issues relevant here in the most manageable form, without taking me too far afield into the whole general question of Chaucer's characterisations. Even so, the critical literature is daunting and can only be very selectively cited here.

By the time that Chaucer came to write the *House of Fame*, he had already written a notable piece of 'clere laude' — the longest and most elaborate, indeed, in all his surviving works. *The Book of the Duchess* is the only one of his poems to address itself clearly to a real here-and-now epideictic occasion: the death in 1368 of the wife of John of Gaunt, Blanche, Duchess of Lancaster, the 'White' of the poem. For Chaucer, as for the author of *Pearl*, the occasion called for praise of the dead. Many elegies meet this traditional requirement quite directly, speaking of the merits of the departed in the poet's own voice, as John Donne does in his *Anniversaries*.[30] Chaucer, though, invents a dream fiction which allows him to attribute all the encomium to the bereaved lover, the Black Knight, a stranger whom the dreamer encounters by chance in the woods. So the Knight's long speech in praise of his dead mistress (ll. 817–1041) is invested with all the authority of personal experience. One critic has spoken of 'the sense of hieratic stiffness — an icon-like quality — in the portrait of the woman';[31] but I do not read

---

[30] See Barbara Kiefer Lewalski, *Donne's 'Anniversaries' and the Poetry of Praise* (Princeton, N.J., 1973).

[31] Helen Phillips, in her edition of the poem, 3rd edn (Durham, 1997), p. 32. On the portrait, see Wolfgang Clemen, *Chaucer's Early Poetry*, trans. C. A. M. Sym (London, 1963), pp. 54–7; and A. J. Minnis, in Minnis *et al.*, *The Shorter Poems*, Oxford Guides to Chaucer (Oxford, 1995), pp. 84–91, with bibliography.

the passage so. Chaucer's primary source, the knight's praise of his lady in Machaut's *Behaigne*, does indeed consist chiefly of a quite regular head-to-toe physical description (*Behaigne*, ll. 302–83). Machaut is here practising his favourite 'louange des dames', and Chaucer felt free to adopt much of this for White – for no man, as Dr Johnson said, is on oath in an epitaph. Yet he breaks up Machaut's sequence with other matter, creating a more fluid and conversational effect. So, after the passage in *Behaigne* about the lady's eyes, referred to above, Machaut goes straight on to her nose, mouth and cheeks, but Chaucer here interleaves a passage about White's behaviour towards others (ll. 878–94) before passing on to her 'visage': 'Therwith hir lyste so wel to lyve, / That dulnesse was of hir adrad'. The voice is the voice of the Black Knight freely recalling his first impressions of the lady and overlaying these with the memory that he now has of her: 'for be hyt never so derk, / Me thynketh I se hir ever moo' (ll. 912–13). Voicing the praise in this way, attributing it to the bereaved lover himself, lays it open to the suspicion of partiality; and the poem notices this when it has the dreamer respond to the Knight's encomium with a touch of polite scepticism:

> I leve yow wel, that trewely
> Yow thoghte that she was the beste
> And to beholde the alderfayreste,
> Whoso had loked hir with your eyen.[32]

'It did indeed seem to you . . . anyone who looked at her through your eyes': this awareness of the source of praise is eminently Chaucerian, and it may cast a shadow of doubt (or more than a shadow) across such utterances, as it does here. 'Who speaks?' is always a question to

---

[32] Lines 1048–51, perhaps suggested by *Behaigne*, l. 1642: 'La plus belle qui vive, a son cuidier' ('The most beautiful woman alive, as he thought').

be asked. But in this case, the doubt suggested is immediately swept
aside by the Knight's reply:

> With myn? Nay, alle that hir seyen
> Seyde and sworen hyt was soo.

Every one agreed that the lady really *was* superlatively good and
beautiful.

Modern interest in Chaucer the ironist or sceptic has tended to
draw attention away from the many places in his work where, as in
the *Book of the Duchess*, the poetry of praise speaks whole-heartedly
and without reservation, as 'clere laude'. The most numerous passages of this kind concern female subjects, such as Alceste, Canacee,
Cecilia, Constance, Emily, Griselda, Nature, the Virgin Mary,
Virginia, as well as 'goode faire White'. The rhetoric of praise in
these passages hardly offers any toehold for ironic interpretation,
however extravagant the language may seem on occasion. Quite
typical is the description of Queen Alceste in the *Prologue* to the
Legend of Good Women:

> So womanly, so benygne, and so meke,
> That in this world, thogh that men wolde seke,
> Half hire beaute shulde men nat fynde
> In creature that formed is by kynde.
>
> G 175–8

In this case, the praise is amplified in the balade that follows, 'Hyd,
Absalon, thy gilte tresses clere' (G 203–23), a poem based entirely
on the epideictic figure of comparison: Alceste is more beautiful
and more virtuous than any of the great examples from Classical or
biblical times. This is *laus feminae* at its most lyrical, drawing on the
language of love poetry; indeed, in the F version of the *Prologue* its
subject is not Alceste but 'my lady'. One may compare the description

of Venus by Mars in *The Complaint of Mars*, ll. 174–81 ('My lady is the verrey sours and welle / Of beaute, lust, fredom, and gentilnesse'), or that of the mistress in *Womanly Noblesse* ('Auctour of norture, lady of plesaunce, / Soveraigne of beautee, floure of wommanhede').

The *Canterbury Tales* also has courtly heroines of this kind, notably Emily in the *Knight's Tale* and Canacee in the *Squire's Tale*. In his description of the latter, the narrator confesses his inability to do justice to such a high subject, which would require all the skills of a rhetorician's *laus feminae*:

> But for to telle yow al hir beautee,
> It lyth nat in my tonge, n'yn my konnyng;
> I dar nat undertake so heigh a thyng.
> Myn Englissh eek is insufficient.
> It moste been a rethor excellent
> That koude his colours longynge for that art,
> If he sholde hire discryven every part.
> I am noon swich, I moot speke as I kan.
>
> V 34–41

Praise of women is an art, with its associated 'colours'. Elsewhere in the *Canterbury Tales*, good women are held up primarily as examples of moral excellence or as objects of religious devotion. Constance, Griselda and Virginia are all, like Canacee, beautiful, but above all they are supremely virtuous (II 155–68, IV 209–31, VI 7–66). The Physician's long opening description of his heroine, in particular, amplifies the theme in the best laudatory style. Virginia's body was formed and painted by Nature to perfection (the *effictio*, VI 7–38); but 'if that excellent was hire beautee, / A thousand foold moore vertuous was she', and the following *notatio* (ll. 41–66) catalogues her virtues in hyperbolic terms. A more specifically Christian ideal of virtuous feminity is represented by St Cecilia in the *Second Nun's Tale*. Following his source, the *Legenda Aurea*, Chaucer here employs an ancient epideictic device, praise by etymology, as Dante does with the names of St Francis and of St Dominic's parents in the *Commedia*.[33] Whichever way you analyse Cecilia's name, it will express her excellence, for she is indeed 'heaven's lily', 'a way for the blind', and the rest (VIII 85–119). This is a learned version of the common use of proper names to signify the character of the bearer, very often *ad bonum* or *ad malum* – most obviously in the case of personifications such as those of Guillaume de Lorris (above, pp. 109–10), but also, a little less obviously, with women's names such as 'White', 'Pearl' or 'Constance'.

The Second Nun's 'Interpretacio nominis Cecilie' has impressed few modern readers, but it is preceded in her *Prologue* by an 'Invocacio ad Mariam' which shows the poetry of praise in a better light. Early in his career, Chaucer wrote his *ABC*, a prayer to the Virgin translated from the French of Guillaume de Deguileville; but since that time he had encountered a much more powerful vernacular kind of *laus Mariae* in the last canto of Dante's *Paradiso* (XXXIII 1–39). Here St Bernard prays to the Virgin, opening with a cluster of ecstatic paradoxes:

> Vergine Madre, figlia del tuo figlio,
> Umile e alta più che creatura,
> Termine fisso d'etterno consiglio,
> Tu se' colei che l'umana natura
> Nobilitasti sì, che 'l suo fattore
> Non disdegnò di farsi sua fattura.

---

[33] *Paradiso* XI 52–4, XII 79–81. On 'Etymology as a Category of Thought', see Curtius, *European Literature and the Latin Middle Ages*, pp. 495–500, observing that 'the etymological evaluation of proper names passed from the eulogies of pagan late Antiquity to Christian poetry' (p. 498). See also Faral, *Les Arts Poétiques*, pp. 65–7, referring to Matthew of Vendôme's *Ars Versificatoria*, 1.78, on the 'argumentum a nomine', where 'per interpretationem nominis de persona aliquid boni vel mali persuadetur' ('through analysis of a name something good or bad about a person is demonstrated'). For an example of etymology *ad malum*, see the Monk on Oliver Mauny, *Canterbury Tales*, VII 2386.

(Virgin Mother, daughter of thy Son, humble and exalted more than any creature, fixed goal of the eternal counsel, thou art she who didst so enoble human nature that its Maker did not disdain to become its creature.)[34]

Chaucer catches something of Dante's concentrated theological wit in the Second Nun's version, though he cannot find an English equivalent for the Italian's clinching play on *fattore* and *fattura*:

> Thow Mayde and Mooder, doghter of thy Sone,
> Thow welle of mercy, synful soules cure,
> In whom that God for bountee chees to wone,
> Thow humble and heigh over every creature,
> Thow nobledest so ferforth oure nature,
> That no desdeyn the Makere hadde of kynde
> His Sone in blood and flessh to clothe and wynde.
>
> VIII 36–42

Dante's great *laudatio* also contributed something to the praise of the Virgin in the Prioress's prologue to the tale which she tells, as she says, 'in laude' of Christ and his mother (VII 460–87).[35] Chaucer assigns both of the Marian passages to nuns, but this outsourcing implies no detachment on his part from the sentiments they express. On the contrary: nowhere in his work does 'clere laude' speak with a more unchallengeable authority.

These *laudes mulierum* are all, or so I believe, clear and above suspicion, including the praises of Alceste in the *Legend of Good Women*. But the same cannot be said of the legends themselves in that strange work. All the stories present their good women in the most laudatory terms, with all but two of them setting off the exemplary truth of women against the evil ways of men. So, in the *Legenda Didonis*

---

[34] *Paradiso* XXXIII 1–6, ed. and trans. Singleton.

[35] VII 474–80, like VIII 50–6 in the *Second Nun's Tale*, follows *Paradiso* XXX 16–21. For an appreciation of these passages, see P. M. Kean, *Chaucer and the Making of English Poetry*, Vol. II: *The Art of Narrative* (London, 1972), chapter 5.

martiris, Dido is highly praised (ll. 1035–43), whilst Aeneas is vituperated as a typical specimen of male deceit and infidelity (ll. 1254–89). Like others of the legends, this one owes much to Ovid's *Heroides*, a poem interpreted by medieval readers as concerned with the praise of virtue and blame of vice.[36] Yet the narrator's circumstances, as represented in the *Prologue*, cast a shadow of doubt across his apparently orthodox performance. His is a penitential task, imposed on him by Alceste because of his earlier failures to honour women and faithful love: where he previously 'mysseyde', he must now 'speke wel' (G 430, 481). So he now writes under instruction, in order to exculpate himself. This situation has understandably prompted some modern critics to look with scepticism at his commissioned *laudes*. One scholar speaks of 'an ironic narrowing of the poet's vision' and of 'the narrator's insistence on creating a clear, black-and-white opposition between the sexes at the expense of truth to his sources and to the complexities of human character'; and another scholar reads the legends as comic travesties of exemplary narrative, which 'distort complex human characters into mere blueprints of "goodness" and "faithfulness" in love'.[37] One might object here that such representations of pure 'white' women, and also of 'black' men, occur frequently enough in Chaucer's other works.[38] Indeed, Jill Mann, arguing against ironical readings, finds in the poem a serious 'riposte to misogyny', for all its 'self-conscious extremism of polemic'.[39] Yet the poem has a recurrent vein of playfulness –

---

[36] On the twelfth-century *accessus* to Ovid's *Heroides*, see above, p. 22.

[37] Citing John M. Fyler, *Chaucer and Ovid* (New Haven, Conn., 1979), pp. 115, 108, and Lisa J. Kiser, *Telling Classical Tales: Chaucer and the 'Legend of Good Women'* (Ithaca, N.Y., 1983), pp. 114–15. For a survey of the critical debate, see A. J. Minnis, in Minnis *et al.*, *The Shorter Poems*, pp. 322–454, with bibliography.

[38] With vituperations in the *Legend* against false men such as Jason (ll. 1368–95, 1580–8) one might compare *House of Fame*, ll. 265–92 (Aeneas), *Anelida and Arcite*, ll. 141–61 (Arcite) and *Squire's Tale*, v 504–20 (the tercelet).

[39] Jill Mann, *Geoffrey Chaucer*, Feminist Readings (Hemel Hempstead, 1991), p. 32.

most evidently when the narrator addresses his lady listeners with 'Trusteth, as in love, no man but me' (l. 2561) – and it is perhaps best understood, following Minnis, as Chaucer's contribution to a 'sophisticated gender game', calculated to amuse and flatter female readers.[40] Its praises are not unconstrained by circumstances, any more than are compliments in ordinary social life; but this does not render them ironic.

Chaucer's praises of women are more numerous and generally more elaborate than his praises of men, and in the latter, modern criticism has found rather more frequent occasion to question his intentions. Before turning to Troilus (and Criseyde), I notice here some passages about men in the *Canterbury Tales*.

Earlier, in my discussion of the 'well-saying' manner of the *General Prologue*, I challenged the ironical reading of the Knight's portrait put forward by Terry Jones. I would rather see the Knight as one of that small group of pilgrims represented in the *Prologue* as model members of their respective estates, along with the Parson, the Plowman and the Clerk.[41] Praise of the Parson is especially whole-hearted, striking a note of unchallengeable gravity and seriousness. It also has a polemical character, not so common in Chaucer, in that it contrasts the Parson's way of life with that of parish priests who are negligent or mercenary. This is not the portrait of a Lollard (though the Host does call him that, II 1173), but the passage evokes an ideal of evangelical simplicity and zeal that has led scholars to suspect the influence of Langland's *Piers Plowman*:

> Wyd was his parisshe, and houses fer asonder,
> But he ne lefte nat, for reyn ne thonder,
> In sikenesse nor in meschief to visite

---

[40] A. J. Minnis, in Minnis *et al.*, *The Shorter Poems*, pp. 443–52, cited from p. 446.
[41] The three last are discussed together as representing 'Estates Ideals' in chapter 3 of Mann's *Chaucer and Medieval Estates Satire*, to which I am indebted in my comments on the Parson.

The ferreste in his parisshe, much and lite,
Upon his feet, and in his hand a staf.

I 491–5

Praise here speaks with a beautiful plainness: the last line would not be out of place in Wordsworth's *Michael*.

Scattered through the tales themselves one finds occasional *laudes* of men: the Clerk on Petrarch (IV 26–38), the Squire on King Cambyuskan (V 12–27), the Monk on Hercules (VII 2095–118). The first of these passages anticipates in little an epideictic type which was to flourish especially in the Early Modern period, poems in praise of other poets. Here it takes the form of a lament for a dead master (as Hoccleve later was to lament Chaucer himself):

Fraunceys Petrak, the lauriat poete,
Highte this clerk, whos rethorike sweete
Enlumyned al Ytaille of poetrie,
As Lynyan dide of philosophie,
Or lawe, or oother art particuler.

IV 31–5

These laudatory passages seem straightforward enough and have attracted little comment; but critics have been exercised by the representations of Duke Theseus in the *Knight's Tale*. The tale opens with Theseus returning in glory from his victory over the Amazons:

Of Atthenes he was lord and governour,
And in his tyme swich a conquerour
That gretter was ther noon under the sonne.
Ful many a riche contree hadde he wonne;
What with his wysdom and his chivalrie,
He conquered al the regne of Femenye.

I 861–6

As lord and governor of Athens, the tale goes on to praise him as 'gentil' (l. 952), 'pitous' (953) and 'wise' (2983); but his wisdom here is associated with his activities as a 'conquerour', and a conqueror of women, at that; so it is no surprise that the glorification of him, like that of his narrator, should be questioned by modern readers. David Aers, in one of the strongest of the critiques, sees Theseus as an absolutist ruler, even a tyrant, who enforces an order based on militarism and violence, riding to destroy Thebes at the beginning of the poem with the image of the warrior-god Mars displayed on his banner.[42] Again, what he offers in his oration at the poem's end is no better, Aers suggests, than a 'ruler's metaphysics', serving to legitimise the order which upholds him and which he himself has upheld by force. I think Aers is right to question the high claims sometimes made for the thought in that final speech ('The Firste Moevere of the cause above') (ll. 2987ff); yet to notice that Theseus speaks, not as a disinterested philosopher, but as a 'governour' is not to condemn him. His arguments are directed to practical ends: to bring Palamon and Emily together in marriage, and thereby to secure the relationship between Athens and Thebes. Since Arcite has died, as all must, 'Thanne is it wysdom, as it thynketh me, / To maken vertu of necessitee' (ll. 3041–2). 'To make virtue of necessity': it is not the highest kind of wisdom, for sure, but then neither is it 'the tyrant's plea', as Aers maintains. Theseus, a man no longer engrossed in private passions like Palamon and Arcite, but not yet reduced to the role of a bystander like his old father Egeus, has the responsibility to deal with public affairs as they arise, making the best of them that he can. If one can understand him so, there will be no

---

[42] David Aers, *Chaucer, Langland and the Creative Imagination* (London, 1980), pp. 174–95. Terry Jones treats Theseus as a tyrant, *Chaucer's Knight*, pp. 192–202, 212–16. By contrast, Jill Mann sees in him 'the fullest development of an ideal of feminised masculinity', displaying the womanly qualities of pity and patience, *Geoffrey Chaucer*, pp. 171–80.

call to look for ironies in the Knight's portrayal of his hero in middle age.[43]

Troilus and Criseyde, far and away Chaucer's longest narrative poem, requires separate comment here. In his discussion of the poem's style, Barry Windeatt calls attention to the 'superlative and hyperbolical' manner in its treatment of its central subject, the progress of the love-affair between Troilus and Criseyde;[44] and it is indeed this extravagance that most strikes all readers – the extremes of hope and fear, joy and despair, experienced by the main characters, especially Troilus himself, but also Criseyde and even Pandarus. When Troilus is at the height of his fortunes, he feels such bliss

> That in his herte he demed, as I gesse,
> That ther nys lovere in this world at ese
> So wel as he.
>
> III 1727–9

But when he first hears of the fatal exchange of prisoners, he becomes 'the wofulleste wyght / That evere was' (IV 516–17); and on the same occasion, Criseyde beats her breast and cries out 'a thousand sithe' for death (IV 752–3), and Pandarus 'Gan wel neigh wood out of his wit to breyde, / So that for wo he nyste what he mente' (IV 348–9). The poem's declared subject, Troilus's dizzy passage 'fro wo to wele, and after out of joie', calls for the strongest auxetic treatment, heightening the joys and deepening the woes.

Where such a long poem is devoted to such a single, uncomplicated plot, one might expect the author to indulge himself extensively

---

[43] See further 'Chaucer's *Knight's Tale* and the Three Ages of Man', in J. A. Burrow, *Essays on Medieval Literature* (Oxford, 1984), pp. 27–48.

[44] Barry Windeatt, *Troilus and Criseyde*, Oxford Guides to Chaucer (Oxford, 1992), pp. 329–32, with observations on 'numerical hyperbolic', i. e. the use of hundreds and thousands as auxetic multipliers.

in descriptive writing (as the *Gawain*-poet does). Yet in fact *descrip-tiones* play only a modest part, relatively speaking, in a narrative that devotes itself at such length to reporting what its three main characters feel, think, say and do. So the poem, for one thing, pays surprisingly little attention to describing the settings within which the love-action takes place – by comparison with Chaucer's dream poems, or with the more dignified Canterbury tales. The great city of Troy, from which the British traced their descent through Brutus, would seem to have invited encomiastic descriptions, such as one finds in the long 'Discripcion of Troye' in the *Gest Hystoriale of the Destruction of Troy*:

> Was never sython under son Cite so large,
> Ne never before, as we fynde, fourmyt in urthe,
> Non so lufly on to loke in any lond oute.[45]

But Chaucer treats the town quite coolly and factually. It has gardens, but of these only Criseyde's is described, and that briefly, not in high-flown poetic terms, but as a well-kept and pleasant place to walk in:

> The yerd was large, and rayled alle th'aleyes,
> And shadewed wel with blosmy bowes grene,
> And benched newe, and sonded alle the weyes.
>
>   II 820–2

The town has temples, settings of importance in Books I and IV, but they are never described at all. Nor is much said about the mansions in which so much of the action takes place, Pandarus's house or the 'paleyses' of Criseyde and Troilus. These buildings, though grand, are treated much like the houses in the tales of the Miller or the Reeve, that is, with just enough description of their internal arrange-ments to plot the comings and goings that occur within them. So, in

---

[45] *The Gest Hystoriale of the Destruction of Troy*, ed. G. A. Panton and D. Donaldson, EETS 39, 56 (1869, 1874), ll. 1539–41. The whole description occupies ll. 1537–1613.

the account of the lovers' first night together in Pandarus's house, Troilus is said to conceal himself in a 'stewe' which has access to the 'closet' where Criseyde sleeps. Again, the description of the dinner party at the house of Deiphebus (which entirely neglects to describe the dinner itself, typically enough) specifies domestic arrangements only insofar as they serve Pandarus's plan to bring the lovers together *à deux* for the first time: a great chamber for the general company, a bed chamber where Troilus can lie 'sick', and access from there down some stairs to a garden so that Deiphebus and Helen can be got out of the way (II 1555ff). Criseyde's own mansion displays rather more auxetic touches: it possesses a paved parlour, a cedar outside her bedroom and even a seat of jasper covered with a gold-embroidered cushion (II 82, 918, 1228–9). But the poem has very few such luxurious details. One might compare the two May-morning wakenings, of the dreamer in the *Book of the Duchess* (ll. 291–342) and of Pandarus here (II 50–70). In the dream poem, a long description of superlative bird-song is followed by a lavish account of the chamber into which the narrator is woken: glass windows picturing the story of Troy, walls decorated with coloured text and images from the *Roman de la Rose*. By contrast, Pandarus is woken by the twittering of a single swallow into a chamber about which nothing is said.

It is almost as if the narrator, inspired by the muse of history, Cleo, whom he invokes at II 8, found his Trojan setting waiting for him and had to do little more than locate the action in it. It was all already there. Something like the same impression is created by the first introductions of Troilus and Pandarus into the action:

> This Troilus, as he was wont to gide
> His yonge knyghtes, lad hem up and down
> In thilke large temple on every side,
> Byholding ay the ladies of the town.
>
> I 183–6

'This same large temple' has already been mentioned, but Troilus has not; so the anaphoric use of *this* in 'this Troilus' is unlike more normal uses as in the *Miller's Tale*, where the parish clerk Absolon, having been first introduced and described, can then figure as 'this Absolon'. In the absence of any such earlier introduction, the anaphora in *Troilus* suggests that the hero 'was already there' before he is first mentioned. A little later, the poem introduces another main character with a similar lack of ceremony, identifying him only as 'a friend':

> A frend of his that called was Pandare
> Com oones in unwar . . .
>
> I 548–9

Familiarities of this sort played no part, though, in the introduction of Criseyde, which has just taken place in the interim. The heroine was described in two substantial passages of praise, first as she appeared to the company in the temple and then as Troilus first set eyes on her there (I 99–105, 169–82). These *descriptiones* are the first in a series of passages devoted, as we shall see, to Criseyde and to 'this Troilus' (never to Pandarus); yet such set pieces of *notatio* and *effictio*, generally eulogistic in character, play a much smaller part in the overall representation of the main actors than they do, say, in the *Knight's Tale*, mainly because *Troilus* offers so much more evidence about what the lovers were like, in its detailed reportings of what they feel, think, say and do. In the face of this wealth of evidence, summary descriptions can hardly fail to strike readers as inadequate and partial. Chaucer himself seems to recognise the fact when, at a very late stage in his poem, he offers what are in effect valedictory portraits of the two lovers, derived chiefly from a 'historical' epic source (v 806–40); for these strangely distant descriptions conspicuously fail to do justice to the persons with whom, by then, we have become very familiar. In particular, the final description of Criseyde there does not at all succeed in setting to rest what is by far the most vexed issue of praise-and-blame in all Chaucer's writings. But before turning to her, let me consider the less difficult case of the hero.

Praises of Troilus sound throughout the poem, sometimes voiced by the narrator and sometimes by Criseyde or Pandarus. What they say may be summed up in the words of a later reader, Sir Francis Kinaston, writing in the 1630s, who describes the hero as 'a most compleat knt. in Armes & Courtshippe, & a faithfull and constant lover'.[46] Prowess in battle, courtesy in society (Kinaston's 'Courtshippe'), and fidelity in love – these are the three topics that recur in his praise. As a lover, he is secret, obedient and above all 'trewe as stiel in ech condicioun' (II 722–8, III 477–8, V 831 etc.); in society, he is 'the frendlieste wight' and the most companionable (I 1079, II 204–7 etc.); and on the battlefield, he is a formidable opponent (I 473–83 etc.). It is this last quality, in fact, that takes pride of place in his final description:

> And certeynly in storye it is yfounde
> That Troilus was nevere unto no wight,
> As in his tyme, in no degree secounde
> In durryng don that longeth to a knyght.
> Al myghte a geant passen hym of myght,
> His herte ay with the first and with the beste
> Stood paregal, to durre don that hym leste.
>
> v 834–40

Chaucer draws here upon the portrait of Troilus in a twelfth-century Latin epic of Troy, the *Ylias* of Joseph of Exeter;[47] and it

---

[46] Kinaston (1587–?1642) translated *Troilus* into Latin verse, publishing the first two books in 1635. His manuscript note on Troilus is printed by Richard Beadle, 'The Virtuoso's *Troilus*', in Ruth Morse and Barry Windeatt (eds.), *Chaucer Traditions: Studies in Honour of Derek Brewer* (Cambridge, 1990), pp. 213–33, on p. 219.

[47] See Windeatt's Oxford Guide, *Troilus and Criseyde*, p. 76. On the *Ylias*, see A. G. Rigg, *A History of Anglo-Latin Literature, 1066–1422* (Cambridge, 1992), pp. 99–102. Joseph

may seem strange that he should end his last *descriptio* of the hero on such an emphatic martial note, stressing his physical strength and his daring; for he has made it clear from the start that his chosen subject is not Troilus the warrior but Troilus the lover, 'In lovynge, how his aventures fellen / Fro wo to wele, and after out of joie' (1 3–4). Accordingly, feats of arms take place mostly off-stage. Criseyde sees Troilus once on his return from combat in a glamorously battered state, being acclaimed by the people as 'holder up of Troye' (II 610–51); but it is only at the end of the poem, after he has despaired of Criseyde's return, that he is described in the act of fighting, and then only in gloomy summary style (v 1751–71, 1800–6). The theme here is indeed Homeric, the Wrath of Troilus, and he is said, with truly epic exaggeration, to kill 'thousands' of Greeks in these battles;[48] but his angry encounters with Diomede prove inconclusive, and he seems almost to have invited his pitiable death at the hands of Achilles. Readers who want more details of the fighting, Chaucer here suggests, should look elsewhere:

> And if I hadde ytaken for to write
> The armes of this ilke worthi man,
> Than wolde ich of his batailles endite;
> But for that I to writen first bigan
> Of his love, I have seyd as I kan –
> His worthy dedes, whoso list hem heere,
> Rede Dares, he kan telle hem alle ifeere.
>
> v 1765–71

Chaucer generally shows little taste for feats of arms as a subject of poetic treatment, and he was no doubt happy enough to sideline

---

describes Troilus as 'Mente Gigas, etate puer, nullique secundus / Audendo virtutis opus' ('A giant in spirit, a boy in years, and second to none in venturing upon deeds of valour') (IV 62–3).

[48] A similar auxetic multiplier seems more at home in the account of his feats in the *Gest Hystoriale*: 'As Dares of his dedis duly me tellus, / A thowsand thro knightes þrong he to dethe / Þat day with his dynttes, of the derffe grekes', ed. Panton and Donaldson, ll. 9877–9.

them here; but his concentration on Troilus the lover, at the expense
of his 'worthy dedes', has contributed to what Jill Mann describes as
those 'irritable and reductive complaints about Troilus's inertia and
weakness so familiar on the lips of Chaucer critics and students'.[49]
There are many varieties of such complaint. Thus D. W. Robertson
writes of the hero's 'neglect of duty': 'Troilus is a "public figure", a
prince whose obligations to his country are not inconsiderable, especially in time of war. But his external submission to Criseyde is based
on an inner submission of the reason to the sensuality . . . And when
sensuality rules him, he can no longer fulfill the chivalric obligations
of his station.'[50] Ida Gordon puts forward a less drastic version of the
critique: 'As a royal prince . . . Troilus has special obligations which
he dishonoured when he resigned his "estat roial" into Criseyde's
hands at the very outset of his love.' In particular, Gordon refers to
the moment when, after the exchange of prisoners has been agreed,
Troilus declares his readiness to abscond with Criseyde, 'without
a thought for the defence of Troy'.[51] There may be some danger
here of blaming the hero for what is in fact the poet's neglect of the
fighting. One should recall how frequently Troilus is said (though
rarely shown) to be a 'holder up of Troy'; and it hardly seems fair
to hold against him his one rather desperate suggestion that he and
Criseyde should abandon the city, prompted as it was by his justified
fears about the consequences of any other course.

Robertson speaks of Troilus's 'submission to Criseyde', and
Gordon suggests that he failed to honour his obligations when he
'resigned his "estat roial" into Criseyde's hands'. Certainly Chaucer's
extended treatment of his behaviour as a lover may test modern readers' patience with the well-known courtly principle that a gentleman

---

[49] Mann, *Geoffrey Chaucer*, p. 110.
[50] D. W. Robertson, *A Preface to Chaucer: Studies in Medieval Perspectives* (Princeton, N.J., 1963), p. 478.
[51] Ida Gordon, *The Double Sorrow of Troilus: A Study of Ambiguities in 'Troilus and Criseyde'* (Oxford, 1970), p. 56.

in love 'most obeye unto his lady heste' (III 1157) – a principle exem-
plified most elaborately in the long scene in Book IV where the lovers
discuss what action to take about the proposed departure of Criseyde
to the Greek camp. For Troilus, faced with his mistress's optimistic
expectations of her early return to Troy, can only in the end humbly
suppress his own well-founded doubts and submit to her judgement,
with unhappy consequences (IV 1254–1631). Yet Jill Mann celebrates
the 'weakness' of Troilus the lover as a prime instance of what she
calls the 'feminised hero' in Chaucer's poetry: 'Troilus is divested
of the coerciveness characteristic of the "active" male, and . . . his
unreserved surrender to the force of love is for Chaucer not a sign of
weakness but of a generous nobility. He is feminised not only in his
reverence for women but also in his vulnerability and sensitivity of
feeling.'[52] Given that Mann goes on to acknowledge also in Troilus
'the conventional attributes of "manhod"' – physical prowess and
bravery – her comments strike me as eminently just. Nor, I believe,
would Chaucer's original readers have found any difficulty with the
contrast between the hero's 'hard' behaviour on the battlefield and
his softness at home. Criseyde praises him for just that:

> For, dredeles, men tellen that he doth
> In armes day by day so worthily,
> And bereth hym here at hom so gentily
> To everi wight, that alle pris hath he
> Of hem that me were levest preysed be.
>
> II 185–9

These lines, coupling the 'worthy' with the 'gentil', give expression
to an idea which underlies and unifies all the praises of Troilus in the
poem, an idea which is encapsulated in a medieval proverb: he is both
a lamb and a lion – a lion in the field and a lamb in the chamber.[53]

[52] Mann, *Geoffrey Chaucer*, p. 166. This study belongs to a series of Feminist Readings.
[53] Bartlett Jere Whiting and Helen Wescott Whiting, *Proverbs, Sentences, and Proverbial Phrases from English Writings Mainly Before 1500* (Cambridge, Mass., 1968), L38.

The qualities are not contradictory but complementary. As Kinaston said, 'a most compleat Knight'.

In the course of her discussion, Mann boldly affirms that 'Chaucer takes pains . . . to present Troilus as admirable throughout'; and Chaucer may be said to have taken pains with his heroine also. There can be no question in her case of 'clere laude', but the poem praises Criseyde while it can and tries to excuse her when it cannot. Book I introduces her with a battery of *laudes*. When her name is first mentioned, the narrator expatiates on her great beauty, in lines glossed by one manuscript as a 'commendacio':[54]

> As to my doom, in al Troies cite
> Nas non so fair, forpassynge every wight,
> So aungelik was hir natif beaute,
> That lik a thing inmortal semed she,
> As doth an hevenyssh perfit creature,
> That down were sent in scornynge of nature.
>
>   I 100–5

This praise of Criseyde's beauty is complemented later by equally high praise of her other qualities. Pandarus is congratulating Troilus on the woman he loves:

> For of good name and wisdom and manere
> She hath ynough, and ek of gentilesse.
> If she be fayr, thow woost thyself, I gesse,
>
> Ne nevere saugh a more bountevous
> Of hire estat, n'a gladder, ne of speche
> A frendlyer, n'a more gracious
> For to do wel.
>
>   I 880–6

Since the eulogy here is voiced by a speaker prejudiced both as uncle of Criseyde and as friend to Troilus, it is open for the reader to

---

[54] *Troilus and Criseyde*, ed. B. A. Windeatt (London, 1984), variants to I 99. Another scribe notes 'Commendacoun of the beaute of Cresseyde'.

discount what he says, perhaps in the light of what the poem has already noticed, the heroine's eventual desertion of her Trojan lover (I 56). Yet one can hardly say that this eventual catastrophe shows Pandarus to be mistaken in the qualities with which he credits her.

Not that Criseyde, even at this early stage, proves easy to sum up. As we see her through the eyes of Troilus and others in the opening scene in the temple, she creates impressions of a rather complex kind. The description at I 169–82 opens with praise of her beauty in her widow's weeds, and continues:

> And yet she stood ful lowe and stille allone,
> Byhynden other folk, in litel brede,
> And neigh the dore, ay undre shames drede,
> Simple of atir and debonaire of chere,
> With ful assured lokyng and manere.
>
> I 178–82

The surprise comes here, not with 'debonaire' – which means something like 'meek' or 'unassuming' – but with the 'ful assured' looking and manner. Although Criseyde cannot help impressing people with her beauty ('Ne under cloude blak so bright a sterre'), she takes up only an unobtrusive position on the temple floor, in fear of the shame that her father has brought to the family by his flight to the Greek camp. Yet she is also entirely self-possessed. Two later stanzas (I 281–91) describe her physical presence in somewhat elusive terms – she is taller than many women, but not in the least 'mannyssh' – and then speak of her demeanour:

> And ek the pure wise of hire mevynge
> Shewed wel that men myght in hire gesse
> Honour, estat, and wommanly noblesse.

There is no call to question this 'guess', and in what follows Criseyde asserts her honourable status with a 'somdel deignous' look as if to say 'What, may I not stand here?' Yet she is then immediately said to adopt a more friendly look, as if to correct any unpleasing impression of arrogance:

> And after that hir lokynge gan she lighte,
> That nevere thoughte hym seen so good a syghte.

Like the great lady in Machaut's poem, with her sharp and sweet looks (above, p. 111), Criseyde well knows how to present herself in society, not least to men.

But what is she really like? In his discussion, Barry Windeatt observes that 'our sense of knowing Criseyde is always accompanied by a sense of what we do not know'; and again, 'Chaucer preserves for her an autonomy, an independence both of other characters in the poem and of the poet and reader.'[55] In a quite different connection, William Empson once commented on how writers can show a subject 'from enough points of view to make one feel something in the real world is being considered';[56] and Criseyde (more so than 'this Troilus') seems to be a case in point. Throughout the first three books of the poem, the reader's 'sense of what we do not know' lends an attractive depth to the many and various representations of the heroine, as if she has a life in the real world far from bounded by the text. So, as she lies in bed with Troilus, she responds to his call 'yeldeth yow!' by saying that she would not be there with him now if she had not already yielded (III 1208–11). But when was that? That bit of her past remains intriguingly off the record.

As things go wrong in the last two books, however, Chaucer calls upon this opacity of hers for different purposes, not to celebrate his heroine but to shield her from 'sklaunder' – the blame that she herself fears from the brass trumpet of Aeolus:

---

[55] Windeatt's Oxford Guide, pp. 281, 282.
[56] Cited in John Haffenden, *William Empson among the Mandarins* (Oxford, 2005), p. 145.

> Allas, of me, unto the worldes ende,
> Shal neyther ben ywriten nor ysonge
> No good word, for thise bokes wol me shende.
> O, rolled shal I ben on many a tonge!
>
>   v 1058–61

Chaucer, of course, cannot evade the central fact of the story he has chosen, that Criseyde proved false, and in the *Legend of Good Women* he has to plead guilty to the charge brought by the God of Love, that the case brings discredit on womankind.[57] But he has no desire to blame ('chide') her any more than the story demands and would excuse her if he could:

> Ne me ne list this sely womman chyde
> Forther than the storye wol devyse.
> Hire name, allas, is publysshed so wide
> That for hir gilt it oughte ynough suffise.
> And if I myghte excuse hire any wise,
> For she so sory was for hire untrouthe,
> Iwis, I wolde excuse hire yet for routhe.
>
>   v 1093–9

The poet cannot be sure about what Criseyde thought and felt at critical junctures, but he can at least entertain the more favourable interpretations of those available to him. Thus, while Criseyde's promises in Book IV to make an early return to Troy may have seemed very optimistic, Chaucer insists that they were offered in all sincerity:

> And treweliche, as writen wel I fynde,
> That al this thyng was seyd of good entente,
> And that hire herte trewe was and kynde

---

[57] *Legend of Good Women*, G 264–66. Chaucer defends himself there by claiming that his intention was 'To forthere trouthe in love and it cheryce, / And to be war fro falsnesse and fro vice', ll. 462–3.

Towardes hym, and spak right as she mente.

IV 1415–18

In the event, Criseyde's decision to go along with the arrangements for the exchange of prisoners – albeit, she insists, for no more than ten days – may come to seem an ominous prelude to her submissive ways in the Greek camp, behaviour which leads to an outcome worse than her lover's worst fears. Yet the narrator does his best to mitigate even that most discreditable part of her history. She did yield to Diomede, but with what kind of love? 'Men seyn – I not – that she yaf hym hire herte' (v 1050). The poet does not know (*not*, that is, *ne wot*). Still less does Chaucer ever commit himself on what it may have been in her nature that led to such a blameworthy outcome. C. S. Lewis singled out the statement that she was 'the ferfulleste wight / That myghte be'; but this remark, offered in passing so early on in the poem (II 450–1), will hardly bear the weight that Lewis attaches to it.[58]

One might look to the big last *descriptio* of Criseyde at v 806–26 for some kind of conclusive summary; but these stanzas prove to be largely devoted to renewed praise of her great beauty and many virtues, just as if nothing significant had happened since the first book. Chaucer's prime source here is again that 'historical' epic of Troy, the *Ylias* of Joseph of Exeter. Joseph wrote: 'Diviciis forme certant insignia morum', that is, 'The riches of her beauty were rivalled only by the excellence of her character.'[59] The curious observation, in this rather disjointed description, that her eyebrows joined in the middle (taken from the *Ylias*) has been understood to imply female weakness, but on this point medieval authorities differed among themselves.[60]

---

[58] C. S. Lewis, *The Allegory of Love* (Oxford, 1936), pp. 185–90.
[59] Text and translation from Windeatt's Oxford Guide, p. 76.
[60] See the note to v 813–14 in the *Riverside Chaucer*.

In fact, the only line that has any clear bearing on her conduct in the latter part of the poem comes at the end of a catalogue of her virtues. She was —

> Charitable, estatlich, lusty, fre;
> Ne nevere mo ne lakked hire pite;
> Tendre-herted, slydynge of corage;
> But trewely, I kan nat telle hire age.

The penultimate line introduces a note of blame not struck by Joseph of Exeter: Criseyde had a 'sliding' heart, that is, her feelings were subject to change. But even here the coupling of 'slydynge of corage' with 'tendre-herted', and with 'pite' in the line before, suggests that the changeability of her feelings had something to do with what was surely a praiseworthy trait, her sympathetic responses to the feelings of others – including, one must admit, Diomede. Well, it may be so. But the following line, the last in the portrait, projects Criseyde back into the real world of history, as a person about whom not everything can be known – least of all perhaps where delicate questions of praise and blame are at stake.

Chaucer was heir to epideictic theories of *oratio poetica*, and also to vernacular traditions of verse (Italian as well as French and English) where auxesis played a major part both in general narrative and in set descriptions. For him, as for Dante, the act of praise might call on all his powers, to display the 'colours longynge to that art'. So his poetry has many passages of strong whole-hearted praise, most often for female subjects like the Virgin Mary or 'goode faire White'. *Laudatio* of this sort is little to modern taste, and I have suggested that recent criticism has sometimes been too ready to find ironies in such passages, as in the case of militant heroes like the Knight and his Theseus in the *Canterbury Tales*. Yet the voicing of praise in Chaucer's poetry – its attribution to a 'narrator' or a character in the fiction – does commonly leave a door open for ironical readings.[61] On occasion the speaker's meaning will be quite unmistakeable, witness the Merchant's encomium on marriage or the Friar's 'laude' of the summoner in the *Friar's Tale*:

> He was, if I shal yeven hym his laude,
> A theef, and eek a somnour, and a baude.
>
> III 1353–4

At other times, especially where it is the narrative voice that speaks, the intentions may be much less clear, as in his portraits of Criseyde in the *Troilus* or the Prioress in the *General Prologue*. It is in the nature of Chaucer's distinctively personal manner of well-saying that it should invite readers to supply the unspoken reservations in these places. Such inflexions toward irony are indeed highly characteristic of his work. Yet, given the dominance of that which has been called a 'hermeneutic of suspicion' in current studies, what seems to need stressing at present is rather his mastery also of 'clere laude'.

---

[61] In his *Textual Subjectivity* (Oxford, 2005), A. C. Spearing questions the part played by 'fallible narrators' in current criticism of medieval poetry. Speaking of the ironic interpretations that often result, he observes: 'Some kind of inadequacy is found in the views or attitudes explicitly expressed in the poem and attributed to the "speaker", while more satisfactory views or attitudes are ascribed to the poet' (p. 202, cf. p. 133).

CHAPTER 5

The decline of praise: two modern instances

The 'decline of praise' in English poetry does not by any means
date back as far as the end of the period with which this study has
been concerned. On the contrary, it was during the following, Early
Modern, period that the poetry of praise was to have its greatest
age. Tudor and Stuart poets produced a wealth and variety of encomiastic writing unmatched by the surviving works of their English
predecessors, and it is only in the course of the seventeenth century
that the impulses can be seen to weaken. This flourishing of *laus* in
Early Modern times has attracted the attention of many scholars, and
I can do little more in this chapter than refer the reader to some of
their studies. Of these, the most wide-ranging known to me is a book
by O. B. Hardison entitled *The Enduring Monument: A Study of the
Idea of Praise in Renaissance Literary Theory and Practice* (Westport,
Conn., 1962). As well as giving a valuable account of the 'theory of
praise' as it was received by poets in the sixteenth century, Hardison
surveys the main encomiastic genres in the English verse of the time:
epic (including Spenser's *Faerie Queene*), lyric (love poetry, hymns)
and occasional poetry (especially elegy, to which he devotes three
chapters). Other books address the subject of praise in particular
writings, such as *The Faerie Queene* and Donne's *Anniversaries*.[1]

---

[1] Thomas H. Cain, *Praise in 'The Faerie Queene'* (Lincoln, Nebr., 1978); Barbara Kiefer
Lewalski, *Donne's 'Anniversaries' and the Poetry of Praise: The Creation of a Symbolic Mode*
(Princeton, N.J., 1973).

The history of praise in English poetry since the Renaissance remains, needless to say, a big and daunting subject, especially for one whose academic competence lies elsewhere; but I have chosen not to overlook it completely here, leaving the modern period aside as if it were no more than what gunners call dead ground. For to notice, albeit sketchily, some of the developments that have occurred there should help in the understanding of our present position as we look back at premodern poetry across the intervening terrain. With this purpose in mind, I select just two types of praise poem for consideration: first, panegyric, mainly as addressed to royalty, and then heroic poetry, mainly about past warriors.

PANEGYRIC: PRAISE OF KINGS

Panegyrics of contemporary rulers represent one of the types of English praise poetry which seems to have flourished more vigorously in the Early Modern period than in the Middle Ages. It is very likely that the scops of Anglo-Saxon England composed many poems of this ancient type, but the monastic producers of the surviving manuscripts saw fit to preserve only very few of them.[2] For many years after the Conquest, again, English poets most commonly chose to address royalty in Latin or in French; and in the fourteenth and even fifteenth centuries, they still fell short of their Tudor and Stuart successors. John Gower, for instance, largely reserved his praise of Henry IV for his Latin verse; and Chaucer directly addressed a reigning monarch only once – and then only in a little petitionary balade celebrating Henry as 'conquerour of Brutes Albyon, / Which that by lyne and free eleccion / Been verray kyng'. Their successors, in particular John Lydgate and his followers, engaged more

---

[2] See pp. 39–40 above, on the poems in the Anglo-Saxon Chronicle.

closely with royal and noble patrons;[3] but their panegyrics are quite surpassed in hyperbolic extravagance by such later Tudor poets as Edmund Spenser.[4] In the proems to all six books of his *Faerie Queene* he praises Queen Elizabeth I, invoking her in the first as 'Goddesse heavenly bright, / Mirrour of grace and Maiestie divine, / Great Lady of the greatest Isle' (1.pr.4); and his narrative adds several encomiastic types of the queen – Una, Belphoebe, Britomart and the Faerie Queene herself – though none of them, Spenser protests, can do justice to the royal original:

> But O dred Soveraine
> Thus farre forth pardon, sith that choicest wit
> Cannot your glorious pourtraict figure plaine
> That I in colour showes may shadow it,
> And antique praises unto present persons fit.
>
> III.pr.3

Panegyric poetry flourished even more vigorously under early Stuart kings, as poets such as Ben Jonson and William Davenant produced 'glorious portraits' of James I and Charles I; and Andrew Marvell's *Horatian Ode* glorifies Oliver Cromwell, albeit in a less straightforward fashion.[5] The restoration of Charles II after the Commonwealth prompted further outbursts. In 1660, John Dryden published *Astraea Redux: A Poem on the Happy Restoration and Return of his Sacred Majesty Charles the Second*, followed in 1661 by his poem *To his Sacred Majesty: A Panegyrick on his Coronation*; and in 1668 Dryden was appointed the first official poet laureate, with

---

[3] On what the author calls 'laureate poetics' in Lydgate and others, see Robert J. Meyer-Lee, *Poets and Power from Chaucer to Wyatt* (Cambridge, 2007).

[4] See the full study by Cain (n. 1 above). I cite in what follows from the edition by A. C. Hamilton (London, 1977).

[5] See Kevin Sharpe, *Criticism and Compliment: The Politics of Literature in the England of Charles I* (Cambridge, 1987); David Norbrook, *Writing the English Republic: Poetry, Rhetoric and Politics, 1627–1660* (Cambridge, 1999), pp. 245–71. Norbrook argues against the over-reading of irony in Marvell's poem.

a yearly fee of one hundred pounds and a butt of canary wine every Christmas.[6]

One might suppose that the establishment of the laureateship promised a bright future for the poetry of royal panegyric, but the outcome proved quite otherwise. It is as if the official hiving off of this particular function to a designated individual encouraged the generality of poets to leave it alone – or indeed, as things turned out, to ridicule it. Dryden himself, according to one scholar, 'came to recognize the futility of writing serious panegyric in Restoration England'.[7] Dryden's time as poet laureate came to an end in 1688; and it was the great event of that year, the Glorious Revolution, which, by sacrificing the claim of the Stuart monarchy to a divine hereditary right, greatly weakened the royal charisma of William of Orange and his successors, not to speak of the Hanoverian kings after 1714. Many Whig poets, including Dryden's successor Thomas Shadwell (ridiculed by Dryden in *Mac Flecknoe*), celebrated William as their liberator; but it can safely be said that royal panegyric was never the same after 1688.[8] Kings were no longer 'mirrors of grace and majesty divine'.

[6] Edmund Kemper Broadus, *The Laureateship: A Study of the Office of Poet Laureate in England, with Some Account of the Poets* (Oxford, 1921), pp. 59–74, on Dryden. Broadus gives a wide survey both of Dryden's unofficial predecessors and of his official successors up to Robert Bridges.

[7] James D. Garrison, *Dryden and the Tradition of Panegyric* (Berkeley, Calif., 1975), p. 198. Cf. A. B. Chambers, *Andrew Marvell and Edmund Waller: Seventeenth-Century Praise and Restoration Satire* (Philadelphia, Pa., 1991), contrasting Waller's celebration of the Duke of York's victory over a Dutch fleet with the debunking sequels by other poets, including Marvell. Richard Helgerson notices the decline in quality once earlier 'self-crowned laureates' were succeeded by the official variety: *Self-Crowned Laureates: Spenser, Jonson, Milton and the Literary System* (Berkeley, Calif., 1983), p. 7 etc.

[8] See John Thomas Rowland, *Faint Praise and Civil Leer: The 'Decline' of Eighteenth-Century Panegyric* (Newark, Del., 1994), observing that 'panegyric acquires pejorative connotations in the late seventeenth and early eighteenth century', although 'panegyrics (of a sort) continue to be written' (p. 17). Rowland, p. 15, cites the definition of panegyric by Thomas Blount in his 1656 dictionary: 'A licentious kind of speaking or oration, in the praise and commendation of Kings, or other great persons, wherein some falsities are joined with many flatteries.'

Throughout the eighteenth century an undistinguished succession of poets laureate turned out birthday and New Year odes in praise of their Hanoverian masters;[9] but in this new world, such encomia won little respect, and serious poets generally preferred to treat the matter ironically. So Alexander Pope, addressing George II in his *Epistle to Augustus*:

> Oh! could I mount on the Maeonian wing,
> Your Arms, your Actions, your Repose to sing!
> What seas you travers'd! and what fields you fought!
> Your Country's Peace, how oft, how dearly bought![10]

'Cuius contrarium verum est', as George's subjects cannot have failed to see. Many years later, in 1822, his successor George III was handled much more roughly by Lord Byron. Byron's *Vision of Judgement* is a burlesque version of a poem of the same name in which the then poet laureate, Robert Southey, glorified the passing of George at his death into the company of other great ones in heaven.[11] In his Preface, Byron speaks of 'the gross flattery, the dull impudence, the renegado intolerance, and impious cant' of Southey's poem, while himself treating the dead king vituperatively, as an 'old, blind, mad, helpless, weak, poor worm' who 'ever warr'd with freedom and the free' (sts 42 and 45).

---

[9] See Broadus, *The Laureateship*, pp. 102–62. He cites Thomas Warton, himself poet laureate, who described the laureateship as 'confessedly Gothic and unaccommodated to modern manners' (p. 154).

[10] *Epistle to Augustus*, ll. 394–7, in *The Poems of Alexander Pope*, ed. John Butt (London, 1963). In Pope's *First Satire of the Second Book of Horace Imitated*, he mocks both royal encomia and contemporary heroic poetry. His interlocutor, F[ortescue], urges him 'if you needs must write, write Caesar's Praise: / You'll gain at least a *Knighthood*, or the *Bays*.' To which Pope replies: 'What? like Sir *Richard*, rumbling, rough and fierce, / With Arms, and George, and Brunswick crowd the verse? / Rend with tremendous Sound your ears asunder, / With Gun, Drum, Trumpet, Blunderbuss & Thunder?' (ll. 21–6).

[11] Broadus, *The Laureateship*, pp. 177–9.

The history of royal panegyric, and indeed of the loyal celebration of public affairs generally, has since Southey's time been undistinguished, with the notable exception of Lord Tennyson. In his long tenure of the laureateship, Tennyson cultivated what he called the 'civic muse' in praise of his queen, her consort and other public figures. One of his earliest laureate pieces, *An Ode on the Death of the Duke of Wellington* (1852), celebrated the burial of the duke alongside Nelson in St Pauls with extraordinary patriotic fervour in a free Pindaric manner. Yet even here 'many of the reviews were hostile'.[12] On the death of Tennyson in 1892, one of the successors proposed was Rudyard Kipling, a poet certainly capable of the full-throated and memorable celebration of royal and public themes.[13] But Gladstone preferred Alfred Austen. It cannot be said that any of the more recent laureates, whatever their other merits, have often succeeded in addressing civic, let alone royal, subjects without embarrassing results. In a poem entitled 'A Model for the Laureate', W. B. Yeats wrote these lines:

> The Muse is mute when public men
> Applaud a modern throne:
> Those cheers that can be bought or sold,
> That office fools have run,
> That waxen seal, that signature.
> For things like these what decent man
> Would keep his lover waiting,
>   Keep his lover waiting?

More than most latterday poets, in fact, Yeats was capable of a grand public rhetoric, as when he celebrated the heroes of his own Ireland –

---

[12] *Tennyson, A Selected Edition*, ed. Christopher Ricks (London, 1989), p. 488.
[13] Broadus, *The Laureateship*, pp. 202, 207. Kipling wrote poems in praise of Queen Victoria (*Ave Imperatrix*) and King Edward VII (*The Dead King*), as well as national heroes like Lord Roberts and Cecil Rhodes.

'MacDonagh and MacBride, / And Connolly and Pearse' – but in the present poem he concludes by expressing what is surely the opinion most widely held today. The Muse has no business joining in applause of a modern throne; poets, like other decent men, will give priority to the private world of the feelings.

HEROIC: PRAISE OF WARRIORS

Earlier chapters here considered some Old and Middle English narratives set in a glorious 'historical' past, Germanic, biblical, British or Classical. The heroes of these poems were typically warriors, and the authors treated them encomiastically (or so I argued) in the main. In the rest of the present chapter, I try to sketch a declining trajectory for this species of praise poetry in modern England, by noticing a main line of long poems from Spenser to Tennyson.

In the first stanza of his *Faerie Queene*, Spenser promises 'For trumpets sterne to chaunge mine Oaten reeds.' He is to turn from pastoral to epic, and praise the 'gentle deeds' of knights and ladies: 'Fierce warres and faithfull loves shal moralize my song.'[14] Accordingly, the ensuing poem magnifies its material in an epical way, commonly devoting to its people, events and places what Spenser's friend Gabriel Harvey called his 'lively Hyperbolicall Amplifications'.[15] Fierce wars bulk large in the poem, most commonly in the form of individual encounters where knights conquer their adversaries, human or otherwise, with sword and spear. These scenes of combat can be long and

[14] 1.pr.1, ed. Hamilton. On the trumpet as the instrument of fame and of epic poetry, see chapter 3 of Alastair Fowler, *Time's Purpled Masquers: Stars and the Afterlife in Renaissance English Literature* (Oxford, 1996), with discussion of Chaucer's *House of Fame* on pp. 90–2.
[15] Harvey is referring to a lost earlier poem of Spenser, *Dreames: Poetical Works*, ed. J. C. Smith and E. de Selincourt (Oxford, 1912), p. 628. On the teaching of amplification in Spenser's time, see Peter Mack, *Elizabethan Rhetoric: Theory and Practice* (Cambridge, 2002), pp. 42–3, 149–54.

glorious, as in Redcrosse's three-day battle with the dragon or Cambell's joust with three brothers (I.xi, IV.iii). It so happens that Spenser derived this Cambell from Chaucer's *Squire's Tale* – speaking of the older poet's 'warlike numbers and Heroicke sound' – but his own epic romance owes much less to native sources than to Classical and Italian poets like Virgil and Ariosto.[16] Yet, considered simply as a poem of fierce wars, *The Faerie Queene* may be said to belong with *Beowulf* or the alliterative *Morte Arthure* as another English poem of 'Heroicke sound'.

The Faerie Queene, however, is very far from devoting itself mainly to praise of heroic warriors, as a reader coming to it from *Beowulf* or the *Morte* cannot fail to appreciate. For one thing, the antique world that Spenser portrays stands at a much wider remove from any conceivable historical or geographical realities. Its central character is indeed Prince Arthur, introduced with an encomium at I.vii.29–36; but we find him, not in Arthurian Britain, but in a land of Faerie, to which the young man has travelled in search of the Faerie Queene, seen by him in a vision (an idea picked up, it seems, from Chaucer's burlesque story of Thopas); and the only other Arthurian person to figure in the action is Tristram, exiled from his native Lyonesse (VI.ii.28–30). Otherwise, Spenser peoples his Faerie land with a very mixed bag of characters, many of them entirely lacking any credentials in earlier stories and bearing names of the poet's own invention such as 'Calidore' and 'Calepine'. In this fantasy world, heroes encounter, not only knightly foes, but also adversaries such as Mammon, Despair and Disdain.

In his letter of explanation to Sir Walter Raleigh, Spenser described *The Faerie Queene* as 'a continued Allegory, or darke conceit'; and it

---

[16] See Colin Burrow, *Epic Romance: Homer to Milton* (Oxford, 1993), with discussion of Spenser in chapter 5.

is here that the difference between his poem and the heroic narratives of the English Middle Ages chiefly lies. At one level of meaning, the persons and events in Faerie land 'shadow', as he puts it, events and persons in his contemporary world, so that the poet's praises can extend from his fictional heroes to notables such as Raleigh, Leicester and above all Queen Elizabeth: 'antique praises unto present persons fit' (III.pr.3). Yet much the most 'continued' and the most significant allegory in the poem concerns not the public but the personal realm, defined by Spenser in his letter to Raleigh as 'that part which they in Philosophy call Ethice, or the vertues of a private man'. It is virtues of this sort that are headlined successively in the six completed books: Holiness, Temperance, Chastity, Friendship, Justice and Courtesy. Each book exemplifies its virtue by a designated hero and also refracted in its varied manifestations by ancillary characters, along with representations of the evils with which that virtue is opposed. Even where the persons are not downright personifications, like Despair, their names commonly speak to the moral theme, as in Book I with its three paynim brothers Sansfoy, Sanjoy and Sansloy, and its two contrasted women, Una and Duessa. Representatives of the virtues will, of course, be portrayed favourably in the main, but the point of the moral allegory, its illocutionary force, is not to praise the fictional characters but to teach the reader by their example – and not least by the example of their occasional failings, as when Redcrosse almost succumbs to Despair or Artegall is ensnared by Radigund (I.xi, v.v). For the moral life, as Spenser shadows it, is not a simple matter of black and white. Heroes can go wrong, and their adversaries are not always distinguishable as such, witness the deceits practised by Duessa and the evil enchanter Archimago.

Heroic narrative and moral allegory were both literary kinds very well established in the Middle Ages, but no English writer then attempted to combine them, as Spenser does in *The Faerie Queene*. Indeed, in their histories of heroes such as Beowulf and Arthur, it is remarkable how little effort they make to address even the simplest of exemplary lessons to their listeners: the *Beowulf*-poet does so very occasionally, but only in short interjected comments ('a man should be like that, a thane at a time of need').[17] The prime intention of these poets, it seems, was not to make moral points but to celebrate old heroes. They would have been surprised, I think, to read what Spenser said to Raleigh about his chief intention in the poem: 'to fashion a gentleman or noble person in vertuous and gentle discipline' by exemplifying 'the twelve private morall vertues, as Aristotle hath devised'. Insofar as the *Faerie Queene* fulfils this intention, the poem represents, I think, a turn away from traditional heroic narrative, with its public rhetoric of praise, towards the private concerns of the individual – in this case, any gentle reader. Later long poems to be considered here make, I shall suggest, their different moves in a like direction.

Near the beginning of Book IX in *Paradise Lost*, John Milton expresses his thoughts about the genre to which the poem belongs.[18] In the past, he remarks, war has been considered the only subject suitable for heroic poetry: 'Wars, hitherto the only argument / Heroic deemed' (IX.28–9). Accordingly the epics of Homer and Virgil portrayed actions prompted by impulses of anger: the wrath of Achilles, the rage of Turnus, the ire of Neptune and Juno (ll. 14–19); and modern romances showed only

> chief mastery to dissect
> With long and tedious havoc fabled knights
> In battles feigned.
>
> ll. 29–31

---

[17] See above, p. 49.
[18] IX.13–47, cited from *Paradise Lost*, ed. Alastair Fowler, 2nd edn (London, 1998).

As a younger man, Milton had planned a poem about Arthur and his knights, and in *Il Penseroso* he expressed his love of the tourneys and enchantments in Ariostan or Spenserian romance;[19] but in the present passage he dismisses the whole glamorous business as 'Not that which justly gives heroic name / To person or to poem' (ll. 40–1). Inspired by a heavenly muse, *Paradise Lost* has a subject 'Not less but more heroic', a 'higher argument'. The poem does find some space for the heroic topics of the past: God and Satan feel anger for each other, and Raphael's account of the war in heaven between them occupies the whole of Book VI – 'battles feigned', and not without long and tedious havoc.[20] But the action of the poem is far from turning on that war, whose outcome proves only too predictable. The crux comes later, in Book IX itself, with the moral conflicts within and between Adam and Eve as they respond to the wiles of the serpent; and that drama, though its outcome carries consequences for all humanity, is played out domestically, in private between a man and his wife.

In the same passage from Book IX, Milton draws a contrast between traditional heroic subjects and what he calls 'the better fortitude / Of patience and heroic martyrdom / Unsung' (IX.31–3). These words, only barely applicable to *Paradise Lost* itself, look forward rather to its successor, *Paradise Regained*. This poem, concerning the temptation of Jesus by Satan in the wilderness, is said to tell 'of deeds / Above heroic, though in secret done' (I.14–15). Jesus has not yet begun his ministry: as Satan says, 'Thy life hath yet been private, most part spent / At home.'[21] The trope of moral conflict as a kind of warfare, which underlies so much of the allegorical action in Spenser's poem,

---

[19] *Mansus*, ll. 80–4, *Epitaphium Damonis*, ll. 162–71, *Il Penseroso*, ll. 109–20: *Complete Shorter Poems*, ed. John Carey, 2nd edn (London, 1997).

[20] Michael condemns the bloodthirsty warfare of the giants of Genesis in Book XI, ll. 641–59, 675–80, 688–99, 788–93.

[21] Ed. Carey, III.232–3. Cf. III.22. At the end of the poem, Jesus 'Home to his mother's house private returned' (IV.639).

figures here only as an occasional metaphor, as in the song of the angels:

> Victory and triumph to the Son of God
> Now ent'ring his great duel, not of arms,
> But to vanquish by wisdom hellish wiles.[22]

Moral victories like this win praise in heaven, but they commonly pass unsung on earth. In Book III, after Satan has attempted to arouse a 'thirst for glory' by recalling great warriors of Antiquity, Jesus responds with the example of Job:

> Famous he was in heaven, on earth less known;
> Where glory is false glory, attributed
> To things not glorious, men not worthy of fame.
> They err who count it glorious to subdue
> By conquest far and wide.[23]

Earthly glory is bestowed by the unthinking masses. 'They praise and they admire they know not what' (III.52), glorifying conquerors as 'Great benefactors of mankind' (III.82), whereas true glory, if it is to be had at all on earth, must be sought rather –

> Without ambition, war, or violence;
> By deeds of peace, by wisdom eminent,
> By patience, temperance.
>
>   III. 90–2

Heroism here is manifested in private by 'deeds of peace'; so, in this last and strictest of Milton's poems, there is no room at all for glorifications of the warrior.

---

[22] 1.173–5. A little earlier, God speaks of how Jesus 'shall first lay down the rudiments / Of his great warfare' (1.157–8), where Carey and Fowler note a Virgilian parallel, 'bellique . . . rudimenta'.

[23] III.68–72. See Barbara Kiefer Lewalski, *Milton's Brief Epic* (Providence, R.I., 1966), on the Old Testament Book of Job as a model for the brief biblical epic, where glory is won by virtues such as patience and temperance rather than by warfare.

It is a long stride from *Paradise Regained* to the next of my stepping-stones, Wordsworth's *Prelude*, for this long poem carries privatisation and demilitarisation (so to speak) further than Milton ever did. *The Prelude* was never published in the author's lifetime, and it was known to him, not by its current title, but as 'the poem to Coleridge', a friend to whom many of its observations are addressed.[24] Its subject is correspondingly personal: 'myself', or 'the history of a poet's mind'. The autobiographical story takes Wordsworth to France in the violent times of the French Revolution, and he encounters there one undoubtedly heroic figure, Captain Michel Beaupuy, a man whom he ranks 'near the worthiest of antiquity' (IX.427); but even Beaupuy is praised, not as the warrior which he was, but as a personal friend loved for his benignity and wisdom (IX.294–437). We are here worlds away from Epic Romance. Yet this highly personal and unwarlike poem does not fail to measure itself against its great predecessors. Early in Book I, Wordsworth recalls his search for a 'noble theme'. Wishing to make some 'yet remembered names . . . inmates in the hearts of men', his mind turned first to 'some British theme, some old / Romantic tale by Milton left unsung' (1.179–80), or to Spenser's world of chivalric adventure. At other times he considered warrior heroes of a kind nearer to his own heart, men like William Wallace who fought for liberty against tyrants and conquerors. Or perhaps, he thought, he might make up a story of his own, 'more near akin / To my own passions and habitual thoughts.' In the event, of course, he abandoned history and fiction altogether, and made his thrilling turn to his own childhood:

---

[24] So, at X.372, Wordsworth addresses Coleridge 'As if to thee alone in private talk'. I cite the 1805 version, from *The Prelude, 1799, 1805, 1850*, ed. Jonathan Wordsworth, M. H. Abrams and Stephen Gill (New York, 1979).

> Was it for this
> That one, the fairest of all rivers, loved
> To blend his murmurs with my nurse's song . . .
>
> I. 271–3

Later in the poem, Wordsworth, like the Milton of *Paradise Regained*, claims the epithet 'heroic' for his chosen subject: 'This is in truth heroic argument, / And genuine prowess' (III.182–3). His history of the poet's mind does indeed deal in high matters, of nature and the human imagination; but 'genuine prowess'? The oddity of the claim betrays the remoteness of Wordworth's subject from any traditional 'heroic argument'.

Wordsworth's contemporaries and successors found other ways of coming to terms with the realities of modern times – what Milton already called 'an age too late' for epic (*Paradise Lost*, IX.44). I refer to Byron's *Don Juan* and Tennyson's *Idylls of the King*.

Lord Byron several times speaks of his *Don Juan* as an epic poem:

> My poem's epic, and is meant to be
> 　　Divided in twelve books; each book containing,
> With love, and war, a heavy gale at sea,
> 　　A list of ships, and captains, and kings reigning,
> New characters; the episodes are three:
> 　　A panoramic view of hell's in training,
> After the style of Virgil and of Homer,
> So that my name of Epic's no misnomer.[25]

Given the reputation of Don Juan, adventures in love naturally bulk very large; but war occupies two whole cantos, which describe the siege and capture of the Turkish town Ismael by Russian forces (Cantos VII and VIII). Byron makes the inevitable comparisons with

---

[25] *Byron*, ed. Jerome J. McGann (Oxford, 1986), Canto I, stanza 200.

Homer's *Iliad* (VII.78–81, VIII.121), but his poem strikes a very modern note in the hatred it evinces for wars – with the exception of honourable wars fought in defence of liberty (VII.40). The Russian assault, prompted by 'mere lust for power', is commanded by a general who 'loved blood as an alderman loves marrow', and, once the town has been taken, his men kill, rape and pillage its inhabitants (VIII.122–32). In the midst of all this havoc, the only warrior to receive full-throated praise is an old Muslim defender who, even after five of his sons have fallen at his side, still refuses to surrender and dies heroically (VIII.104–19). Young Don Juan fights on the Russian side courageously, but his courage is of a more impetuous kind, prompted by occasions that arise in the heat of battle, as when 'after a good deal of heavy firing, / He found himself alone, and friends retiring' (VIII.27). Like Tolstoy's *War and Peace*, Byron's epic does full justice to the sheer chaos of the killing fields, beyond the control of combatants and commanders alike.

Despite his more dramatic adventures in both love and fighting, Byron's hero bears some resemblance to Tom Jones in Fielding's 'prosai-comic-epic' novel.[26] Both young men belong in a latterday modern world where true heroes in the old style are no longer to be looked for:

> Cervantes smiled Spain's Chivalry away;
> A single laugh demolished the right arm
> Of his own country; – seldom since that day
> Has Spain had heroes.[27]

Like Fielding, too, Byron himself occupies a commanding position in his work. As he says, 'I rattle on exactly as I'd talk' in 'this sort of

---

[26] Ulrich Broich, *The Eighteenth-Century Mock-Heroic Poem*, trans. D. H. Wilson (Cambridge, 1990), discusses Fielding and Byron on pp. 177–9.

[27] XIII.11. See also I.1–5 on the difficulty of finding a hero in the present age. IV.6 dismisses the heroes and heroines of chivalric romance as 'obsolete': 'I choose a modern subject as more meet.'

desultory rhyme' (xv.19–20). The story of Juan's exploits must have prompted contemporary readers to look for parallels with the life of its notorious author; and there are many passages of 'desultory' comment and reflection where Byron expresses his personal opinions about modern life and society – in the main sceptically, as in *The Vision of Judgement*. So he follows his account of the siege of Ismael with an ironical attack on a modern English warrior-hero, the Duke of Wellington, as an upholder of tyrannic regimes abroad (ix.1–9). With some justice, indeed, Byron could describe his poem as 'this epic satire' (xiv.99). Its very personal tone of amused detachment – sometimes tolerant, sometimes not – leaves little scope for straight heroic amplification. Its hero is an engaging fellow, a 'broth of a boy' (viii.24); but in the accounts of his romantic exploits, jokes are never very far away:

> Then for accomplishments of chivalry,
>   In case our lord the king should go to war again,
> He learn'd the arts of riding, fencing, gunnery,
> And how to scale a fortress – or a nunnery.
>
> 1.38

The twelve books that make up Tennyson's *Idylls of the King* treat episodes from the history of King Arthur and his knights from their glorious beginnings to their tragic end. It was very late in the day for such a romance of chivalry, and readers of Malory or of the alliterative *Morte Arthure* will notice how 'literary' the narratives seem, not least in their treatment of the inevitable battles with sword and lance. As Wordsworth ruefully said of one of his own narrative projects, 'the whole beauteous fabric seems to lack / Foundation, and withal appears throughout / Shadowy and insubstantial.'[28] It is not easy, in fact, to take any of Tennyson's knights quite seriously as *warrior*

---

[28] *The Prelude*, i.226–8.

heroes, though he turns their shadowy insubstantiality to good effect
in his highly atmospheric descriptions of the last tournament and the
last battle:

> The sudden trumpet sounded as in a dream
> To ears but half-awaked, then one low roll
> Of Autumn thunder, and the jousts began:
> And ever the wind blew, and yellowing leaf
> And gloom and gleam, and shower and shorn plume
> Went down it.[29]

In the jousting that follows, one recalls only the narrow face of
Modred, a chief agent in the moral decline of the Round Table,
glimpsed 'like a vermin in its hole' (*The Last Tournament*, 165–6).
The sense of an ending is even more overpowering in Tennyson's
account of Arthur's 'last, dim, weird battle of the west' (*The Passing
of Arthur*, 90–117). This takes place in a 'deathwhite mist'. 'Friend
and foe were shadows in the mist.'

   Hallam Tennyson said that his father 'has made the old legends
his own, restored the idealism, and infused into them a spirit of
modern thought and an ethical significance'.[30] Tennyson himself
complained that reviewers of the *Idylls* 'have explained some things
too allegorically, although there is an allegorical or perhaps rather a
parabolic drift in the poem'.[31] By comparison with the *Faerie Queene*,
the *Idylls* is hardly allegorical at all, nor does it articulate anything
like that system of virtues and vices that Spenser's poem inher-
ited from Antiquity and the Middle Ages. Yet the two poems have
in common their orientation of romance towards personal moral
issues – by tracing, in Tennyson's case, the exemplary moral

---

[29] *The Last Tournament*, ll. 151–6, from *Tennyson, A Selected Edition*, ed. Christopher Ricks
     (Harlow, 1989).
[30] Cited from the Ricks edition, p. 667.   [31] From the Ricks edition, p. 670.

history of the Round Table. *Idylls* opens with King Arthur swearing
his knights to a life of high virtue:

> my knights are sworn to vows
> Of utter hardihood, utter gentleness,
> And, loving, utter faithfulness in love,
> And uttermost obedience to the King.
>
> (*Gareth and Lynette*, ll. 541–4)

Thereafter this ideal order is progressively corrupted by the fleshly
Vivien, the treacherous Modred and especially the adultery of Guinevere with Lancelot. So in his last conversation with the queen,
towards the end of the poem, Arthur declares that his knightly following is now only the 'loathsome opposite' of what it once was
(*Guinevere*, l. 488). Late in life, Tennyson recalled that 'I intended
Arthur to represent the Ideal Soul of Man coming into conflict with
the warring elements of the flesh.'[32] His Arthur is neither the young,
questing prince of the *Faerie Queene* nor the formidable battle-leader
of the alliterative *Morte*. Indeed, between his initial conquest of the
rival kings in *The Coming of Arthur* and his last battle, he does very
little fighting at all, apart from his campaign against the Red Knight
in the north; and there the encounter with his adversary ends without
a blow struck, when the drunken knight falls off his horse into the
mud (*The Last Tournament*, ll. 457–70). Tennyson celebrates Arthur
rather as a patient, just and merciful ruler of men. In his final interview
with Guinevere, his reproaches for her 'shameful sin' with Lancelot
are suffused with love and pity, and he leaves her with a blessing
(*Guinevere*, l. 580). It is an impressive scene; yet it cannot be said that
King Arthur commands the central position that Tennyson certainly
planned for him.[33] Merlin describes him as a 'blameless King and

---

[32] Ed. Ricks, p. 671.
[33] The poem is headed with an epigraph from Joseph of Exeter, 'Flos Regum Arthurus'
('Arthur, Flower of Kings').

stainless man' (*Merlin and Vivien*, l. 777), but such an Ideal Soul,
virtuous and forebearing, seems an unlikely kind of hero even in
this latterday version of Arthurian romance, partially demilitarised
though it is.

Another text from Tennyson's time clearly speaks to a similar
extension of the 'heroic' in favour of civilian, non-military values.
When Thomas Carlyle in 1840 delivered his six lectures on 'Heroes,
Hero-Worship and the Heroic in History', he distinguished six types
of hero, roughly in historical order: Divinities (Odin), Prophets
(Mahomet), Poets (Dante, Shakespeare), Priests (Luther, Knox),
Men of Letters (Dr Johnson, Rousseau, Robert Burns) and Kings
(Cromwell, Napoleon).[34] Warriors figure in only one of these categories, as 'Kings'. The rest are all heroes of the religious or the literary
life, to be considered 'heroic' only in a distinctly non-Homeric sense
of the term. Carlyle acknowledged as much when he came, in his
fifth lecture, to the Men of Letters who represent heroism in the
eighteenth century. In that age of 'Triviality, Formulism and Com-
monplace', he says, the hero 'has had to cramp himself into strange
shapes' (pp. 155, 140). Strange shapes indeed: Johnson, Rousseau and
Burns.[35] Nor were things any better in 1840. Carlyle speaks of the
'sad state' of hero-worship in his own day, 'an age that as it were
denies the existence of great men; denies the desirableness of great
men' (pp. 103, 111). The examples of Cromwell and Napoleon do
nevertheless encourage him to suppose that the tide may be turning:
'I prophesy that the world may once again become *sincere*; a believing world; with *many* heroes in it, a heroic world!' (p. 160). Yet his

[34] *Carlyle's Lectures on Heroes, Hero-Worship and the Heroic in History*, ed. P. C. Parr (Oxford, 1910).
[35] On the domestication of the hero in the eighteenth century, see Robert Folkenflik (ed.), *The English Hero, 1660–1800* (Newark, Del., 1982).

prophecy has hardly been fulfilled, certainly not by any revival of warrior heroes in English poetry.

Since the early twentieth century, 'War Poetry' has been taken chiefly to denote the poems of the First World War, composed by Wilfrid Owen and the rest. The experiences of these men on the Western Front found expression in poetry which – like Byron's, but more so – exposed the horror and futility of war; and this view has been widely shared since, not least by literary scholars, both male and female. The introduction to a recent collection of scholarly essays on medieval literary responses to war opens with two epigraphs, one taken from Malory's account of Arthur's last and most bloody battle, and the other from a poem by Siegfried Sassoon:

> But the past is just the same – and War's a bloody game . . .
> Have you forgotten yet? . . .
> Look down and swear by the slain of the War that you'll
>   never forget.[36]

It is hardly surprising that this 'bloody game' should have failed to attract contemporary poets as a heroic argument for narrative verse. However, I refer finally to one exceptional case: the sequence *War Music* by the contemporary poet Christopher Logue.[37]

War Music is the latest in a long line of Englishings of Homeric and Virgilian epic, represented in the past by poets such as Gavin Douglas, George Chapman, John Dryden and Alexander Pope.

---

[36] *Writing War*, ed. Corinne Saunders, Françoise Le Saux and Neil Thomas (Cambridge, 2004), p. 1. It may be that the experiences of J. R. R. Tolkien on the Western Front played some part in his criticisms of Byrhtnoth, Beowulf and the Arthur of *Sir Gawain* for risking lives by their misplaced 'chivalry': see above, pp. 42 and 54.

[37] Five of the projected six volumes have so far been published: *War Music* (1981), *Kings* (1991), *The Husbands* (1994), *All Day Permanent Red* (2003) and *Cold Calls* (2005). Revised texts of the first three of these were published in one volume as *War Music: An Account of Books 1–4 and 16–19 of Homer's 'Iliad'* (London, 2001).

Logue's version of Homer's *Iliad* is very far from being a straight, continuous translation – the author describes it as 'a poem in English dependent upon whatever, through reading and through conversation, I could guess about a small part of the *Iliad*' (*War Music*, p. 8) – but it does full justice to Homer's warlike subject. With a technique owing much to film ('Cut to the fleet'), the poem invites readers to visualise as distinctly as possible the battlefield, the fighting and the warriors themselves, as in this *descriptio* of the chief hero, Achilles:

> Observe his muscles as they move beneath his skin,
> His fine, small-eared, investigative head,
> His shoulder's bridge, the deep sweep of his back
> Down which (plaited with Irish gold)
> His never-cut redcurrant-coloured hair
> Hangs in a glossy cable till its tuft
> Brushes the combat-belt gripping his rump.
>
> *Husbands*, p. 16

Not all the warriors are as glamorous as that, but most of them are heroically strong and skilful fighters, looking for death or glory on the battlefield like their Homeric originals. Hector says to King Priam:

> We are your heroes.
> Audacious fameseekers who relish close combat.
> Mad to be first among the blades.
>
> *Kings*, p. 52

Yet war also figures in this poem as a kind of madness, killing and maiming its participants, often in horrible ways. One section of the first volume is headed 'GBH', police shorthand for Grievous Bodily Harm (*War Music*, p. 41); and the whole sequence has many unsparing records of sheer violence. Here Menelaos dispatches a young Trojan:

Offhandedly the bitter Greek reached up
And hooked the tendon around Thackta's neck
And smashed his downwards moving cry against his knee,
And poached his eyes, and smashed and smashed
That baby face, loose as a bag of nuts.

War Music, p. 45

Heroes can do such things without ceasing to be heroes, here as in Homer.

The *War Music* sequence is much too engrossed in evoking the physical realities of its people and events to spare much time for expressions of authorial opinion. So I wrote to Christopher Logue asking him if he would comment on his treatment of war in the poem. I am grateful to him for his reply:

My attitude to war is ambivalent. It is a human habit and it is, mostly, a poor habit, but it is endemic to humans and it is extremely interesting. It shows a kind of male animal behaviour . . . [it is] a very curious affair – extraordinary things occur, noble and bestial things, the mind is completely preoccupied, there is excitement, sexual tension and a sense of comradeship, of being psychologically linked to others.[38]

Something not unlike this 'ambivalence' may be found in the *Iliad* itself. Perhaps it is only under the aegis of such a Classical original that a contemporary English poet could do justice, as Logue does, to what he calls the nobility as well as the bestiality of war. As for excitement, sexual tension and the sense of comradeship – for these, we nowadays commonly look, not to poetry, but to fiction or film.

---

[38] Since the author was ill at the time, his wife Rosemary Hill very kindly noted down his thoughts and conveyed them to me in her letter. For an uncompromisingly modern and pacifist view of the *Iliad*, see the essay that Simone Weil published in 1940, translated by Mary McCarthy as 'The *Iliad*, or the Poem of Force', in Simone Weil and Rachel Bespaloff, *War and the Iliad* (New York, 2005), pp. 1–37. Weil writes that 'heroism is but a theatrical gesture and smirched with boastfulness' in a poem that presents 'a picture of uniform horror, of which force is the sole hero' (pp. 22, 27).

If English poets have generally moved away from praise of warrior heroes, this is a development which reflects changes in their society at large – as does the decline, already noticed, in their cultivation of royal panegyric since 1688. The sociologist Max Weber long ago laid stress on the differences between the modern fighting force and those of earlier periods. He characterised the modern standing army as a body of men governed by a military discipline which imposes uniformity (and a uniform) upon its members. The discipline has as its object 'the consistently rationalized, methodically trained and exact execution of the received order', so that 'the actor is unswervingly and exclusively set for carrying out the command'.[39] Such 'bureaucratic' control of warriors tells against freedom of action by the individual, and it leaves little room for what Weber calls the 'personal charisma' of old-style heroes and their pursuit of honour in the field. To illustrate the difference, Weber draws a contrast between the Ironsides of Oliver Cromwell, with their close and disciplined formations, and the impetuous Cavaliers, always ready to break ranks in pursuit of the enemy (pp. 256–7). Weber's account may be rather highly coloured, but one can see that the modern, 'Roundhead', way of fighting will much reduce the opportunities for poets to celebrate the heroic feats of individual warriors. So it is that changes in warfare, like changes in kingship, must count among the very many developments in English life – too many to consider here – that have contributed to the 'decline of praise' since Renaissance times.

---

[39] Translated from Weber's *Wirtschaft und Gesellschaft* (1922) in H. H. Gerth and C. Wright Mills (eds.), *From Max Weber: Essays in Sociology*, 2nd edn (London, 1991), p. 253. See further pp. 253–61 and 221–3.

CHAPTER 6

Praise and its purposes

In poems, as in other kinds of utterance, praise serves a variety of purposes, some obvious and others not. The intention is most plain to see where a poet addresses praise to another person in the hope of some benefit to come, or in acknowledgement of a benefit already received. Such occasions arose quite commonly in the case of what Nagy called here-and-now praisings. This kind of praise-writing has attracted much unfavourable comment in modern times, as when Byron accused Southey of gross flattery in his laureate poem on George III; but it played a reputable part in societies more traditional than our own. Such societies worked on what anthropologists call a 'gift-exchange system'. This system (not altogether strange to us) imposed reciprocal obligations on giving and receiving and repaying; and in exchanges of this kind, poetic praise played a part, as Leslie Kurke has argued in her book about Pindar entitled *The Traffic in Praise*. 'Praise poetry', she observes, 'is by its very nature a gift exchanged.'[1] Poetic praise, that is, may be offered in exchange for the excellences of the person celebrated, and the poem in its turn will call for gifts from that person to its author.[2]

---

[1] Leslie Kurke, *The Traffic in Praise: Pindar and the Poetics of Social Economy* (Ithaca, N.Y., 1991), pp. 103–4.
[2] Compare Gregory Nagy on Pindar, writing in his foreword to Kurke's book: 'The athlete's ordeals ... are viewed as requiring the compensation of the poet's creative efforts as realized in the performance of the victory ode, which in its turn, as praise poetry, requires honorific material compensation for the poet' (pp. vii–viii).

Much medieval praise poetry of the here-and-now kind can be understood in terms of such an 'exchange economy of praise' (Kurke, p. 101). There must, for one thing, have been many more poets in England than we know of who composed encomia of secular lords in return for benefits, in the Pindaric way – scops like Widsith in Anglo-Saxon times, or poets associated with the courts of the last medieval centuries. In the earlier period, the evidence for such panegyric is very sparse, by comparison with the early Welsh or Scandinavian material. In the limited corpus of Old English verse, only the report in *Beowulf* of the Danish scop's song in praise of the hero allows one to guess what form such *lof-sang* actually took at the time.[3] There are no surviving texts at all like the face-to-face encomium to King Offa imagined by Geoffrey Hill in *Mercian Hymns*. In the later period, it is easier to see the exchange economy at work, in praise poetry addressed to kings and lords, and especially where the poet couples his praises with complaints about his own circumstances and petitions for a remedy, as Chaucer does in his little balade addressed to Henry IV (above, p. 151). Chaucer's follower Thomas Hoccleve, for example, composed several poems of this kind, some explicitly petitionary and some not. He reserves his most hyperbolical praise for his master Henry V, whom he welcomed back from France with an epideictic balade:

> What may we seyn / or what may we yow calle?
> We can for noon aart þat may happe or falle
>   Your worthy deedes / as us oghte / preise;
>   They been so manye / and so mochil peyse.[4]

Servants of royalty such as the Privy Seal officer Hoccleve or William Dunbar at the court of James IV of Scotland had very

---

[3] See above, pp. 50–1. Neither *The Battle of Brunanburh* nor the other Chronicle poems appear to have been addressed at their royal subjects.

[4] *Minor Poems*, ed. Gollancz, no. IX, ll. 18–21. Cf. *Minor Poems*, ed. Furnivall, nos. V, XV, IX (to the Duke of York) and XII (to the Chancellor).

pressing reasons for ensuring that they continued to enjoy the favour of those upon whom they depended for their living. Other praise poems seek favours of a less tangible kind, whether from a mistress or from the Virgin Mary. In love poems, praise of the beloved commonly goes along with a plea for her to take pity on the sufferings of which the lover complains, as in this little four-line instance:

> O kendly creature of beute perle3,
> Glorious merrour of alle clernesse,
> Sum sygne of love, y pray you with humblenesse,
> To shewe your servant in gret distresse.[5]

Unlike the court petitions of Hoccleve or Dunbar, these poems specify no object of their addresses, and their highly conventional praises bear little or no relation to what an individual lover might have felt about an individual woman. Rather, they represent what any lover might offer up to any woman in the hope of being rewarded with 'some sign of love' from her in return.[6] So, when Lydgate composed a love poem 'at þe request of a squyer þat served in loves court' (above, p. 66), he was content to supply the young man with a standard courtly *laus feminae*: 'Fresshe lusty beaute Ioyned with gentylesse . . . etc.' Such epideictic eloquence, by virtue of its very lack of particularity, could play a part in the exchanges – praise for favour – between any lover and his mistress.[7]

Praise serves a rather similar purpose in religious poems that express a petitionary intention, as those addressed to the Virgin

---

[5] No. 153 in *Secular Lyrics of the XIVth and XVth Centuries*, ed. Robbins, with music in the manuscript.

[6] Andreas Capellanus lists 'copiosa sermonis facundia', copious eloquence, among the five ways of winning a lady's love: *Andreas Capellanus on Love*, ed. and trans. P. G. Walsh (London, 1982), I.vi.1.

[7] Lydgate's squire might have used the poem like that other squire, Aurelius, in Chaucer's *Franklin's Tale*, to 'wreye / His wo, as in a general compleynyng' (*Canterbury Tales*, V 944–5): cited by John Stevens in his discussion of courtly lyric, *Music and Poetry in the Early Tudor Court* (Cambridge, 1979), p. 216.

commonly do. These offer *laudes Mariae* for the use of any devotee who wishes to enjoy her favour.[8] As in the love poems, the praise takes very conventional forms and may be understood, in part at least, as an offering made to Mary in the hope – or rather, in this case, the lively expectation – of a favourable response. So a thirteenth-century poet writes: 'Mi swete levedi, her mi bene / And reu of me ȝif þi wille is' ('My sweet lady, hear my prayer and take pity on me, if it is your will to do so').[9] In Marian poetry, the gift-exchange system extends more widely than in love poems, for Mary is commonly appealed to as a mediatrix between the poet and her son, as if she were an eirenic Queen Mother in the court of heaven. So the same thirteenth-century poet appeals to her: 'Help me to mi lives ende, / And make me wið þin sone isauȝt' ('Help me until the time of my death and reconcile me with your son') (ll. 39–40). The same principle of reciprocity that governs the relations between the poet and Mary also governs her relations with Christ, for he will surely grant favours to his mother, benefits which may then be passed by her down the line to the author of her *laudes*.

Unlike panegyric, love poetry or the devotional lyric, narrative poems played little part in the 'exchange economy of praise' during the English Middle Ages. There are no flattering dedications to patrons here, and only rarely does a poet slip in a compliment to some contemporary grandee.[10] So one must look elsewhere for the purposes of praise in these narratives. The traditional explanation, handed down from Antiquity, held that amplifications of

---

[8] Rosemary Woolf, speaking of the 'abnegation of individuality' in medieval religious lyrics, draws a contrast between them and the more personal writing of later times: 'Whereas the seventeenth-century poets show the poet meditating, the medieval writers provide versified meditations which others may use', *The English Religious Lyric in the Middle Ages* (Oxford, 1968), p. 6.

[9] *English Lyrics of the XIIIth Century*, ed. Brown, no. 60, ll. 7–8.

[10] As the *Beowulf*-poet perhaps does with his reference to King Offa (above, p. 48 n. 39) and Chaucer very probably does with an allusion to Queen Anne (*Troilus* I 171–72).

praise – and of blame – served a didactic end. Their function was
to persuade readers to follow the good examples and shun the evil
ones.[11] It is this that was said to justify poets in pushing to extremes
both the *laus* and the *vituperatio* of their characters, as they so commonly do. Vincent of Beauvais states the general case baldly, in a
passage already cited from his *Speculum Doctrinale*:

> The special business of poetry is, by its utterances, to make people imagine
> something to be more beautiful and repulsive than it really is, in such a way
> that the hearer, believing, will either shun or seek it. Although it is certainly
> not so in truth, yet the minds of the listeners will be roused either to shun or
> seek what they imagine.[12]

Certainly the stories of Beowulf, Arthur, Alexander and the like
offered many conspicuous examples of conduct, good and bad, by
which individuals might be guided in their own lives.[13] Yet, quite
unlike Spenser in the *Faerie Queene*, medieval English narrative poets
generally take little explicit account of any such didactic intention.
Indeed, most of them display rather less interest in general moral
issues than do the modern scholars who write about them. What
they more clearly do offer to their readers is the sheer pleasure
of narrative texts in which not just the people but also most other
things surpass ordinary expectations – the buildings, gardens, feasts,
armour and all the rest. That is the kind of thing which, according to

---

[11] Aristotle noticed the kinship between epideictic oratory and the deliberative type (concerned
with future actions) in his *Rhetoric*, 1367b–1368a. Cf. Quintilian: 'the same things are usually
praised in the former as are advised on in the latter', *Institutio Oratoria*, III.vii.28. Hardison
stresses the prominence of didactic considerations in Renaissance discussion of poetic praise:
'Priest, philosopher, educator and critic proclaimed that the record of noble deeds preserved
in great poetry is of inestimable value in teaching fortitude, liberality, patriotism . . .', *The
Enduring Monument*, p. 191.

[12] See above, pp. 17–18, and the references in n. 39.

[13] One scholar finds 'an erosion of the authority of exemplary figures' already in the later
Renaissance: Timothy Hampton, *Writing from History: The Rhetoric of Exemplarity in
Renaissance Literature* (Ithaca, N.Y., 1990), p. x.

the prologue to the *Wars of Alexander*, audiences 'fain would hear': stories of notable saints, lovers, kings and knights from the great days of the past.[14] In Northrop Frye's terminology, medieval taste in narrative favoured 'romance' or the 'high mimetic' rather than that 'low mimetic' mode which required narrators to observe 'the same canons of probability that we find in our own experience'.[15]

The history of narrative poetry in English broadly supports Frye's account of a 'centre of gravity' moving downwards through these modes towards the lowest, the 'ironic' mode of recent times. Such a downward tendency may be observed, not only in the case of heroes, but also in the general manner of such poems. Most of the narratives considered in this book employ a persistently auxetic style, with many laudatory epithets, often in superlative form, as well as protestations by the poet that his subject is inexpressible or incomparable, and other such rhetorical figures and commonplaces. Archaic poetic traditions, Greek and Germanic alike, wove such praises into the whole fabric of their narratives, and the rhetoricians' teachings about epideictic eloquence later supervened to very similar effect. Epithets in this style rarely draw attention to themselves, for they are most often formulaic or generic (brave warriors, beautiful women, magnificent buildings); but they serve to build up that high or 'golden' world of poetry that gave pleasure to Philip Sidney in a later age. Since then, in more modern times, this kind of 'magnification', as a default style, has increasingly come to be considered naive and sub-literary, and mainstream narrative in verse and prose has largely abandoned it to

---

[14] Lines from the prologue are cited above, p. 71. Although *Wars* was surely not recited after dinner, the prologue serves to mark it as entertainment. On poetry for pleasure, see Glending Olson, 'The Profits of Pleasure', in Minnis and Johnson (eds.), *The Cambridge History of Literary Criticism*, pp. 275–87, and the same author's book, *Literature as Recreation in the Later Middle Ages* (Ithaca, N.Y., 1982).

[15] Frye, *Anatomy of Criticism*, p. 34.

such more popular forms as romance fiction, where heroines can still
simply be very beautiful and heroes very brave.[16]

In my last chapter, I spoke of a 'privatisation' to be observed in
long narrative poems since the Middle Ages, and it seems that similar
developments play a part in the more general decline of auxesis in
post-medieval English poetry. Where modern poets write for private
readers, the manner of their English predecessors was adapted to
common use – narrative poems for any listening audience, devotional
poetry for any devotee, love-lyrics for any lover. What one rarely
hears is the voice of a poet speaking in privacy, as Chaucer does in
his two extraordinary balades addressed to his friends Scogan and
Bukton. So premodern poets, in England as elsewhere, most often
speak a language of praise that strikes a modern ear as too predictable
in its vocabulary and too high in its volume – like the *laus* then taught
by practitioners of that other public art, epideictic rhetoric. Indeed,
the decline of this style of narrative in mainstream writings seems
to have gone along with the decline of rhetoric, a tradition of public
praise which was losing its vitality by the later eighteenth century
and especially after the coming of Romanticism; so that Thomas De
Quincey, writing in 1828, could declare that 'the age of Rhetoric,
like that of Chivalry, has passed among forgotten things'.[17] These
are among the developments, noticed in the present study, that have
distanced us from the old poetry of praise and created difficulties in
the understanding and appreciation of it.

[16] A measurable index of the decline of such magnification would be the reducing frequency
of superlative adjective forms – calculable, perhaps, with the aid of computors.
[17] On the decline of rhetoric in modern times, see Vickers, *In Defence of Rhetoric*, pp. 196–213,
citing De Quincey on p. 197.

Bibliography

TEXTS

Ad Herennium De Ratione Dicendi, ed. and trans. Harry Caplan, Loeb Classical Library (Cambridge, Mass., 1964).

Alcuin, *Dialogus de Rhetorica et Virtutibus*, in *Patrologia Latina*, Vol. 101, cols. 919–50.

Alexander and Dindimus, ed. W. W. Skeat, EETS e.s. 31 (1878).

Andreas Capellanus, *Andreas Capellanus on Love*, ed. and trans. P. G. Walsh (London, 1982).

Anglo-Irish Poems of the Middle Ages, ed. Angela Lucas (Dublin, 1995).

Anglo-Saxon Poetic Records, ed. G. P. Krapp and E. V. K. Dobbie, 6 vols. (New York, 1931–42).

Aristotle, *Poetics*, trans. D. A. Russell and M. Winterbottom, in their *Classical Literary Criticism* (Oxford, 1989).

Aristotle, *Rhetoric*, trans. George A. Kennedy, *Aristotle on Rhetoric: A Theory of Civic Discourse* (Oxford, 1991).

Augustine, *De Doctrina Christiana*, ed. and trans. R. P. H. Green (Oxford, 1995).

Averrois, *Middle Commentary on Aristotle's 'Poetics'*, trans. O. B. Hardison, in Alex Preminger, O. B. Hardison and Kevin Kerrane (eds.), *Classical and Medieval Literary Criticism: Translations and Interpretations* (New York, 1974), pp. 341–82.

Bede, *Bede's Ecclesiastical History of the English People*, ed. and trans. Bertram Colgrave and R. A. B. Mynors (Oxford, 1969).

Benvenuto da Imola, *Comentum super Dantis Aldigherij Comoedium*, ed. J. P. Lacaita, 5 vols. (Florence, 1887).

Beowulf, ed. Bruce Mitchell and Fred C. Robinson (Oxford, 1998).

The Brut, ed. F. W. D. Brie, EETS 131, 136 (1906, 1908).

Byron, George Gordon, Lord, *Byron*, ed. Jerome J. McGann (Oxford, 1986).

Carlyle, Thomas, *Carlyle's Lectures on Heroes, Hero-Worship and the Heroic in History*, ed. P. C. Parr (Oxford, 1910).

Chaucer, Geoffrey, *The Book of the Duchess*, ed. Helen Phillips, 3rd edn (Durham, 1997).

Chaucer, Geoffrey, *The Minor Poems*, The Variorum Edition of Chaucer, Vol. v, Part One, ed. George B. Pace and Alfred David (Norman, Okla., 1982).

Chaucer, Geoffrey, *The Nun's Priest's Tale*, The Variorum Edition of Chaucer, Vol. ii, ed. Derek Pearsall (Norman, Okla., 1984).

Chaucer, Geoffrey, *The Riverside Chaucer*, 3rd edn, general editor L. D. Benson (Boston, Mass., 1987).

Chaucer, Geoffrey, *Troilus and Criseyde*, ed. B. A. Windeatt (London, 1984).

Cicero, *De Inventione*, ed. and trans. H. M. Hubbell, Loeb Classical Library (Cambridge, Mass., 1949).

Dante Alighieri, *The Divine Comedy*, ed. and trans. Charles S. Singleton, 6 vols. (Princeton, N.J., 1970–5).

Dante Alighieri, *Le Opere di Dante*, ed. M. Barbi *et al.*, 2nd edn (Florence, 1960).

Douglas, Gavin, *Virgil's Aeneid Translated into Scottish Verse*, ed. David F. C. Coldwell, 4 vols., Scottish Text Society (1957–64).

Dunbar, William, *The Poems of William Dunbar*, ed. Priscilla Bawcutt, 2 vols. (Glasgow, 1998).

Encomium Emmae Reginae, ed. Alastair Campbell, with supplement by Simon Keynes (Cambridge, 1998).

English Lyrics of the xiiith Century, ed. Carleton Brown (Oxford, 1932).

Faral, E. (ed.), *Les Arts Poétiques du xiie et du xiiie Siècle* (Paris, 1924).

Geoffrey of Monmouth, *The Historia Regum Britannie of Geoffrey of Monmouth*, 1, Bern, Bürgerbibliothek MS 568, ed. Neil Wright (Cambridge, 1984).

Geoffrey of Vinsauf, *Poetria Nova*, ed. E. Faral, *Les Arts Poétiques*, pp. 194–262.

The Gest Hystoriale of the Destruction of Troy, ed. G. A. Panton and D. Donaldson, EETS 39, 56 (1869, 1874).

Greene, Richard Leighton, ed., *The Early English Carols*, 2nd edn (Oxford, 1977).

Hermann the German, *De Arte Poetica cum Averrois Expositione*, ed. L. Minio-Paluello, Corpus Philosophorum Medii Aevi: Aristoteles Latinus XXXIII, 2nd edn (Leiden, 1968).

'Hermogenes', *Progymnasmata*, trans. C. S. Baldwin, in his *Medieval Rhetoric and Poetic* (New York, 1929).

Hill, Geoffrey, *Mercian Hymns* (London, 1971).

Hill, Geoffrey, *The Triumph of Love, A Poem* (Harmondsworth, 1999).

Historical Poems of the XIVth and XVth Centuries, ed. Rossell Hope Robbins (New York, 1959).

Hoccleve, Thomas, *Minor Poems*, ed. F. J. Furnivall, EETS e.s. 61 (1892), and ed. I. Gollancz, EETS e.s. 73 (1925); revised reprint in one volume, 1970.

Hoccleve, Thomas, *The Regiment of Princes*, ed. Charles R. Blyth (Kalamazoo, 1999).

Huygens, R. B. C. (ed.), *Accessus ad Auctores: Bernard d'Utrecht, Conrad d'Hirsau Dialogus super Auctores* (Leiden, 1970).

Isidore of Seville, *Etymologies, Book II*, ed. and trans. Peter K. Marshall (Paris, 1983).

John of Garland, *The 'Parisiana Poetria' of John of Garland*, ed. and trans. Traugott Lawler (New Haven, Conn., 1974).

Joyce, James, *Ulysses* (London, 1937).

Laȝamon, *Brut*, ed. G. L. Brook and R. F. Leslie, 2 vols., EETS 250, 277 (1963, 1978).

Laȝamon, *Lawman: Brut*, trans. Rosamund Allen (London, 1992).

Laȝamon, *Laȝamon's 'Arthur'*, ed. and trans. W. R. J. Barron and S. C. Weinberg (Harlow, 1989).

The Life of the Black Prince by the Herald of Sir John Chandos, ed. and trans. Mildred K. Pope and Eleanor C. Lodge (Oxford, 1910).

Logue, Christopher, *War Music: War Music* (London, 1981), *Kings* (London, 1991), *The Husbands* (London, 1994), *All Day Permanent Red* (London, 2003), *Cold Calls* (London, 2005).

Lorris, Guillaume de, *Le Roman de la Rose*, ed. Félix Lecoy, CFMA, Vol. I (Paris, 1965).

Lybeaus Desconus, ed. M. Mills, EETS 261 (1969).

Lydgate, John, *Poems*, ed. John Norton-Smith (Oxford, 1966).

Lydgate, John, *Troy Book*, ed. H. Bergen, EETS e.s. 97, 103, 106, 126 (1906–20).

Machaut, Guillaume de, *Le Jugement du Roy de Behaigne and Remede de Fortune*, ed. James I. Wimsatt and William W. Kibler, The Chaucer Library (Athens, G., 1988).

Matthew of Vendôme, *Ars Versificandi*, ed. E. Faral, *Les Arts Poétiques*, pp. 106–93.

Menander, *Menander Rhetor: Edited with Translation and Commentary*, ed. and trans. D. A. Russell and N. G. Wilson (Oxford, 1981).

Milton, John, *Complete Shorter Poems*, ed. John Carey, 2nd edn (London, 1997).

Milton, John, *Paradise Lost*, ed. Alastair Fowler, 2nd edn (London, 1998).

Morte Arthure, ed. John Finlayson (London, 1967).

Morte Arthure, *The Morte Arthure: A Critical Edition*, ed. Mary Hamel (New York and London, 1984).

The Owl and the Nightingale, ed. and trans. Neil Cartlidge (Exeter, 2001).

The Parlement of the Thre Ages, ed. M. Y. Offord, EETS 246 (1959).

Pearl, ed. E. V. Gordon (Oxford, 1953).

Pindar, *The Odes*, ed. and trans. Sir John Sandys, Loeb Classical Library (Cambridge, Mass., 1915).

Pope, Alexander, *The Poems of Alexander Pope*, ed. John Butt (London, 1963).

Proust, Marcel, *Within a Budding Grove, Part Two*, trans. C. K. Scott Moncrieff (London, 1949).

Puttenham, George, *The Arte of English Poesie*, ed. G. Gregory Smith, in his *Elizabethan Critical Essays*, 2 vols. (Oxford, 1904), Vol. II, pp. 1–193.

Quintilian, *Institutio Oratoria*, ed. and trans. Donald A. Russell as *The Orator's Education*, 5 vols., Loeb Classical Library (Boston, Mass., 2001).

Religious Lyrics of the xvth Century, ed. Carleton Brown (Oxford, 1939).

Rhetorica ad Herennium, ed. and trans. Harry Caplan, Loeb Classical Library (Cambridge, Mass., 1964).

Secular Lyrics of the xivth and xvth Centuries, ed. Rossell Hope Robbins (Oxford, 1952).

Sidney, Sir Philip, *An Apology for Poetry*, ed. G. Gregory Smith, in his *Elizabethan Critical Essays*, 2 vols. (Oxford, 1904), Vol. I, pp. 148–207.

Sir Gawain and the Green Knight, ed. J. R. R. Tolkien and E. V. Gordon, revised Norman Davis (Oxford, 1967).

Sir Orfeo, ed. A. J. Bliss, 2nd edn (Oxford, 1966).

Spenser, Edmund, *The Faerie Queene*, ed. A. C. Hamilton (London, 1977).

Spenser, Edmund, *Poetical Works*, ed. J. C. Smith and E. de Selincourt (Oxford, 1912).

Tennyson, Alfred, Lord, *Tennyson, A Selected Edition*, ed. Christopher Ricks (London, 1989).

Vincentius Bellovacensis [Vincent of Beauvais], *Speculum Doctrinale* (Dvaci, 1624, facsimile, Graz, 1965).

Wace, *Wace's Roman de Brut: A History of the British*, ed. and trans. Judith Weiss (Exeter, 1999).

The Wars of Alexander, ed. Hoyt N. Duggan and Thorlac Turville-Petre, EETS s.s. 10 (1989).

Wilson, Thomas, *Arte of Rhetorique*, ed. Thomas J. Derrick (New York, 1982).

Wordsworth, William, *The Prelude, 1799, 1805, 1850*, ed. Jonathan Wordsworth, M. H. Abrams and Stephen Gill (New York, 1979).

STUDIES

Aers, David, *Chaucer, Langland and the Creative Imagination* (London, 1980).

Allen, Judson Boyce, *The Ethical Poetic of the Later Middle Ages* (Toronto, 1982).

Anderson, R. Dean Jr, *Glossary of Greek Rhetorical Terms* (Leuven, 2000).

Anderson, William, *Dante the Maker* (London, 1980).

Baldwin, C. S., *Medieval Rhetoric and Poetic* (New York, 1929).

Barron, W. R. J., *'Trawthe' and Treason: The Sin of Gawain Reconsidered* (Manchester, 1980).

Beadle, Richard, 'The Virtuoso's *Troilus*', in Ruth Morse and Barry Windeatt (eds.), *Chaucer Traditions: Studies in Honour of Derek Brewer* (Cambridge, 1990), pp. 213–33.

Benskin, Michael, 'The Style and Authorship of the Kildare Poems – (1) *Pers of Bermingham*', in J. Lachlan Mackenzie and Richard Todd (eds.), *In Other Words: Transcultural Studies in Philology, Translation and Lexicology Presented to H. H. Meier* (Dordrecht, 1989), pp. 57–75.

Benson, Larry D., *Art and Tradition in Sir Gawain and the Green Knight* (New Brunswick, N.J., 1965).

Benson, Larry D., 'The Beginnings of Chaucer's English Style', in Theodore M. Andersson and Stephen A. Barney (eds.), *Contradictions: From 'Beowulf' to Chaucer: Selected Studies of Larry D. Benson* (Aldershot, 1995), pp. 243–65.

Blake, Norman, *The English Language in English Literature* (London, 1977).

Boitani, Piero, *Chaucer and the Imaginary World of Fame* (Cambridge, 1984).

Bradley, S. A. J. (trans.), *Anglo-Saxon Poetry* (London, 1982).

Brewer, D. S., 'The Relationship of Chaucer to the English and European Traditions', in D. S. Brewer (ed.), *Chaucer and Chaucerians* (London, 1966), pp. 1–38.

Broadus, Edmund Kemper, *The Laureateship: A Study of the Office of Poet Laureate in England, with Some Account of the Poets* (Oxford, 1921).

Broich, Ulrich, *The Eighteenth-Century Mock-Heroic Poem*, trans. D. H. Wilson (Cambridge, 1990).

Burgess, Theodore C., *Epideictic Literature* (New York, 1987), originally published in *University of Chicago Studies in Classical Philology*, 3 (1902), 89–261.

Burrow, Colin, *Epic Romance: Homer to Milton* (Oxford, 1993).

Burrow, J. A., *The Ages of Man: A Study in Medieval Writing and Thought* (Oxford, 1988).

Burrow, J. A., 'Chaucer's *Knight's Tale* and the Three Ages of Man', in J. A. Burrow, *Essays on Medieval Literature* (Oxford, 1984), pp. 27–48.

Burrow, J. A., 'William Dunbar', in Priscilla Bawcutt and Janet Hadley Williams (eds.), *A Companion to Medieval Scottish Poetry* (Cambridge, 2006), pp. 133–48.

Cain, Thomas H., *Praise in 'The Faerie Queene'* (Lincoln, Neb., 1978).

Cannon, Christopher, 'Chaucer's Style', in Piero Boitani and Jill Mann (eds.), *The Cambridge Companion to Chaucer*, 2nd edn (Cambridge, 2003), pp. 233–50.

Cannon, Christopher, *The Grounds of English Literature* (Oxford, 2004).

Cary, George, *The Medieval Alexander*, ed. D. J. A. Ross (Cambridge, 1956).

Chadwick, H. Munro, and N. Kershaw Chadwick, *The Growth of Literature*, Vol. I: *The Ancient Literatures of Europe* (Cambridge, 1932).

Chambers, A. B., *Andrew Marvell and Edmund Waller: Seventeenth-Century Praise and Restoration Satire* (Philadelphia, Pa., 1991).

Chism, Christine, *Alliterative Revivals* (Philadelphia, Pa., 2002).

Clemen, Wolfgang, *Chaucer's Early Poetry*, trans. C. A. M. Sym (London, 1963).

Cooper, Helen, *The Canterbury Tales*, Oxford Guides to Chaucer (Oxford, 1989).

Crow, Martin M., and Clair C. Olson (eds.), *Chaucer Life-Records* (Oxford, 1966).

Curtius, E. R., *European Literature and the Latin Middle Ages*, trans. Willard R. Trask (London, 1953).

Dahan, Gilbert, 'Notes et Textes sur la Poétique au Moyen Âge', *Archives d'Histoire Doctrinale et Littéraire du Moyen Âge*, 47 (1980), 171–239.

Finnegan, Ruth, *Oral Literature in Africa* (Oxford, 1970).

Finnegan, Ruth, *Oral Poetry: Its Nature, Significance and Social Context* (Cambridge, 1977).

Fitzgerald, William, *Agonistic Poetry: The Pindaric Mode in Pindar, Horace, Hölderlin, and the English Ode* (Berkeley, Calif., 1987).

Folkenflik, Robert (ed.), *The English Hero, 1660–1800* (Newark, Del., 1982).

Fowler, Alastair, *Time's Purpled Masquers: Stars and the Afterlife in Renaissance English Literature* (Oxford, 1996).

Frye, Northrop, *Anatomy of Criticism* (Princeton, N.J., 1957).

Fyler, John M., *Chaucer and Ovid* (New Haven, Conn., 1979).

Garmonsway, G. N., 'Anglo-Saxon Heroic Attitudes', in Jess B. Bessinger and Robert P. Creed (eds.), *Franciplegius: Medieval and Linguistic Studies in Honor of Francis Peabody Magoun, Jr.* (New York, 1965), pp. 139–46.

Garrison, James D., *Dryden and the Tradition of Panegyric* (Berkeley, Calif., 1975).

Gillespie, Vincent, 'From the Twelfth Century to c. 1450', in Minnis and Johnson (eds.), *Cambridge History of Literary Criticism*, pp. 145–235.

Gneuss, Helmut, '*The Battle of Maldon* 89: Byrhtnoð's *ofermod* Once Again', *Studies in Philology*, 73 (1976), 117–37.

Godden, Malcolm, 'Biblical Literature: The Old Testament', in Godden and Lapidge (eds.), *Cambridge Companion to Old English Literature*, pp. 206–26.

Godden, Malcolm, and Michael Lapidge (eds.), *The Cambridge Companion to Old English Literature* (Cambridge, 1991).

Goldsmith, Margaret, *The Mode and Meaning of 'Beowulf'* (London, 1970).

Göller, Karl Heinz (ed.), *The Alliterative Morte Arthure: A Reassessment of the Poem* (Cambridge, 1981).

Gordon, Ida, *The Double Sorrow of Troilus: A Study of Ambiguities in 'Troilus and Criseyde'* (Oxford, 1970).

Greenfield, S. B., 'Beowulf and the Judgement of the Righteous', in Michael Lapidge and Helmut Gneuss (eds.), *Learning and Literature in Anglo-Saxon England: Essays Presented to Peter Clemoes* (Cambridge, 1985), pp. 393–407.

Haffenden, John, *William Empson among the Mandarins* (Oxford, 2005).

Hamel, Mary, 'The Dream of a King: The Alliterative *Morte Arthure* and Dante', *Chaucer Review*, 14 (1980), 298–312.

Hampton, Timothy, *Writing from History: The Rhetoric of Exemplarity in Renaissance Literature* (Ithaca, N.Y., 1990).

Hardison, O. B. Jr, *The Enduring Monument: A Study of the Idea of Praise in Renaissance Literary Theory and Practice* (Westport, Conn., 1962).

Helgerson, Richard, *Self-Crowned Laureates: Spenser, Jonson, Milton and the Literary System* (Berkeley, Calif., 1983).

Jacobs, Nicolas, '*The Owl and the Nightingale* and the Bishops', in Myra Stokes and T. L. Burton (eds.), *Medieval Literature and Antiquities: Studies in Honour of Basil Cottle* (Cambridge, 1987), pp. 91–8.

Jones, Terry, *Chaucer's Knight: The Portrait of a Medieval Mercenary* (London, 1980).

Kean, P. M., *Chaucer and the Making of English Poetry*, Vol. I: *Love Vision and Debate*; Vol. II: *The Art of Narrative* (London, 1972).

Keen, Maurice, 'Chaucer's Knight, the English Aristocracy and the Crusades', in V. J. Scattergood and J. W. Sherborne (eds.), *English Court Culture in the Later Middle Ages* (London, 1983), pp. 45–61.

Kelly, H. A., 'The Non-Tragedy of Arthur', in Gregory Kratzmann and James Simpson (eds.), *Medieval English Religious and Ethical Literature: Essays in Honour of G. H. Russell* (Cambridge, 1986), pp. 92–114.

Kennedy, George A. (trans.), *Aristotle on Rhetoric: A Theory of Civic Discourse* (Oxford, 1991).

Kennedy, George A. (ed.), *The Cambridge History of Literary Criticism*, Vol. I: *Classical Criticism* (Cambridge, 1989).

Kennedy, George A., 'The Genres of Rhetoric', in Stanley E. Porter (ed.), *Handbook of Classical Rhetoric in the Hellenistic Period, 330 B.C.–A.D. 400* (Leiden, 1997), pp. 43–50.

Kiser, Lisa J., *Telling Classical Tales: Chaucer and the 'Legend of Good Women'* (Ithaca, N.Y., 1983).

Kurke, Leslie, *The Traffic in Praise: Pindar and the Poetics of Social Economy* (Ithaca, N.Y., 1991).

Lewalski, Barbara Kiefer, *Donne's 'Anniversaries' and the Poetry of Praise* (Princeton, N.J., 1973).

Lewalski, Barbara Kiefer, *Milton's Brief Epic: The Creation of a Symbolic Mode* (Providence, R.I., 1966).

Lewis, C. S., *The Allegory of Love* (Oxford, 1936).

Leyerle, John, 'Beowulf, the Hero and the King', *Medium Aevum*, 34 (1965), 89–102.

Lord, Albert B., *The Singer of Tales* (New York, 1965).

Lynch, Andrew, '"Peace is Good after War": The Narrative Seasons of English Arthurian Tradition', in Saunders, Le Saux and Thomas (eds.), *Writing War*, pp. 127–46.

Mack, Peter, *Elizabethan Rhetoric: Theory and Practice* (Cambridge, 2002).

Mann, Jill, *Chaucer and Medieval Estates Satire: The Literature of Social Classes and the 'General Prologue' to the 'Canterbury Tales'* (Cambridge, 1973).

Mann, Jill, *Geoffrey Chaucer*, Feminist Readings (Hemel Hempstead, 1991).

Matthews, William, *The Tragedy of Arthur* (Berkeley, Calif., 1960).

Meyer-Lee, Robert J., *Poets and Power from Chaucer to Wyatt* (Cambridge, 2007).

Minnis, Alastair, *Magister Amoris* (Oxford, 2001).

Minnis, A. J. (ed.), *Gower's 'Confessio Amantis': Responses and Reassessments* (Cambridge, 1983).

Minnis, A. J., and Ian Johnson (eds.), *The Cambridge History of Literary Criticism*, Vol. II: *The Middle Ages* (Cambridge, 2005).

Minnis, A. J., and A. B. Scott, *Medieval Literary Theory and Criticism, c. 1100–c. 1375: The Commentary Tradition* (Oxford, 1988).

Minnis, A. J., with V. J. Scattergood and J. J. Smith, *The Shorter Poems*, Oxford Guides to Chaucer (Oxford, 1995).

Murphy, J. J., 'The Arts of Poetry and Prose', in Minnis and Johnson (eds.), *Cambridge History of Literary Criticism*, pp. 42–67.

Mustanoja, Tauno F., *A Middle English Syntax*, Part I (Helsinki, 1960).

Nagy, Gregory, 'Early Greek Views of Poets and Poetry', in Kennedy (ed.), *Cambridge History of Literary Criticism*, pp. 1–77.

Niles, John D., *Beowulf: The Poem and its Tradition* (Cambridge, Mass., 1983).

Norbrook, David, *Writing the English Republic: Poetry, Rhetoric and Politics, 1627–1660* (Cambridge, 1999).

O'Keefe, Katherine O'Brien , 'Heroic Values and Christian Ethics', in Godden and Lapidge (eds.), *Cambridge Companion to Old English Literature*, pp. 107–25.

Olson, Glending, 'The Profits of Pleasure', in Minnis and Johnson (eds.), *Cambridge History of Literary Criticism*, pp. 275–87.

Opland, Jeff, *Anglo-Saxon Oral Poetry: A Study of the Traditions* (New Haven, Conn., 2005).

Orchard, Andy, *A Critical Companion to 'Beowulf'* (Cambridge, 2003).

Patterson, Annabel M., *Hermogenes and the Renaissance: Seven Ideals of Style* (Princeton, N.J., 1970).

Patterson, Lee, *Negotiating the Past: The Historical Understanding of Medieval Literature* (Madison, Wis., 1987).

Pearsall, Derek, *The Canterbury Tales* (London, 1985).

Pearsall, Derek, *John Lydgate* (London, 1970).

Porter, Elizabeth, 'Chaucer's Knight, the *Alliterative Morte Arthure*, and Medieval Laws of War: A Reconsideration', *Nottingham Medieval Studies*, 27 (1983), 56–78.

Porter, Stanley E. (ed.), *Handbook of Classical Rhetoric in the Hellenistic Period, 330 B.C.–A.D. 400* (Leiden, 1997).

Preminger, Alex, O. B. Hardison Jr and Kevin Kerrane (eds.), *Classical and Medieval Literary Criticism: Translations and Interpretations* (New York, 1974).

Putter, Ad, 'Finding Time for Romance: Medieval Arthurian Literary History', *Medium Aevum*, 63 (1994), 1–16.

Ransom, D. J., *Poets at Play: Irony and Parody in the Harley Lyrics* (Norman, Okla., 1985).

Reynolds, Suzanne, *Medieval Reading: Grammar, Rhetoric and the Classical Text* (Cambridge, 1996).

Reynolds, Suzanne, '*Orazio Satiro* (*Inferno* IV, 89): Dante, the Roman Satirists, and the Medieval Theory of Satire', in Z. G. Baranski (ed.), *Libri Poetarum in Quattuor Species Dividuntur: Essays on Dante and 'Genre'*, Supplement to *The Italianist*, 15 (1995), 128–44.

Rigg, A. G., *A History of Anglo-Latin Literature, 1066–1422* (Cambridge, 1992).

Robertson, D. W., *A Preface to Chaucer: Studies in Medieval Perspectives* (Princeton, N.J., 1963).

Robinson, Fred C. *'Beowulf' and the Appositive Style* (Knoxville, Tenn., 1985).

Rowland, John Thomas, *Faint Praise and Civil Leer: The 'Decline' of Eighteenth-Century Panegyric* (Newark, Del., 1994).

Russell, D. A., and M. Winterbottom (trans.), *Classical Literary Criticism* (Oxford, 1989).

Saunders, Corinne, Françoise Le Saux and Neil Thomas (eds.), *Writing War: Medieval Literary Responses to Warfare* (Cambridge, 2004).

Schlauch, M., 'An Old English *Encomium Urbis*', *Journal of English and Germanic Philology*, 40 (1941), 14–28.

Sharpe, Kevin, *Criticism and Compliment: The Politics of Literature in the England of Charles I* (Cambridge, 1987).

Shippey, T. A., *Beowulf* (London, 1978).

Shippey, T. A., 'Boar and Badger: An Old English Heroic Antithesis', *Leeds Studies in English*, n.s. 16 (1985), 220–39.

Shippey, T. A., *Old English Verse* (London, 1972).

Simpson, James, *Reform and Cultural Revolution*, The Oxford English Literary History, Vol. II, 1350–1547 (Oxford, 2002).

Sisam, K., *The Structure of 'Beowulf'* (Oxford, 1965).

Spearing, A. C., *Textual Subjectivity: The Encoding of Subjectivity in Medieval Narrative and Lyrics* (Oxford, 2005).

Stemmler, Theo, 'The Problem of Parody: *Annot and John*, for Example', in Piero Boitani and Anna Torti (eds.), *Genres, Themes, and Images in English Literature: The J. A. W. Bennett Memorial Lectures* (Tübingen, 1988), pp. 156–65.

Stevens, John, *Music and Poetry in the Early Tudor Court* (Cambridge, 1979).

Tolkien, J. R. R., 'The Homecoming of Beorhtnoth Beorhthelm's Son', *Essays and Studies 1953* (1953), 1–18.

Turville-Petre, Thorlac, *England the Nation: Language, Literature, and National Identity, 1290–1340* (Oxford, 1996).

Vickers, Brian, *In Defence of Rhetoric* (Oxford, 1988).

Webb, Ruth, 'Poetry and Rhetoric', in Porter (ed.), *Handbook of Classical Rhetoric*, pp. 339–69.

Weber, Max, *From Max Weber: Essays in Sociology*, ed. H. H. Gerth and C. Wright Mills, 2nd edn (London, 1991).

Weinberg, Bernard, *A History of Literary Criticism in the Italian Renaissance*, 2 vols. (Chicago, 1961).

Whitelock, Dorothy, *The Audience of 'Beowulf'* (Oxford, 1951).

Whiting, Bartlett Jere, and Helen Wescott Whiting, *Proverbs, Sentences, and Proverbial Phrases from English Writings Mainly before 1500* (Cambridge, Mass., 1968).

Wilde, Geert de, 'The Stanza Form of the Middle English Lament for the Death of Edward I: A Reconsideration', *Anglia*, 123 (2005), 23–45.

Windeatt, Barry, *Troilus and Criseyde*, Oxford Guides to Chaucer (Oxford, 1992).

Woolf, Rosemary, *The English Religious Lyric in the Middle Ages* (Oxford, 1968).

Index

CAMBRIDGE STUDIES IN MEDIEVAL LITERATURE